Soldiers of Misfortune

Studies in the
Postmodern Theory of Education

Joe L. Kincheloe and Shirley R. Steinberg
General Editors

Vol. 25

PETER LANG
New York • Washington, D.C./Baltimore • Boston
Bern • Frankfurt am Main • Berlin • Vienna • Paris

Valerie L. Scatamburlo

Soldiers of Misfortune

The New Right's Culture War
and the Politics
of Political Correctness

PETER LANG
New York • Washington, D.C./Baltimore • Boston
Bern • Frankfurt am Main • Berlin • Vienna • Paris

Library of Congress Cataloging-in-Publication Data

Scatamburlo, Valerie L.
Soldiers of misfortune: the New Right's culture war and the politics
of political correctness / Valerie L. Scatamburlo.
p. cm. — (Counterpoints; v. 25)
Includes bibliographical references and index.
1. Conservatism—United States. 2. Political correctness—
United States. 3. Education—Social aspects—United States. I. Title. II. Series:
Counterpoints (New York, N.Y.); vol. 25.
JC573.2.U6S33   320.52'0973—dc21   96-37016
ISBN 0-8204-3012-9
ISSN 1058-1634

Die Deutsche Bibliothek-CIP-Einheitsaufnahme

Scatamburlo, Valerie L.:
Soldiers of misfortune: the new right's culture war and the politics of political
correctness / Valerie L. Scatamburlo.–New York; Washington, D.C./Baltimore; Boston;
Bern; Frankfurt am Main; Berlin; Vienna; Paris: Lang.
(Counterpoints; Vol. 25)
ISBN 0-8204-3012-9
NE: GT

Cover design by James F. Brisson.

The paper in this book meets the guidelines for permanence and durability
of the Committee on Production Guidelines for Book Longevity
of the Council of Library Resources.

© 1998 Peter Lang Publishing, Inc., New York

Printed in the United States of America.

For my parents, Renato and Pierina Scatamburlo

and to the memory of my grandmothers

Genoeffa Caverzan and Clara Scatamburlo

We realize all the more clearly what we have to accomplish in the present—I am speaking of a *ruthless criticism of everything existing*, ruthless in two senses: The criticism must not be afraid of its own conclusions, nor of conflict with the powers that be.

-Karl Marx, *Letter to Arnold Ruge*, 1843

The emotion of hope goes out of itself, makes people broad instead of confining them . . . The work of this emotion requires people who throw themselves actively into what is becoming . . . Hopelessness is itself, in a temporal and factual sense, the most insupportable thing, downright intolerable to human needs.

-Ernst Bloch, *The Principle of Hope*

Sometimes you have to follow the opposite course: Distrust agreement and find in dissent the confirmation of your own intuitions. There is no rule; there is only the risk of contradiction. But sometimes you have to speak because you feel the moral obligation to say something.

-Umberto Eco, *Travels in Hyperreality*

Table of Contents

Acknowledgements   xi

Preface   xiii

Introduction   1

1.   **Backlash: Old Strategies, New Times**   25
       Clear and Present Danger?: Political Correctness
         and the Academy   25
       The Birth of the New Right: From "Remnants"
         to Rabble-Rousers   30
       The Legacy of the Sixties   36
       The Sixties Under Siege: The Rise of
         Neoconservatism   42
       The Conservative Counter-revolution   46
       Funding the New Right Agenda   53
       Notes   66

2.   **Products of the "Ideas Industry"**
     and Other (Not So) Great Books
     of the Culture Wars   75
       The New Right Goes to School   75
       The Canon and the Politics of Knowledge   78
       Say What?? Speech Codes and the Politics of
         Verbal Hygiene   92
       Feminists, "Special Interests" and Other
         Politically Correct Bogeymen   102
       For Whom the Bell Tolls   112
       Notes   125

3.   **P.C. in the Media**   **133**
    Media Culture   133
    Manufacturing the Crisis: The P.C. Menace   136
    Dispelling the Myths   143
    Unreliable Sources   153
    Notes   156

4.   **Theory Wars and Cultural Strife**   **159**
    1968 and After   159
    The Cult of Theory   163
    The Ruse of "Truth"?   175
    Identity Politics and the Politics of
       Representation   182
    "Whiteness" and the Politics of Resentment   188
    Beyond the Last "Post"   195
    Cultivating Common Dreams   203
    Notes   210

5.   **Conclusion: Towards a (P)olitically (C)ommitted Pedagogy**   **221**
    Is "Teaching the Conflicts" Enough?   221
    Beyond the Ivory Tower   227
    Notes   231

References   233

Index   263

Acknowledgements

This book would not have been possible without the support and encouragement of many people. First and foremost, I am indebted to my parents, Renato and Pierina Scatamburlo, whose unwavering support, love, patience and understanding made this a goal worth striving for. There are simply no words which could express my gratitude. To my many relatives who have encouraged my intellectual pursuits over the years, I simply wish to say "Thanks"—your support has meant the world to me. I also owe a great debt of gratitude to my "Brigantino" family—Sam, Emilia, Domenico, Vincenzo and Manuela Ambrosio—for being there for me, time and time again, and whose friendship I cherish dearly.

In preparing this manuscript, several people graciously provided me with suggestions and inspiration. I want especially to thank: Rhonda Hammer who provided guidance and friendship from the get-go; Douglas Kellner who generously gave of his time to provide a number of invaluable insights and whose work continues to be a source of inspiration; James Winter for his input in the formative stages of this project and for his continued encouragement; Amir Hassanpour and Sharhzad Mojab for their friendship and intellectual stimulation; Peter McLaren for the insights his work provides; my editors, Joe Kincheloe and Shirley Steinberg, for their patience and for supporting my efforts; and the fine staff at Peter Lang Publishing.

Finally, I must thank the following people for their friendship and moral support over the years: Linda Amato, Himani Bannerji, Klaudia Capalbo, Erika and Andrew Dallabona, Ioan and Diane Davies, Sara Didone, Cathy and Robert Greco, Lauren Langman, and Lana Mancini.

Preface

Douglas Kellner

Valerie Scatamburlo's *Soldiers of Misfortune: The New Right's Culture War and the Politics of Political Correctness* provides the first systematic account of the linkage between the right-wing attack on political correctness and its assault on education as part of a conservative offensive in the culture wars that have been raging since the 1960s. During the 1960s, a wide array of progressives challenged every aspect of North American societies from education to military policy. As a response to these struggles, conservative forces launched a counterattack against what they perceived to be the "excesses" of that decade. Through the amalgamation of various right-wing groups and the benevolence of big business, the New Right was born. With vast financial resources at its disposal, it was able to engage in a series of culture wars over everything from the family and abortion to the educational curricula and policy.

Scatamburlo traces the trajectory of the New Right from its earliest roots in the 1950s and 1960s to the early 1990s and analyzes the events, circumstances and social conditions which spawned its formation. She provides a detailed account of the corporate sponsorship undergirding the culture wars and the right-wing attack on the so-called "politically correct" zealots who are allegedly attempting to impose the edicts of political correctness on unassuming students and curtailing freedom of speech and inquiry in their efforts to legislate "correct" thought and language.

According to Scatamburlo, the war on "political correctness" must be understood contextually as part of the much broader, systematic attempt to roll back the progressive changes wrought by the struggles of the 1960s and 1970s. Her analysis suggests that the rightist assault on P.C. is partly ironic and partly hypocritical since it has traditionally been the Right that has attacked the thought and speech of its opponents and critics. Indeed, during the Cold War McCarthy era, thousands of radicals were purged from the universities for their alleged "communist" ideas or affiliations. Scatamburlo shows that, more recently, a number of right-wing groups have engaged in attempts to target professors with "left-leaning" or "subversive" tendencies and are thus themselves practicing a new form of McCarthyism.

Scatamburlo also provides a genealogy of the phrase "political correctness" and points to the fact that it was once used ironically among leftists to designate those who showed excessive concern for verbal and symbolic purity. In the hands of the New Right, however, P.C. has been turned on its head, stripped of its good-natured humor and denuded of its original context. As a result, it has become a label for allegedly intolerant and oppressive attempts to squelch sexist, racist, homophobic, and other offensive forms of thought and behavior.

While one could happily welcome a genuine defense of academic freedom by our conservative colleagues, I fear that their attacks on P.C. exhibit a large dose of political hypocrisy and that the whole issue is a smokescreen for an attack on critical multiculturalism and other progressive initiatives which would expand and reform the academic curricula and bring in voices and cultures excluded in standard curricula, thus providing access to ideas and material that conservatives oppose. Therefore, I think that right-wing "Political Hypocrisy" (P.H.) is what we should really be on the watch for, rather than the P.C. that our conservative colleagues malign.

Putting the campaign against P.C. in its historical and social context, Scatamburlo provides a detailed study of the media, academic, and political campaigns to undermine progressive ideals and initiatives both inside and outside of the academy. In her study, she engages some of the major texts made popular in the New Right's culture war by ideologues such as Allan Bloom, Dinesh D'Souza, Roger Kimball, Camille Paglia, and others, and provides an ideological critique of their underlying presuppositions and biases. Scatamburlo also depicts the mainstream media's complicity in promulgating anti-P.C. discourse and analyzes the rhetorical strategies employed by the media in their coverage of P.C.

While Scatamburlo looks at the role of the Right in creating the "myth" that a campaign to repressively impose an agenda of political correctness is endangering academic freedom and education, she also critiques the P.C. ethos, which while over exaggerated by the Right for rhetorical effect, has nonetheless permeated some Left constituencies and led to overzealous attacks on "politically incorrect" discourse and behavior, which in turn have been endlessly propagated and exaggerated by the Right and in the media.

Scatamburlo locates the P.C. phenomenon both theoretically and politically between the linguistic turn in social theory and the rise of identity politics. In doing so, she is able to discern many of the current problems that plague leftist thought and politics in general—problems and contradictions which have made the right-wing vision of contemporary campus politics all the more palatable to the general public. She argues that in many instances, the discursive skirmishes over P.C. language and the representational purism of identity politics amount, in the end, to a form of ludic politics, in that so much of P.C. has been concerned solely with language and gestures, while ignoring more substantive issues. For Scatamburlo, P.C. politics are critiqued not for being too radical, but for not being radical enough, for being in some sense a form of pseudo-radicalism, that restricts politics to the linguistic and/or textual domains.

Thus, Scatamburlo critiques both the right-wing campaign against P.C. as well as the left-wing tendencies that generated and made plausible some forms of rightist criticism. She takes a critical look at dominant trends in leftist theory and politics with the intent of moving beyond political correctness, identity politics, the postmodern descent into discourse, and liberal forms of multiculturalism in order to preserve what she sees as more emancipatory and progressive theoretical and political perspectives. Since the struggle over P.C. continues unabated and because one expects that the culture wars will continue well into the next millennium, this is an extremely timely and provocative study that addresses an issue of utmost importance. For those who want to know what the P.C. controversy is all about, this is the book.

Introduction

The "Newt" Amerika

The tradition of the oppressed teaches us that the 'state of emergency' in which we live is not the exception but the rule. (Benjamin, 1969:257)

Toto, I have the feeling we're not in Kansas anymore. (Dorothy, in *The Wizard of Oz*)

Walter Benjamin's rivetting observation provides a reminder that the "state of emergency" and the conditions of degradation and subordination are pervasive. They are, in short, the rule rather than the exception. However, even a cursory glance at the contemporary social landscape seems to suggest that the state of emergency has somehow intensified. As we approach the dawning of a new millennium, the Dickensianization of our society is becoming all the more apparent—while the financial pundits of *Fortune* and *Business Week* boast about the record profits of corporate enterprise and the net worth of capitalist moguls, the material conditions of large sectors of the population continue to deteriorate. At the present historical juncture, in excess of thirty million Americans live below the poverty line; more than seven million are unemployed;[1] real wages for average workers are plummeting;[2] homeless figures are on the rise[3] and the chasm between rich and poor continues to widen.[4] For countless citizens, the everyday struggles for mere sustenance have been vitiated by the greed of a predatory global capitalism which lurks furtively in search of its next victim in the form of restructuring, downsizing, and flexible specialization.

Everyday in America, the world's wealthiest nation, one out of four children is born into poverty (Sklar, 1995:113). For millions of disillusioned and disenfranchised youth, the hope of attaining the American dream of yesteryear has become a living nightmare[5] Increasingly, today's teens, impelled by intense feelings of alienation, turn to suicide; others escape temporarily to drug-induced utopias and still others find comfort in gangs—the new havens in an otherwise heartless world.[6] Record numbers of disaffected White youth have joined citizen militias and white supremacist organizations (McLaren, 1997:9) in their search for a secure and meaningful identity in an era marked by uncertainty and ambiguity. Too many of them are able to find meaning only in their capacity to hate non-whites so they have donned the blood-stained sheets and adopted the hateful bravado of their Klan forefathers. Violence has become such a pervasive feature of our social topography that saying we inhabit a "predatory culture" is hardly an over-statement.[7]

Of course, social relations of oppression and alienation have always existed. But what makes this moment particularly invidious is the resurgence of the New Right[8] armed with initiatives designed to exacerbate the already deplorable circumstances of millions of Americans.[9] New Right Gingrichites are seeking, through the introduction of measures more Draconian than any of those initiated during the heyday of the Reagan-Bush administration, to lead the American public down a path that will be golden for a few and perilous for most. In the guise of fiscal restraint and deficit reduction, the New Right has launched an all-out assault on what remains of the social safety net by targeting programs intended to assist the disadvantaged. All the while, it remains conspicuously silent about the $5 billion spent weekly on military operations.[10]

The *Contract With America* or, as it has been more aptly labelled, the *Contract On America*, is devised to benefit those who already profit from the ravages of capitalism—profits garnered from the misery of large sectors of the population. In addition to fortifying what Chomsky (1995) calls the hidden welfare state for the rich, the *Contract* also epitomizes the regressively sexist, homophobic, xenophobic, and racist agendas of the New Right—a loose but lethal coalition of Christian fundamentalists, intellectual provocateurs, think-tank policy analysts, and cultural conservatives.

With an estimated 1.7 million members, 1425 local chapters, a budget in excess of $25 million and substantial control over the Republican apparatus in at least thirty-one states, Ralph Reed's Christian Coalition represents a formidable presence in contemporary American politics. The religious Right's catapulting of the Republicans to Capitol Hill and its recent unveiling of the *Contract with the American Family* poses a serious threat to civil rights, the arts, and education as the Coalition and Republicans seek to restore the "Law of the Father" to the seditious and immoral wasteland created by the dark forces of liberalism,[11] popular culture, rap music, and Hollywood film.[12]

In keeping with a long-standing conservative tradition, the hobgoblin of the 1960s and its "excesses" has once again emerged as the latter-day equivalent of the Red Menace. The wrath once directed outwards toward Communists and their sympathesizers has been redirected inwards toward women, minority groups, and "radical intellectuals." Conservatives, vowing to end the alleged "reverse discrimination" engendered by affirmative action, are currently dismantling equity initiatives. Pete Wilson's successful bid to end affirmative action at the University of California has already spawned similar measures at other institutions. The targeting of affirmative action is but one of several ploys in a right-wing agenda that aims to push the buttons of racial prejudice, and a deep-rooted racial animosity has been a major motivating factor in the backlash against the democratic gains of the civil rights movement. In short, affirmative action has become the Willie Horton of contemporary politics.[13]

Moreover, the wars on welfare and crime amount, in the end, to little more than thinly veiled attacks on racial and ethnic minorities and the poor. Capitalizing on the widespread "white panic," promulgated largely by the mainstream media, the New Right has successfully demonized nonwhites as drug addicts, welfare cheats, gang warriors, and undesirable, criminal elements.[14] This panic and the concomitant paramilitary approach to law and order have, in turn, lent themselves to a reconfiguration of social space in the form of "guarded" communities.[15] This militarization of urban life, so hauntingly described by Mike Davis (1990), has more recently been accompanied by the growth of a prison industrial complex. In fact, the building of prisons seems to be the New Right's answer to the lack of adequate public housing. As education and social

assistance budgets are being brutally slashed, the "crime industry" has gained momentum even though crime rates have
not changed significantly in the last two decades.[16] What *has*
escalated, however, is the infatuation with incarceration, which
is unmatched almost anywhere in the world or at any other
time in American history (Chomsky, 1995; Davis, 1995). In fact,
the United States is number one when it comes to incarcerat-
ing its own citizens—especially Black and Latino males—many
of whom are victims of the racially biased "war on drugs."[17]
This obsession, however, must be understood in broader terms,
as a predictable manifestation of the *criminalization* of non-
whites and the regnant social and cultural practices of constructing the "*other*" as violent, irrational and treacherous.[18] In
the endless barrage of mass media images, ranging from Hollywood films, pseudo-docudramas such as *Cops* and mainstream
reportage of crime, racial coding plays a pivotal role in the
criminalization and stigmatization of non-whites (especially
Black males).[19]

Yet it is precisely this distorted collective "common sense"[20]
which enables racist scholarship such as that expounded in
Charles Murray and Richard Herrnstein's 845-page tome, *The
Bell Curve*, and more recently in Dinesh D'Souza's *The End of
Racism*, to receive widespread, and even respectable attention.[21]
While the resurgence of overtly racist viewpoints (parading
under the guise of scientific empiricism) is disturbing, it cannot be interpreted as a sudden and isolated aberration, for the
mind-set of neocolonialism continues to shape the "underlying metaphors of white capitalist patriarchy" (hooks, 1994:6).
Despite the shifting terrain of racist articulations and the various spheres where they are manifest, they nonetheless have
their anchorage in what Goldberg (1990:301) calls the
"preconceptual grounds of racist discourse" which consists of
"those factors of power . . . that directly enable the expression
of racist discourse."

That *The Bell Curve* was released shortly before the November 1994 elections should come as no surprise for it is the
perfect ideological accoutrement to a political and social
agenda which embraces anti-immigration policies such as Pete
Wilson's Proposition 187, fiscal conservatism, anti-affirmative
action campaigns, "three strikes and you're out" policies and

prison culture. Furthermore, the findings of Murray and Herrnstein and their barnacled appeals to eugenics and genetic determinism are being used by New Right mandarins to attack government educational programs designed to assist disadvantaged students, housing policy, and social welfare. Quite simply, eugenicist arguments are being used to justify regressive social policy initiatives[22] The most disturbing aspect of this campaign of hate politics is that so many Whites are buying into the rhetoric in increasingly alarming numbers (Hacker, 1995).

Many have dubbed the *Newt-onian* coup the "white man's revolution," and it is hard to deny that White hostility is indeed a growing cultural phenomenon. The hostility is, by and large, grounded in economic uncertainty, the fear of un- and under-employment among segments of the disillusioned and demoralized working and middle classes, and a profound mistrust of government. Nevertheless, the New Right has secured its hegemony over public opinion on red-button issues (i.e. affirmative action, immigration, crime) by manipulating the realm of *cultural* politics. By using buzzwords, images, and sound bites, the New Right has proven its mastery at exploiting simmering resentments and scapegoating women, minorities, and the poor. The ever-shrewd and perceptive Patrick Buchanan once remarked that:

> Culture is the Ho Chi Minh trail of power; you surrender that province and you lose America.[23]

Buchanan's statement epitomizes the strategies of the New Right which, for some time, have relied upon the cultural and ideological demonization of ideas that could loosely be described as leftist or liberal.[24] Indeed, railing against the 1960s has been a pillar of the Right's agenda for more than two decades.[25] In many respects, this backlash mentality informs the Republican assault on the Clinton administration. Clinton is projected as the Sixties incarnate—a product of that decade who smoked pot (but of course, never inhaled) and dodged the draft; whose wife, Hilary, is the epitome of the feminist movement gone awry; and whose supposed commitment to a "multicultural" cabinet are the embodiment of Sixties-style radicalism.[26] Despite the fact that Clinton has moved even further to the Right in the last few years, the subtext of the right-wing offensive clearly reveals their fixation on anything which could even remotely be related to the 1960s.

In *The Ideology of the New Right*, Ruth Levitas (1986) argues that the conservative attempt to control the cultural sphere is motivated by economics. Indeed, the backbone of conservative ideology is rooted in economics and the ideas of personal responsibility, individualism, and markets; however, as Gramsci (1971) perceptively noted many years ago, the creation of consent (or willing assent) to a particular ideology or socio-political vision is often played out in the cultural terrain. For conservatives, culture and economics are inextricably intertwined, since their correlation is necessary for both the efficient functioning of capitalism and the hegemony of White, patriarchal ideology. The New Right, however, has consciously moved away from an exclusive emphasis on economics to an emphasis on culture and the acknowledgement that the "politics that carry us into the twenty-first century will be based . . . on culture."[27] One need only look to Rush Limbaugh's latest book *See, I Told You So*, where he quotes Antonio Gramsci speaking of the "long march through the institutions" (especially educational institutions) and expounds the importance of the cultural arena (Limbaugh, 1994:87).[28] As McLaren (1995) has aptly pointed out, the agenda of the New World Order necessitates the creation of a new "moral order at home," and culture inevitably becomes the battlefield upon which the struggle for control over collective consciousness is ultimately waged.[29]

To this end, attacking the 1960s provides an effective rhetorical strategy. Indeed, back in 1964, Ronald Reagan was pontificating about the long-hairs on campuses; twenty-seven years later, George Bush was chastising the political correctness of tenured radicals in his infamous University of Michigan address; at a recent conference sponsored by the right-wing *Accuracy In Academe*, Bob Dole was expounding on anti-Americanism in education; and at the 1995 Christian Coalition's "Road To Victory" jamboree, Pat Buchanan brought down the house by deriding the "secular humanists in sandals and beads" who run the Department of Education (which conservatives want to disband).[30] Time and circumstances may have changed, but the song, as they say, remains the same.

Sixties bashing is by no means restricted to the sacrosanct corridors of Washington, for it is manifest in the broader terrain of popular culture. It is estimated that an audience of twenty million "Dittoheads" delight in Rush Limbaugh's daily harangues against "femi-Nazis," "tree-hugging environmentalists," "homosexuals," "long-haired dope smoking peace pansies," and other sordid "limousine liberals" whose politics allegedly crystallized during the murky mayhem of the 1960s. Limbaugh's brand of populism and his bombastic manner have made him the spokesperson, par excellence, for the "average Joes" allegedly abandoned by the liberal elite and Big Government—a remarkable feat for a man whose estimated income over the last two years was $25 million. That most of Limbaugh's devotees are disaffected white males is no surprise, for he provides ready-made simplistic explanations, gives form to their resentments, provides them with a basis for a new shared "identity," and preys upon their insecurities about employment prospects. Undoubtedly, these concerns are very real in the bleak Hobbesian climate of late capitalism but creating *enemies within* and making them scapegoats is, after all, far simpler and more entertaining than explaining the structural shifts in global capitalism largely responsible for the precarious job market and actual declines in income.[31] The appeal of "shock jock" Howard Stern also rests on a form of pro-big business, right-wing libertarian, cultural populism and an antediluvian nostalgia for the days when women (unless they are Stern groupies) and minorities knew their place. From the garishness of Limbaugh and Stern to the intellectual dishonesty of Charles Murray, Richard Herrnstein, and Dinesh D'Souza, the New Right has seized the airwaves and the best-seller lists by promoting a rather brutish brand of reactionary politics and offering a return to a mythical pre-1960s Shangri-La—a retreat into social amnesia. Should anyone doubt the romantic nostalgia which undergirds the New Right's agenda, one need only point to Paul Weyrich, one of the major architects of cultural conservatism, and his appeals for a 1950s America.[32]

Like the "Know-Nothings" of the mid-nineteenth century, whose call to arms was a defence of "real" Americans against the invasion of immigrants, the strategy of today's New Right relies on similar methods of demonizing and dehumanizing the "other(s)" and exploiting the "natural *fear of difference*"—a strategy that Umberto Eco (1995:58) equates with the early stages of fascism. The success of talk radio bigots and reactionary agendas is, of course, rooted largely in what Goldstein (1995) and others have called the "angry white male syndrome"—a factor which played a decisive role in the 1994 elections. As Goldstein (1995:25) claims:

> there have always been angry white men. What's new is their emergence as a political bloc. These guys are on a well-publicized rampage, howling about their loss of power, casting themselves as victims and everyone else as their oppressors.

The angry cry of the White male underlines the populist strategy utilized in the discourses of politicians and "entertainers" like Limbaugh and Stern who, no longer content with simply maintaining the status quo which has benefitted their ranks for years, are on a mission to roll back many of the gains won by the social movements of the 1960s and 1970s. More frightening still are the patriotically zealous invitations by radio personalities like G. Gordon Liddy to use violence to defend hearth and home. Of course, the most radical manifestation of the angry White male syndrome is the current growth of militia movements, whose violent tendencies were most tragically displayed in the Oklahoma City bombing.

These tendencies, however, must be understood in relation to the New Right's populist underpinnings and its successful ideological attempts at representing itself as on the side of the little people, the common folk, against the forces of big government and the so-called liberal establishment. Ideologically, New Right mandarins have positioned themselves, not only against "them," but perhaps more disturbingly as part of an imagined community of "us."[33] In this case, the "us" refers to "real" Americans—White, conservative, God-fearing, citizens.

Despite this sobering context and the urgent need to cultivate a progressive coalitional politics, we are witnessing the entrenchment of conservatism in the public. Significantly of late, this has been accomplished through the use of anti-"political correctness" rhetoric.[34]

P.C. Hysteria

The popularity currently enjoyed by reactionaries and their policies must be understood not only in the broader context of the assault on the 1960s, but also as the culmination of another hysteria which began in the early 1990s: the P.C. scare, itself a carefully crafted indictment of the 1960s, Left activism and multiculturalism. Having launched P.C. into mainstream consciousness with the help of the media, the New Right prepared the ground for the current proliferation of reactionary agendas. Now that the epithet P.C. can be easily summoned to describe any and all who object to the regressive politics touted by the New Right, conservatives have in their possession a master trope, which enables them to summarily dismiss criticism and quell dissent. Furthermore, the anti-P.C. rhetoric, cultivated by conservative gurus in the parlours of corporate sponsored think-tanks and sensationalized by the media, has enabled the Right to project itself as moderate and objective in relation to Left-wing lunatics still enamoured with Sixties-style idealism. Despite the varied shortcomings of Robert Hughes's assessment of the culture wars in *Culture of Complaint*, he accurately points out that in recent years, conservatives have had complete, almost unopposed "success in labelling as left-wing ordinary agendas and desires that, in a saner polity, would be seen as ideologically neutral" (1993:34)[35] Moreover, the negative connotations that P.C. has assumed since its appropriation by the Right has enabled them to win the hearts and minds of many "liberals." Merely to utter one's disdain about the persistence of social injustice invites the label of P.C. and the contempt of liberals and conservatives alike. P.C., however, is increasingly used to condone the most racist of sentiments in the name of free speech and free inquiry. The brouhaha that emerged following the release of Murray and Herrnstein's *The Bell Curve* is a case in point. Arguing that the topics of genes, intelligence and race were taboo given the P.C. atmosphere, several conservative and even liberal commentators claimed that the "findings" of the authors would never be granted the airing they deserved because of left-wing thought police (the book, of course, became a national best-seller and was debated and discussed in the media extensively—so much for the forces of P.C.!).[36] That such an explanation has become hegemonic or common sensical is indicative of the power exerted by the Right over the media and public opinion.

Indeed, in the early 1990s even casual attention to the mainstream media was enough to discover that an unruly cabal of "leftists" had taken over campuses and turned them into hotbeds of radicalism.[37] Decrying the dissolution of objectivity, the decline of standards, the attack on the "Western" tradition (as though that existed as a monolithic construct) and the "fascist" control of academic institutions, conservative intellectuals and media cognoscenti managed to paint a picture of campus life reminiscent of Hieronymus Bosch's vision of hell. Suddenly, the Left—a catch-all phrase encompassing feminists, multiculturalists, deconstructionists, gays, and others—was demonized as a coterie of propagandists; as Orwellian dragoons of group-think intent on silencing free expression and imposing the edicts of "correctness." In a paradoxical shift, it was claimed that those who had once marched for the right to free speech were now vigorously creating mini "ministries of truth" that were springing up like pernicious weeds and choking out the flowers of free expression on campuses.

The headlines have waned considerably and P.C. has since found a comfortable home in the lexicon of popular parlance, describing everything from sandwiches to crayons. The phrase now floats unfettered within the culture and has been the topic of satirical *Saturday Night Live* skits, *Murphy Brown* episodes, a *Beavis and Butt-Head* segment and even a Hollywood film. While these more or less trivial instances of its invocation attest to its fashionable currency, P.C., more often than not, is invoked to stifle critical discourse. As an ideological code, P.C. operates as a device which mediates perception in the relations of public discourse—progressives and critics are now viewed as social oddballs, elements of a lunatic fringe and politically threatening extremists.

The currency of P.C. also enables it to be summoned and used in ways that decontextualize the practices and social relations that governed its design as a pejorative term. In other words, the right-wing appropriation of the term, which led to the transformation of P.C. from its original ironic use among

Leftists to a category of "deviance," is obscured. That this transformation was made possible with the assistance of right-wing think-tanks, conservative ideologues, and acquiescent journalists is rendered invisible. Hence, when critics attack policies or practices designed to further disenfranchise particular constituencies, the Gingrichs and Limbaughs of the world can claim that their ideas and views are falling prey to P.C. "special interests," while at the same time passing themselves off as representatives of the "common" interest. This, more than anything, is the potency of P.C.

While greatly exaggerated accounts of P.C. were abundant in the early media flurry, recycled from the hysterical anecdotes provided by the likes of Dinesh D'Souza, Roger Kimball, George Will, and others, it would be misleading to characterize the anti-P.C. onslaught as merely another manifestation of the backlash phenomenon. This is not to suggest that anti-P.C. does not belong to that genre; undoubtedly it does, but some of the ridiculous excesses of P.C. described in caricature by conservatives and embellished by the media were evident on some campuses. Amid the P.C. ballyhoo, the proclivity evident in some circles, of equating verbal uplift with veritable change not only provided the fuel for sensationalistic coverage but also deflected attention away from far more substantive issues.

Furthermore, there *has* been a tendency towards an excessive moralism among some leftists which has had the effect of curtailing critical and open dialogue. Both Barbara Epstein (1995) and bell hooks (1994) have described classroom situations where students are often reluctant to speak for fear of saying the "wrong" thing or being branded as racist, sexist, or homophobic. In addition, both discuss situations in academic circles where conformity is an unspoken rule imposed upon intellectual exchange. In particular, hooks (1994) speaks of the ostracism she was subjected to by her feminist comrades after writing an essay on the Anita Hill-Clarence Thomas proceedings and the "dissing" she received from some Black intellectuals after critiquing the views of some prominent Black thinkers. Epstein (1995) registers a similar complaint about some feminists reactions to Alice Echol's *Daring To Be Bad: Radical Feminism in America, 1967-1975.* Epstein explains that while the book is dedicated to the goals of radical feminism, it provides a critical, historical account of some of the ideological rigidities that characterized the movement under the slogan the "personal is political." She describes how some feminists suggested that anything critical of the movement should not be condoned and that any account that cast "women, especially feminists, in a bad light was sexist" (Epstein, 1995:9). Such simplistic, essentialist, knee-jerk responses certainly have no place in social movements which, as hooks and Epstein maintain, should be committed to providing the space for constructive contestation and confrontation.

Therefore, dismissing P.C. as a fantasy or assuming that the charges are false or do not exist simply because it is proclaimed by the Right undermines the possibility for a long-overdue project of critical reflection among self-proclaimed "Leftists." Thus far, many have responded to the attacks by closing ranks or calling their critics intellectual charlatans. However, if progressives hope to chart a course for political action a sincere effort must be made to engage those issues that continue to divide them, namely, the fragmentation engendered by various forms of identity politics and multiculturalism, as well as academic practices and theoretical tendencies that have widened the chasm between Left intellectuals and the world outside the academy. These issues are subsequently addressed in these pages.

The Left Writes Back?

During the apex of the conservative assault on P.C. and in the midst of the media frenzy, Left intellectuals scrambled to respond to the onslaught of charges launched against them. Many of these statements are now encapsulated in books and collections, which have proliferated in recent years. But, as is argued here, many of the ripostes to the right-wing charge of P.C. have been limited or partial at best, in terms of their weaving together of the myriad issues raised by the debate, and most have been sorely lacking in critical self-evaluation of current "Left" scholarship and practices. Overall, and at the risk of overgeneralization, these limitations can be placed into four rather loosely defined categories.

(i) ***Dismissive****:* In what I deem dismissive narratives, it is suggested that anti-P.C. rhetoric represents the "white man's last gasp" at power.[38] Such a formulation is limited in several fundamental regards. First (and perhaps inadvertently), it implies that the White male establishment has indeed forfeited the reigns of power, when in fact, the top echelons of academic institutions are still, by and large, occupied by them. Second, even if conservative white males had succumbed to feminists, multiculturalists, and radicals in the academy (which they have not), White male dominance in all other institutional spheres (government, corporate culture, media) continues unabated.[39] Furthermore, the "last gasp" explanation seriously compromises an understanding of contemporary academic and political culture. It also ignores the fact that the backlash itself has been cultivated by a large and powerful network of think-tanks and foundations lavishly funded by corporate sponsors. The financial figures and the commitment made by groups such as the National Association of Scholars to a long and protracted journey aimed at revamping higher education, implies that the anti-P.C. forces represent much more than a mere last gasp at controlling the reigns of power.

Finally, a number of texts have sought to demonstrate the "myth" of P.C. as though it existed only in the imaginations of P.C. bashers. Certainly, the Right has manipulated and exaggerated its charge of P.C., but one cannot ignore that there have been instances where a rigid orthodoxy has taken form both inside and outside the academy. Therefore, to dismiss P.C. as a myth or to treat it as a red herring created by the Right ignores an important set of questions and simultaneously closes off the possibility of exploring them.

(ii) ***Decontextualized****:* Many of the reports in circulation treat the anti-P.C. insurrection as though it had suddenly sprung up in response to Leftist overtures in college classrooms, while others treat it solely as an attack on the university—which it is, but it is much more than that. These narratives fail to acknowledge that the campaign against P.C. was anything but reactive; rather, it was part of a much broader right-wing counterrevolution designed to restore conservatism to higher education and other spheres, an effort that began long before P.C. became a household word. Corporate-funded think-tanks and conservative groups began mapping out their plans to "reclaim the academy" in the early 1980s. Right-wingers assumed the role of policing the education system by creating an apparatus of power-knowledge (through its network of think-tanks and media links) which sought to establish the boundaries within which "normal," "moral" and "socially responsible" education would be defined. They merely began to promulgate their private agenda for education publicly in the early 1990s.

Indeed, the "victory" in the Gulf War made the early 1990s the most opportune time to thrust P.C. into national consciousness.[40] Riding high on a renewed sense of patriotism at a time when many Americans were still strangling themselves with yellow ribbons and revelling in a sea of "New World Order" jingoism, the New Right seized the moment to create a new enemy within. Having kicked the "Vietnam syndrome," what better way to discredit and undermine any "dangerous" memories of the 1960s than to initiate "Operation Campus Storm," and attack those few who were allegedly still clinging to the egalitarian idealism of that decade—the P.C. tenured radicals. For conservatives, anything even remotely related to the 1960s— affirmative action, civil rights, the women's movement—became the targets for censure. These "new" enemies were, in the paranoid minds of conservatives like George Will, more insidious than the threat posed by Saddam Hussein himself.[41] And now as the culture wars continue to rage, one can see the efficacy of P.C. in demonizing all those who dare dissent from the "patriotically correct" agenda of the New Right. Quite simply, the campaign against P.C. has been one of the most successful ideological exercises in the history of the Right.

(iii) *Depoliticized:* There has also been a tendency to treat P.C. merely as an attack on the university. Undoubtedly it is, but it represents something much more insidious than skirmishes over curricular inclusion and exclusion. Unfortunately, many have chosen to deal with the implications of P.C. and the culture wars solely in terms of academic practices, rather than addressing them in much broader political and social terms. In such narratives, the struggles in the university are hermeneutically sealed off from the broader struggles of everyday life and the battle over textual representation in the curriculum becomes the be-all and end-all of politics.

In many respects this logic informs the pedagogical prescription to "teach the conflicts." In fact, this position was one of the most widely touted pedagogical "solutions" offered as a way out of the impasse generated by the "culture wars." This liberal formulation, however, reveals a number of shortcomings, not least of which is its inability to adequately contextualize and historicize these "conflicts." Suggestions to "teach the conflicts" tend to treat both sides (the liberal pluralists and the conservative traditionalists) as though they are equally weighted in terms of political power, thereby obscuring real power differentials. This posturing also ignores the fact that there are other "sides" which do not fit so easily into neat categorizations such as liberal pluralism versus conservative traditionalism. Many radical critics of current educational practices cannot be categorized under the umbrella of liberal pluralism. Indeed, several would eschew such a label.

Another rather limited formulation has involved the championing of liberal forms of multiculturalism in the name of "diversity." In these discourses, "difference" is managed and classified into fixed and rigid categories which actually serve to subvert the differences within "difference." In other instances, lip service is paid to cultural distinctions and, in the interest of inclusion, "multicultural" texts are "added-on" to an already existing schema which continues to be Eurocentric at its core. This tolerance of "difference" advocated in the name of some benevolent liberal principle represents, as Audré Lorde (1984:111) states, the "grossest reformism." On the other hand, there has also been a tendency in some "leftist" camps to espouse a sort of terminological or representational purism that often gets articulated under the rubric of "identity politics." Here, the political is often equated with the practice of destabilizing or decentering dominant systems of representation, or reduced to a form of metaphorical displacement—an advocacy of certain verbal and symbolic behaviors. In these formulations, "difference" is fetishized to such an extent that it is often assumed that there exists an authentic "female" or "African-American" experience or being-in-the-world, and that one's experience or social location offers a special authority from which to speak. In its most essentialist manifestations, it is assumed that a group's culture or collective experience cannot be understood by an "outsider," or as McLaren (1995:125) puts it, "one is asked to show one's identity papers before dialogue can begin." This pattern of essentialist posturing and the separatist tendencies it engenders has not and cannot provide a base for a viable political project. As such, both the depoliticized and politically disabling tendencies of current formulations are addressed.

(iv) *Defensive:* Of all possible rejoinders, the "defensive" best describes the posture assumed by several intellectuals who have attempted to respond to the charges of academic treachery and theory fetishism lodged against them, and it is by far the most disturbing. Here, the attack on P.C. is perceived simply as a form of anti-intellectualism by people who really just don't know any better. Intellectuals, responding to what is basically a "legitimation" crisis, assume a defensive stance, lamenting the "war against theory," the gross "misrepresentations" of their scholarship, and the rising tide of anti-intellectualism which they blame for their woes. Surely, anti-intellectualism has strong roots within American culture, a tendency most extensively addressed by Richard Hofstadter (1962); however, a simple appeal to the forces of anti-intellectualism as the *only* plausible explanation for the success of the anti-P.C. campaign is merely a convenient excuse for some Leftist intellectuals whose careerism has superseded any effort to reach a public other than their own academic cohort. Indeed, some rebuttals informed by this stance have bordered on arrogance and have merely reinscribed the self-serving binary opposition of "us" (the in-the-know intellectual aristocracy) and "them" (the hoi polloi outside the fray of high falutin theorizing).

Moreover, merely blaming the forces of anti-intellectualism does not adequately address *why* the New Right has been winning the culture wars, *why* their version of events has been so widely accepted, and *why* their regressive agenda has been readily embraced by large sectors of the population. These are questions that must be explored and they require not indignant, self-aggrandizing defences of "theory" or the "life of the intellect," but thoughtful, sustained and self-critical examinations of the dominant currents in Leftist thought and politics. Unfortunately, rather than engaging in honest self-evaluations about what may be deficient, extreme, ridiculous or just plain irrelevant in their own theoretical and political discourses, many Leftists simply responded by closing rank and dismissing those unable to see the political relevance of deconstructing "texts." This observation, however, should not be read as an indictment of theory, but it would seem that adequate theorizations of the present must address not only the "textual" dimension esteemed by the literati, but material conditions and the social, political, and economic circumstances which impact everyday life.

This text, therefore, represents an effort to address some of the shortcomings and tendencies outlined above. Chapter One foregrounds an analysis of P.C. in relation to the New Right's broader "war of position," provides an historical overview of the New Right and examines the network of corporate-sponsored think-tanks undergirding their project of cultural conservatism. Chapter Two examines the ideological propensities of some of the major texts made popular by the New Right's "ideas industry" and explores the rhetorical strategies employed by conservative authors in their defence of the "Western tradition." In addition, it engages the issues raised by the debates over speech codes; explores the demonization of feminism and multiculturalism by anti-P.C. forces, and addresses the recent controversy spawned by the publication of Herrnstein and Murray's *The Bell Curve* and D'Souza's *The End of Racism*. Chapter Three provides an analysis of the mainstream media's complicity in propagating anti-P.C. sentiment by focussing on the unarticulated presuppositions that informed the media's (and more specifically, *Newsweek*'s) coverage of P.C. Far from providing an "objective" account of campus politics, the media figured prominently in promoting the myth of a left-wing takeover of universities and were instrumental in making P.C. a household term. Chapter Four takes up current theoretical, pedagogical and political issues which have been hotly debated among leftists, including the "linguistic turn" in social theory, identity politics, and multiculturalism. While this may seem like a neat and functional categorization, it is in some ways deceiving, for the themes discussed in each of the chapters are inextricably intertwined since I believe that many of the New Right's current successes must be understood in relation to some disturbing developments in both leftist thought and leftist politics in general.

Nonetheless, I do not purport to provide definitive answers, irrefutable proof or tidy solutions to theoretical foibles and political woes, for such an effort would be an exercise in futility. Rather this book must be read as an attempt to re-contextualize the issues raised by P.C. and to explore the sorts of questions leftists might want to start exploring in light of the New Right's recent resurgence. The purpose or pattern which connects the diverse strands of this treatise is to draw attention to the need for progressive leftists to reassess their role as public intellectuals and cultural workers and, more important, to rethink the relationship between theory and practice. In this conservative era, the goal of Left cultural workers must be, not merely to decenter existing knowledges or re-vamp curricula, but to find ways to use educational institutions to create social change. Those committed to such goals must now embark upon the task of creating "activist" knowledge rather than mere "academic" knowledge. Michael Apple (1995) reminds us that there is a danger on the Left of losing a sense of collective memory, of forgetting the hard work and political *organizing* which it took to put even a limited vision of equality on the social and educational agenda. To that end, this book is offered, in part, as an attempt to reclaim those "dangerous" memories.

Notes

1. According to Sklar (1995:125-126), official statistics indicate that some 7.5 million people are unemployed and 2.5 million people who worked full-time, year round, in 1994, still found themselves below the official poverty line.

2. Todd Gitlin (1995:225) points out that between 1973 and 1994, average real wages fell by 18.8 percent.

3. Although ascertaining the number of homeless is somewhat difficult, according to official statistics, it is estimated that two million or more are forced to live on the streets or in makeshift shelters and the numbers continue to escalate (Parenti, 1996:8).

4. In his attempt to illuminate the vast difference between the rich and the poor in the United States, Chomsky (1995:22) points out that the gap between them within the United States is "surpassed only by a group of 70 households in a former leper colony in Hawaii." Similarly, Sklar (1995:113) maintains that the United States is now experiencing the highest rate of economic inequality since 1929.

5. · In his book, *Fugitive Cultures*, Henry Giroux describes the plight of today's youth in disturbing detail and reveals the hypocrisy of the New Right, which despite its "family values" rhetoric, is currently waging a vicious assault on American youth. Furthermore, Giroux argues that the American dream of past generations has become the nightmare of contemporary youth. He writes:

    > The dreams of a better life that were on the horizon for earlier generations of youth appear dysfunctional within a declining economy that condemns a vast number of working-class white and black youth to minimum-wage, low-skill, part-time work. Youth between the ages of fifteen and twenty-nine not only have the highest unemployment rate in the labor market, but polls further indicate "that 75% think they will be worse off than their parents" (Giroux, 1996:12).

6. For a disturbing, yet eye-opening examination of the situation of contemporary youth, see Ferguson (1994); Foster (1994); Rodriguez (1994); Ventura (1994); and Vogel (1994).

7. For a provocative look at the predatory tendencies in contemporary culture, see McLaren's (1995) introduction to his book, *Critical Pedagogy and Predatory Culture*.

8. Throughout this treatise, I make reference to the New Right and a fragmented Left. For some this demarcation may intimate some kind

of binary opposition and as such requires some degree of clarification. I am *not* suggesting that the New Right is homogenous, united, or conflict-free for that would be a naive assertion. In fact, there are many factions within the New Right, ranging from the ultra-conservatism of the religious Right, the libertarian zealotry of right-wing militia movements, to the more moderate conservatism espoused by various members of the Republican party. Despite these differences, there is nonetheless, some agreement that the New Right consists of (1) a loose amalgam of different sets of interests that is held together by a sometimes contradictory and uneasy blend of many strands of political thought (see Chapter One), and (2) that it demonstrates a ready capacity for developing forms of populist, political rhetoric that both produce and play upon popular concerns and discontents (Apple, 1989; Cohen et al., 1986; Kenway, 1990; Levitas, 1986). There is and has always been a more coherent, unifying strategy among right-wing conservatives, while the contemporary Left has been distinguished by its incoherency, especially since the advent of identity-based politics.

9.   In the November, 1994 election, Republicans gained fifty-two house seats, eight senate seats, eleven governorships, and 472 state legislative seats, signalling the largest single transfer of power from a majority party to a minority party in the twentieth century.

10. According to the Center for Defence Information (CDI), the military budget of the United States is nearly as large as the military budgets of all the other nations in the world combined. The country spends $5 billion every week, $700 million per day—on military expenditures, and Congress is currently attempting to increase that figure. This figure becomes all the more ludicrous when one analyzes it comparatively. In 1994, the federal government spent $17 billion on Aid to Families with Dependent Children (AFDC), child support enforcement and child care—all of which have been targeted by the Republican Congress for cutbacks—yet $31 billion will be spent to build twenty more unneeded B-2 bombers (Sklar, 1995:127).

11. The November 1994 elections saw the largest turnout of religious voters in modern American history. Exit polls showed that 33.3 percent of all voters were self-identified born again evangelicals or pro-family Roman Catholics. Of that 33.3 percent more than 70 percent voted Republican (Reed, 1995).

12. Writing in *The Nation*, Katha Pollitt (1995:9) referred to Senator Dole's speech about the evils of popular culture as the most discussed "piece of political oratory since Mark Antony's eulogy for Julius Caesar." Dole's tirade against media culture for depicting lascivious sex and raucous violence, however, was carefully measured and selective to ensure that high-profile Republican celebrities were not branded with

Dole's righteous fireiron. For example, fellow Republican Arnold Schwarznegger's *True Lies*–a film replete with violent imagery and massive carnage—was listed by Dole as a family friendly film.

13. William Robert Horton, nicknamed "Willie" by white news commentators during the 1988 presidential campaign, became a widely known symbol of the "menacing black criminal" (Feagin & Vera, 1995:114). During the 1988 presidential campaign, Horton had been released on a weekend furlough in the state of Massachusetts (the home state of Democratic presidential candidate, Michael Dukakis). During his furlough, Horton murdered a young gas station manager. Shortly thereafter Republicans began to run a series of paid television advertisements about crime which many argue played unnecessarily upon racial fears. In their book *White Racism*, Feagin and Vera (1995) devote almost an entire chapter to the Willie Horton fiasco and persuasively argue that the selection of Horton as poster-boy for the war against crime clearly reveals racist undertones. The image of Horton still resonates within American popular culture and, as several commentators have suggested, the recent attacks on affirmative action invoke those resonant images. Indeed, Raskin (1995:33) points out that the Republican Party, decided to ride White resentment by making affirmative action "the Willie Horton of 1996," while another pundit quipped that the attack on affirmative action was the equivalent to Willie Horton's "gonna get your alma mater."

14. I am appropriating the phrase "white panic" from Henry Giroux (1995:12), who argues that the "elements of this panic are rooted . . . in a growing fear among the white middle class over the declining quality of social, political and economic life." In American culture, where racial coding plays a significant role in constructing the evil Other(s), non-whites are scapegoated as the source of problems which actually stem from structural relations.

15. For a discussion of this trend, especially in multiracial and multiethnic states like California, see Maharidge (1994).

16. In a lengthy article written for *Z Magazine*, Noam Chomsky (1995) argues that the increase in the number of people incarcerated in the United States is indicative of a policy intended to control what he calls the "surplus" population.

17. The racially biased nature of the war on drugs is particularly evident when one considers the fact that while three out of every four drug users are white, it is non-whites who make up the bulk of those arrested and convicted for drug-related offenses. Sklar (1995:129) points out that the number of those convicted of drug offenses as a share of the federal prison population skyrocketed from 16 percent of inmates in 1970 to 61 percent in 1993, and is expected to grow to 72 percent by 1997.

18. The Oklahoma tragedy is a telling example of such practices. In the early reportage of the bombing incident, it was *assumed* that the blast was the work of Middle Eastern terrorists. That the individuals responsible for the carnage in Oklahoma could be home-grown, all-American white boys, escaped the collective consciousness of white America. Patricia Williams (1995:782) also documents how the media coverage of the event moved from speaking about "those people," "Middle Eastern," "thuggish, terrorist types" to a flowery discourse which cautioned against stereotyping and castigating all militias and their "individual" members.

19. This was particularly evident in the weeks following O.J. Simpson's arrest for the double murder of his ex-wife, Nicole Brown and her friend, Ronald Goldman when *Time* ran a feature story with Simpson's "darkened" complexion emblazoned on the cover. While the magazine eventually apologized for embellishing the photograph, it is obvious that the attempt to make Simpson appear "blacker" is evidence of the mainstream media's practice of racial coding.

20. This phrase is being employed here in a Gramscian sense. For an enlightening account of the ways in which media have contributed in making racist ideology part of collective "common sense," see Feagin and Vera (1995) and Giroux (1996).

21. *The Bell Curve* and *The End Of Racism* are discussed in greater detail in Chapter Two.

22. The Pioneer Fund, an organization known for funding eugenicist tracts, including those authored by Philippe Rushton, has also been a vigorous supporter of Proposition 187 in California. The fund helps to publish research which is then used and invoked as justification to cut social programs, especially those geared towards minorities and the poor.

23. Patrick Buchanan, cited in Berube, 1994.

24. In *The Hard Road To Renewal*, Stuart Hall (1988) discusses how this strategy of ideological demonization was employed by Margaret Thatcher in Britain.

25. Of course, this does not insinuate that conservatives did not have a target for contempt prior to the 1960s. Conservatives of yesterday shared a disdain for the liberalism spawned by Roosevelt's New Deal. Today, the New Right attacks both the economic and social programs created during the 1930s as well as the cultural changes engendered by the social movements of the 1960s and the counterculture.

26. One is reminded of Newt Gingrich's smear of Bill Clinton as a "countercultural McGovernite." In addition, this posturing was particularly evident during the 1996 presidential campaign. Republicans, capitalizing on a recent report about an increase in drug use among

teens, repeatedly summoned Clinton's "marijuana smoking" days and Clinton's draft-dodging was often contrasted to Bob Dole's allegedly sterling service record.

27. Quoted from *Cultural Conservatism: Toward A New Agenda* (Washington, D.C.: Institute for Cultural Conservatism/Free Congress Research and Educational Foundation), 1987, p. 1.

28. The initial print run of two million copies for Limbaugh's second book *See, I Told You So*, set a publishing industry record and rushed to the top of the best-seller charts after its first week in stores (Bertsch, 1994).

29. Paradoxically, while the New Right has come to appreciate the interrelationship between cultural and economic imperatives, there has been a tendency in many Leftist quarters to neglect political economy and to valorize a form of cultural politics that limits it to the realm of the discursive and the textual—a development addressed in Chapter Four.

30. For further commentary on the Christian Coalitions "Road To Victory" gathering, see Diamond 1995(c).

31. For discussions of Limbaugh's right-wing populism, see Ivins (1995); Talbot (1995); and Wilentz (1995). See also *FAIR's* publication *The Way Things Aren't: Rush Limbaugh's Reign of Error* (1995).

32. See Weyrich's letter to the editor in *Mother Jones* (Jan/Feb.1996), p. 3.

33. For a discussion of symbolically constructed "imagined communities," see Anderson (1983).

34. Political Correctness will hereafter be referred to as P.C.

35. While Hughes's pretense that any agenda could ever be ideologically *neutral* relies too heavily on a form of positivist rationality which presumes that certain ideas exist outside and above the throes of ideology, his statement is nonetheless indicative of the contemporary climate of American politics.

36. See Genovese's "Living With Inequality" in *The Bell Curve Debate: History, Documents, Opinions* (New York: Random House), 1995. Genovese, a renowned Marxist historian, has recently veered to the Right and has emerged as one of the most vocal opponents of P.C. Genovese, like other intellectuals such as Christopher Lasch (prior to his untimely death), have joined the neoconservative chorus condemning the "excesses" of Sixties radicalism.

37. Conservatives, of course, have charged Leftists with "politicizing" education; yet it seems that conservatives are not immune to charges of politicization. Indeed, the recent Newt Gingrich fiasco (in which he was charged with ethics violations) is a clear indication of this prac-

tice for it was revealed that Gingrich used his course "Renewing American Civilization" as a tool to recruit students to the Republican Party and GOP Action Committees.

38. At a conference held at the University of Michigan in November, 1991 entitled *"P.C."*: *What's Behind The Frame-Up*, a number of scholars, journalists, and activists gathered to debate the P.C. controversy. One of the participants, newspaper columnist and Berkeley Afro-American Studies scholar Julianne Malveaux suggested that P.C. was the embodiment of white male fear and that the campaign against P.C. represented the "white man's last gasp." Echoing these sentiments in the *Los Angeles Times*, Ruth Rosen (Jan. 20, 1991) referred to P.C. as the "old guards last moan at the passing of a coherent world view." This stance has also been articulated in several forums and essays by Catherine Stimpson.

39. The Glass Ceiling Commission, created by George Bush's Secretary of Labor, Elizabeth Dole, revealed that White men occupy 97 percent of senior management positions in Fortune 1000 and Fortune 500 corporations. African-Americans occupy approximately one-half of one percent of these top positions, with even fewer Hispanics and Asian-Americans. Overall, in the private sector, African-American males with professional degrees still earn less than their white counterparts and the situation is even worse for African-American women (Raskin, 1995:33-41).

40. Of course, media attention to P.C. preceded the Gulf War, but the aftermath of the "victory" fury initiated a more intense round of P.C. bashing, especially after George Bush's speech at the University of Michigan.

41. In an article entitled "Literary Politics," George Will (1992:25) suggests that Lynne Cheney, then the chair of the National Endowment for the Humanities had a more difficult job than her husband Dick Cheney, then Secretary of Defence for George Bush. Will refers to Lynne Cheney as the "secretary of domestic defence" and further suggests that the "foreign adversaries" are "less dangerous, in the long run, than the domestic forces" which are "fighting against the conservation of the common culture that is the nation's cement."

Chapter 1

Backlash: Old Strategies, New Times

Clear And Present Danger?:
Political Correctness and the Academy

> This country is being systematically communized, perhaps uncon-
> sciously through its educational institutions. These institutions are
> instruments through which left-wing theories and philosophies may
> be and are taught to large groups of people by persons whom they
> respect and trust—their instructors. That process has been going on
> for years, in an insidious manner.[1]

These sentiments, expressed by Representative George
Dondero of Michigan in 1946, resound with apodictic famil-
iarity and are hardly indistinguishable from the conservative
charges launched against "left-leaning" educators during the
P.C. frenzy of the early 1990s. With the Cold War over and the
threat of "communism" buried in the graveyard of history, the
New Right and its crusading army of Norman Rockwell proto-
types set out to fabricate a stand-in for the Evil Empire. Redi-
recting the wrath once reserved for commies and pinko com-
patriots, the New Right concocted a new adversary comprised
of Left intellectuals and multicultural sympathizers, and em-
barked upon an ideological struggle to reclaim the last bas-
tion allegedly controlled by radicals—the academy. The war
waged against leftists, however, was not one of weapons, but
one of ideas. Rather than soldiers, the New Right's armies
consisted of conservative ideologues, media pundits, and academic associations such as the National Association of
Scholars.

The enemy of course, was P.C. Insisting that left-wing vigilantes were overrunning campuses all across America, the New Right sounded a "red" alert warning that higher education was being *politicized* by those attempting to impose the edicts of P.C. on unassuming faculty and students. Suddenly, those intellectuals who had begun to speak out against sedimented forms of racism, debilitating practices of patriarchy, and xenophobia were cast as anti-democratic and anti-Western. Conservatives interpreted demands for inclusive curricula, canon revision, and pedagogical reform as signals that Western civilization itself was under siege by the "new" barbarians clamoring at the gates. The menace of multiculturalism supplanted the red menace.

Those who had hoped that P.C. would disappear from public consciousness once the media onslaught subsided are undoubtedly disappointed for P.C. has become even more entrenched in the memory banks of conventional wisdom. Whether or not P.C. is the large-scale pogrom conservatives charge that it is, is quite besides the point for the label has entered the popular lexicon and is used mockingly to dismiss critical commentary and progressive initiatives, both inside and outside the walls of academe.

P.C., a phrase once used among Leftists as a form of self-mockery, has, in its right-wing appropriation, been turned on its proverbial head. Tim Brennan maintains that the Right's commandeering of the term

> follows a now familiar practice of theft—as in the singing of "We Shall Overcome" by anti-choice activists as they were carried away from abortion clinics; or in the CIA manual of covert operations in Nicaragua, which lifted the phrases of Che Guevara to support a US mercenary army. In this way, a costly history of protest is simply erased from the books, making the powerful appear to be the underdogs. (Brennan, 1991:18)

Various genealogies of the phrase have located its origins in everything from the Leninist-Left, Chairman Mao's little red book, the Black Power movement, and the New Left. In the hands of right-wing ideologues, however, P.C. has been denuded of its original ironic subtext and emptied of its historical specificity.[2] To the extent that it had any referent prior to its current application, the term was a "self-deprecating in-

joke among leftists who sometimes teased one another for con-
fusing radical gestures with radical politics" (Raskin, 1992:31).
Politically correct thus applied, in a delicately chastizing way,
to people who thought of radical political engagement as the
willingness to embrace ascetic language conventions and symbolic behaviors without assuming active political engagement.
In this sense, P.C. described a frozen politics of hollow gestures. The politically correct were criticized not for being too
radical, but for not being radical enough. Ironically then, the
phrase P.C. was first used as a sarcastic reference to those on
the Left whose political activity demonstrated a greater concern for the *form* of oppression rather than its *substance*. Apart
from that esoteric context, P.C. had no ecumenical value and
did not imply a rigid set of political positions. In other words,
P.C. never existed as a unified manifesto of ideas, viewpoints,
or ideological presuppositions.

The phrase, however, has since been seized by the New Right
and has assumed an entourage of defining characteristics.
Enforcers of today's status quo now use the term to describe
any position that challenges the virtuosity of capitalism, the
nobility of right-wing cultural values, or the notion that oppressive relations of racism and sexism are still pervasive in
America. The right-wing appropriation of the term has enabled
P.C. to become a catchall phrase for a variety of conservative
targets, embracing every imaginable cause even remotely associated with the Left. Indeed, P.C. permeates our cultural
sphere like no other soundbite in recent history. More importantly, P.C. operates as an ideological code:

> Ideological codes operate as a . . . form of control in the relations of
> public discourse. They can replicate anywhere. They organize talk,
> thinking, writing and the kinds of images and stories produced . . .
> Ideological codes may be, and perhaps often are, components of ideo-
> logical "master frames". They operate as "outriders" of that frame,
> carrying it into discursive sites where the ideology itself might be
> unassimilable . . . they operate pretty independently as devices, car-
> rying the effects but not the body of the master frame that governed
> their design. This is their power . . . this is their utility to the right-
> wing industries of ideology . . . Of course the production and opera-
> tion of ideological codes is not new, nor is it an exclusively right-wing
> device . . . But "political correctness" is specialized to focus on regu-
> lating the authority of participants in public discourse and hence re-

stricting who can be part of the making of its topics and relevances
and hence the social forms of consciousness.(Smith, 1995:27-31)

From the debates around multiculturalism and curricular reform through to affirmative action and equity incentives, P.C.
has become the master trope used to decontextualize issues,
undermine critique and circumscribe the "bounds of the expressible."

Although the Right has managed to create the illusion of a
monolithic group of P.C. crusaders, criticisms of existing pedagogical practices and power relations have been launched from
a number of various sources. Many contemporary theoretical
discourses have sought to contest, decenter and otherwise disrupt the epistemological and ontological presuppositions of
Western thought. Concomitantly, new social movements and
the development of identity-based politics have raised a series
of questions about hegemonic power/knowledge relations.
Marginalized constituencies have sought to make curricula and
education in general, more inclusive and less Eurocentric. Of
course, these demands often extend far beyond the walls of
academe and may manifest themselves in the wider social context and find their expression in the ongoing struggles for
equality and social justice. These challenges, however, have
met with vehement resistance by the self-proclaimed guardians of Western civilization.

According to conservative pundits, P.C. is the program of a
generation of campus radicals whose formative years were the
1960s and who have since achieved positions of academic influence as "tenured radicals." They claim that P.C. thought
police on American campuses are conducting witch hunts
against people with whom they disagree: conservative students,
right-wing lecturers, or professors who uphold the "canon" of
Western literature and thought. Once the crusade of far-right
crackpots, the attack on P.C. has become one of the center-
pieces in the conservative social agenda.[3] Interestingly enough,
when the P.C. "debate" is examined in terms of political power,
it no longer appears to be an "equal" struggle between the
Left and the Right, but rather the dominance of conservative
forces. The fervor of the anti-P.C. campaign, the attention accorded to the conservative stance in the mainstream media as
well as the influence of texts such as Roger Kimball's *Tenured*

Radicals and Dinesh D'Souza's *Illiberal Education,* has brought
to light both the scope and strength of conservative hegemony.
Furthermore, there is a disturbing irony in the conservative
charges of witch hunts and egregious activities on the part of
the Left, for it has been right-wing groups such as *Accuracy In
Academia* that have led concerted campaigns of harassment
against left-wing professors. Indeed, since the AIA's founding
in 1985, the organization has actively "recruited classroom
spies" and has compiled a "data base on professors" it labels
"left-wing propagandists" (Diamond, 1995[b]:26). While some
conservatives denounced the AIA after it was initially established,[4] the organization has enjoyed an increase in popularity
since the onslaught of alleged P.C. abuses have been publicized en masse in the popular press. The AIA's bulletin *Campus Report* is mainly used as a forum for recounting tales of
left-wing repression and ideological indoctrination. In 1991,
the AIA sponsored a conference in Washington, D.C. entitled
"Politically Incorrect: Fighting the Campus Thought Police"
which featured workshops such as "Affirmative Discrimination
on Campus," "Marxist Indoctrination in the Academy" and
"Fighting Liberal Fascism on Campus."[5] In January 1995, Peter LaBarbera, the executive director of AIA, promised that
the organization and its bulletin would again return to spy
tactics and increase efforts to expose the malfeasance of tenured radicals.[6]

Furthermore, conservative intellectuals, administrators and
students have routinely engaged in crusades aimed at exacer-
bating intolerance and inciting hatred. Predictably, these incidents have not attracted the degree of media attention accorded
to the "P.C. movement." One of the most notorious examples
of abuse is John Silber. A staunch right-winger, the Boston
University president has a lengthy history of tyrannical behavior ranging from unlawful firings of faculty members and head-
ing campaigns to expunge Left intellectuals to censoring student publications.[7] His egregious breaches of free speech and
acceptable conduct are well documented in a fact book compiled by concerned faculty and students from Boston University. During the apex of the P.C. brouhaha, Silber encouraged
his conservative comrades to abandon any semblance of civility toward scholars whose work they deemed "political." Given

Silber's current status as the highest paid university president in the United States, one could safely conclude that "left-wing" radicals have not taken over Boston University.

Despite the P.C. horrors endlessly recycled by conservatives, a survey cited in *The Chronicle of Higher Education* found that very few educational institutions had reported instances of campus disruptions by the "forces" of P.C.[8] Other surveys have indicated that the number of professors who identify themselves as "radical" or "Leftist" is between four and six percent, a statistic that has remained relatively constant for the last thirty years (Ohmann, 1992/93). In addition, the claims that the teaching of canonical texts has been abandoned in universities are patently false as a number of observers have demonstrated.[9] Given these circumstances, it is indeed a remarkable feat that the Right's version of campus affairs has been so readily accepted as truth, but this acceptance has less to do with the facts and more to do with the scope and strength of the New Right's apparatus. This situation therefore warrants an historical overview of the roots of the New Right, that begins, as it were, from its beginnings.

The Birth of the New Right:
From "Remnants" to Rabble-Rousers

The assault on P.C., framed by the New Right[10] and the media as a challenge to the enforced orthodoxy, one-sided debate, and brainwashing by tenured radicals is, in fact, part of a broader assault on liberal and leftist ideas in general.[11] Although conservatives have charged leftists with infiltrating campuses and wreaking havoc, it has been the *organized* presence of the Right that has sought, for several years, to refashion the academy in its own image. To break the perceived "liberal" stranglehold on the academy and other public spheres, the Right has, for the last two decades, been vigorously creating their own counter-establishment, which has grown increasingly influential within policy making circles and the mainstream media.

From the 1955 establishment of the *National Review* through to the conservative organizing of the 1960s and 1970s, what had begun as a conservative "remnant" was, by the 1980s, a powerful rabble-rousing presence on American campuses and in American politics. A large network of corporate-funded foundations and think-tanks were established in the 1970s, and by the 1980s and early 1990s, they commanded a large cache of resources enabling them to shape public opinion on several key issues, not least of which was education.[12] Now, in what may be a case of collective transference, the Right has projected its own desire to control universities onto the so-called Left-leaning politically correct. Yet the right-wing wish to control the academy has been a motivating feature of the conservative agenda for decades.

Lamenting the success of the New Deal and the creation of the welfare state, Albert Jay Nock mourned the condition of conservative politics in a 1937 essay entitled *Isaiah's Job*. Nock described what he called the conservative "remnant"—an "obscure," "inarticulate," and "unorganized" world view which, with the correct guidance and nurturing, would ultimately triumph and "come back and build a new society." What was needed, however, was a prophet who could lead "the Remnant out of its cloisters" (Blumenthal, 1988:13). That prophet, as history demonstrates, was William F. Buckley, Jr., the man often called the father of modern conservatism.

In 1951, William F. Buckley, Jr., then a mere twenty-four years old, published *God and Man at Yale: The Superstitions of "Academic Freedom"* in which he chastized the idea of academic freedom (for communists and liberals) and the independent academy. Buckley inveighed against the alleged "atheism" and secularism of professors, and suggested that universities should embrace one value system and seek to inculcate it in their students. The value system that Buckley advocated was one that would extol the virtues of capitalism and Christianity.

Given his predilection, it is not surprising that three years later, in 1954, Buckley and his brother-in-law Brent Bozell penned *McCarthy And His Enemies,* a defence of the Wisconsin Senator's illustrious career and his activities. At the tender age of twenty-eight, Buckley had become one of the most outspoken anticommunist intellectuals, and was always quick to express his disdain for what he saw as a "collectivist," "Liberal" orthodoxy in American higher education. Bemoaning the hegemony of liberals and leftists, Buckley began to sow the seeds

of a conservative counterrevolution—an enterprise whose legacy
has provided the P.C. bashers of today with both the intellectual and financial basis for their successful anti-P.C. campaign.
In the early 1950s, after his return from a short-lived stint with
the CIA,[13] Buckley began raising funds for his vision. What
was needed, in his opinion, was a publication that would provide a forum for the articulation of a conservative world view.
With a $100,000 donation from his father, a Texas born oil
wildcatter, and a little help from some of Herbert Hoover's
friends, Buckley published the first issue of *National Review* in
1955. While it shared some affinities with previous conservative publications like Albert Nock's *The Freeman*, Blumenthal
(1988:26) points out that the *National Review* was "wholly new"
and represented the views of "free-marketers, ex-Communists
and cultural conservatives." In short, it epitomized the
"fusionist" ideology which conservatives had forged. It was also
a journal where the "protracted struggle" against the Soviets
abroad and the dissidents at home was a recurring theme.
Rehashing arguments from *McCarthy And His Enemies*, Buckley
used the magazine as a vehicle for promulgating his rabid anticommunism, his contempt for liberalism and freedom of
expression. Given his intellectual history, it is farcical that
Buckley should emerge recently as a conservative spokesperson condemning leftists for stifling freedom of speech on campuses.[14] Aside from Buckley's intellectual trickery, what is more
significant is the role that he has played in establishing a firm
base of conservative ideology and in cultivating what is now a
vast network of think-tanks and foundations that generously
support and disseminate conservative scholarship.

Before Buckley's emergence as the Svengali of conservatism,
there was no "common designation for people on the right"
(Blumenthal, 1988:30). This is not to suggest that American
conservatism did not exist before the 1950s, for it did; however, it was during that decade that conservatives began the
task of reconstructing their ideology and building a long-term
movement to gain political power. It was also the first time
they agreed on the label "conservative" to identify themselves
and their agenda. The construction of a new ideology entailed
a merger of two differing, but not unrelated, strains which
had been the hallmarks of conservative and right-wing schol-

arship: a libertarianism that accentuated freedom and individualism and a traditionalism that emphasized moral order and community.[15] Coupled with the then-emergent anticommunism of the Right, this new ideology was referred to as "fusionism." Sara Diamond (1995 [a]:29) claims that:

> Fusionism . . . was the historical juncture at which right-wing activists and intellectuals focused, diversely, on the libertarian, moral-traditionalist, and emerging anticommunist strains of conservative ideology, recognized their common causes and philosophies, and began to fuse their practical agendas.

Not surprisingly, one of the leading proponents of fusionism, along with Frank Meyer and Russell Kirk, was none other than Buckley.

Taken together, Buckley's ability to articulate a vision for what would eventually be labelled conservatism and the establishment of *National Review* helped to lay the foundations for the conservative movement. Prior to the establishment of the *National Review,* conservatives had no central outlet for debate among themselves, nor for expounding their views to the unconverted. Ultimately, the *National Review* provided an instrument to unite what had been a disparate ensemble of conservative "remnants" and provided a centre from which to delineate a more coherent brand of conservative philosophy. As Blumenthal (1988:30) maintains:

> *National Review* . . . was largely responsible for giving the believers an identity as "conservatives" . . . the conservative label enabled conservatives to gloss over their incoherence by providing a convenient rubric under which to file everything. Identification as "conservative" also gave the conservatives a self-consciousness as a movement aspiring to power.

From the onset, *National Review* projected itself as a renegade publication—one designed to combat the hegemony of "liberalism" and pull mainstream thinking in a conservative direction. Buckley was adamant about the need for conservatives to think *strategically* and urged them to engage in a systematic propagation of anti-liberal ideology. The expressed purpose of the *National Review* was, among other things, to attack the following:

(i)   "the growth of government"
(ii) the "cultural menace" of "conformity of the intellectual cliques" in education and the arts (another aspect which is strikingly similar to the anti-P.C. jeremiads which have sought to challenge what they perceive to be group-think tendencies among the so-called politically correct);
(iii) the communist threat described as the "most blatant force of satanic utopianism";
(iv) "politically oriented unionism"; and
(v)   "the fashionable concept of world government, the United Nations . . . and internationalism."[16]

While the last category was clearly intended to challenge American foreign policy at the time, the strident nationalistic undertones are similar to those expressed by the detractors of "multiculturalism." Indeed, the orchestrated attack on multiculturalism reflects a deeply rooted and unsettling assumption about the nature of national identity and "Americanness."[17]

Buckley was subsequently instrumental (along with one of his mentors Frank Chodorov) in creating the Intercollegiate Society of Individualists which was eventually renamed as the Intercollegiate Studies Institute (ISI)—the first national conservative organization of its kind—in 1952. Buckley and his fellow comrades at the *National Review* and the ISI belonged to what Hart (1987) has deemed the First Generation of conservatives. This first generation, among them the editors and contributors to *National Review,* exuded a "Burkean reverence" for yesteryear and saw themselves more as intellectual guardians of a longed-for cultural past (a posture epitomized in the phrase "Western civilization") than political activists. Diamond claims that the construction of the Right

> was largely the work of conservative intellectuals, as opposed to a more grassroots-based echelon of activists . . . Initially, it was a group of conservative intellectuals who viewed with trepidation the expansion of the welfare state and some seemingly related trends: racial minorities' nascent demands for civil rights, the spread of secularism, and the growth of mass, popular culture. (Diamond, 1995[a]:21)

These intellectuals sought, through various means, to advance conservative philosophy and free-market ideology and began to establish the intellectual base for the subsequent conservative movement. Although many first generation conservatives were more inclined to philosophize rather than organize, by the late 1950s and early 1960s, the ISI had successfully introduced conservative clubs on dozens of college campuses and had helped to establish "a loose confederation of student conservatives, groups and individuals" (Evans, 1961:71) which would eventually provide a foundation for student organizing.[18]

The major consequence of this organizing was the Young Americans For Freedom (YAF)—an organization whose 1960 founding meeting was held at Buckley's Great Elm estate and whose stated intent was to mobilize support among American youth for conservative political candidates and policy initiatives. It was at that meeting of ninety-three student activists that the YAF drafted its conservative manifesto—the Sharon Statement, which, among other things, chastised government intervention in the economy and avowed the YAF's commitment to fighting the menace of "Communism".[19] The establishment of the YAF marked a definitive shift in conservatism, from a focus on abstract economic and legal theory to a concrete interest in practice, and helped pave the way for the Second Generation conservatives. In addition, whereas the older conservatives of the first generation emphasized anticommunism and free enterprise, the second generation supplemented these concerns with more populist and moralistic themes. From its inception, YAF sought to promulgate its views and enlarge its membership by holding rallies and hosting highly publicized speeches by major right-wing pundits.[20]

YAF provided guidance to young conservatives interested in organizing and helped to form chapters on campuses throughout America. Although conservatives often lament the 1960s and movements such as the SDS, it is imperative to note that the 1960s were also a period of creative ferment for the conservative movement. This conservative ferment prompted one observer to write about a "new revolt" on campuses and to predict that many of the campus conservatives of the 1960s would eventually emerge as some of the most prominent opinion makers in the United States.[21]

The next major project for the YAF was garnering support for Barry Goldwater's run for presidency. Goldwater began his ascent to national prominence by speaking all across the country between 1954 and 1960. While initially reluctant to run for political office, his book *Conscience of a Conservative*,[22] ghost-written by Buckley's brother-in-law Brent Bozell in 1960, made him hugely popular among young conservatives and he assumed the leadership of the conservative movement.[23] The 1964 Goldwater campaign, while unsuccessful, nonetheless laid the foundations for the New Right. Besides producing a noteworthy base of right-wing activists with the know-how necessary for coalition building, the campaign also provided training in political mobilization and fundraising tactics to a new generation of conservatives. The Goldwater campaign provided the basis for the cohort of conservatives who would eventually form the backbone of the right-wing organizations established during the 1970s and 1980s. More importantly, it provided the backdrop for the launching of Ronald Reagan's political career, thereby setting the stage for the age of Reaganism.

One of the conservatives involved in the Goldwater campaign was Richard Viguerie who, in his capacity as YAF's account executive, compiled a list of Goldwater supporters which he used to set up his own direct-mail firm.[24] By the 1970s, Viguerie's outfit, known as RAVCO, had mushroomed and his direct-mail scheme for solicitation of funds helped to cultivate a powerful conservative infrastructure. In addition, by the early 1970s, YAF's membership exceeded 50,000 people and *National Review's* readership exceeded the 100,000 mark (Himmelstein, 1990:67-70). The seeds for the conservative counter-revolution were being sown and the second generation was well on its way to formulating a coherent body of political and cultural ideas, which set the stage for the establishment of think-tanks and policy institutes devoted to a conservative vision of education and society. Whereas the Old Right had anticommunism and the attack on New Deal policies as its unifying principles, the second generation of conservatives targeted the liberal establishment, and "the Sixties" became its nemesis.

The Legacy of the Sixties

In recent years there has been a burgeoning interest in the 1960s. Many historians, sociologists, social movement scholars and journalists have written extensively on the events of the decade and more specifically on the counterculture, the New Left and the civil rights movement (Diggins, 1992; Gitlin, 1987; Lee and Schlain, 1985; Miller, 1987; Peck, 1985). Still others have taken up the task of problematizing how the history of the 1960s has been "remembered" in many of the aforementioned narratives.[25] Remarkably, few have commented extensively on the critiques of the university which emerged in that decade's various movements, and how those very challenges enraged not only conservatives but members of the "Old Left" to such an extent that they swung violently to the Right. It is therefore necessary to briefly summarize some of the more pivotal challenges launched against the culture of academe in order to best contextualize the rise of neoconservatism.

Protests on campuses in the 1960s brought about a considerable rethinking of educational practices, especially those which condemned the student to a purely passive role. While the official rhetoric used in defining what education should entail embodied the notion that the process be one that foster the development of free, autonomous and critical thinking individuals—the "citizen" in the most democratic sense of the word—the educational system, with its academic division of labor and its separation of facts from values, was failing the expectations of students and faculty alike.[26]

By the end of 1962, the membership of *Students For A Democratic Society* (SDS) had grown substantially, and under the auspices of Tom Hayden, the Port Huron Statement—one of the most pivotal documents of the New Left—was drafted between June 11-15, 1962.[27] The statement was a passionate examination of the moral, economic, and political deficiencies of the most powerful country in the world. It appealed for the development of consciousness and for political activity against the ideology of the Cold War era, and helped to popularize the idea of "participatory democracy," an idea which had a profound influence on the radical politics of the New Left. Based in large part on the experience of the civil rights movement,[28] the politics of the polyglot known as the New Left were decisively detached from the norms which had characterized the Old Left and previous communist movements. Participatory democracy was defined by a "charge to action" and to "active participation" and "citizenship."[29] The concepts of political

participation and an educated citizenry symbolized the underlying philosophy of the radical student movement, and the Port
Huron Statement indicted the university, academics and the
curriculum:

> Our professors and administrators sacrifice controversy to public re-
> lations; their curriculums (*sic*) change more slowly than the living
> events of the world; their skills and silence are purchased by investors
> in the arms race; passion is called unscholastic. The questions we
> might want raised—what is really important? can we live in a different
> and better way? if we wanted to change society, how would we do it?—
> are not thought to be questions of a "fruitful, empirical nature," and
> thus are brushed aside. (Students For A Democratic Society, 1962:10)

The statement not only exuded a disdain for the positivist rationality that permeated the university, it also spoke to the
necessity of making the curriculum relevant to temporal practical relations. Furthermore, the statement was the first document to "focus on the university as an institution not of cultural transmission but of social change" (Diggins, 1992:228).
Contrary to the conservative indictments of the 1960s, student
radicals were not calling for the dissolution of intellectual
rigour; rather, they were demanding that the very foundations
of culture, society, and the educational system be vigorously
and unrelentingly interrogated.

The growth of the SDS and other campus groups had the
establishment concerned about further insurrections and many
institutions took steps to limit campus activism, but the rules
they sought to impose did little to curb protest. In fact, they
provided the impetus for even more fervent organizing. Drawing upon the radical lessons of the civil rights movement, the
Free Speech Movement started at Berkeley in 1964 as a protest
against new directives designed to prohibit the use of a twenty-
six-foot strip of university property for on-campus solicitation
of funds and planning and recruitment of off-campus social
and political action.[30] The FSM was a groundbreaking event as
students asserted their right to organize politically on campus. Within three months, the protest movement, which had
succeeded in promoting boycotts of classes and a sit-in at the
university's administration building, gradually expanded its
demands to insist on the elimination of all university restric-
tions of political activity on campus. The movement, ostensi-

bly nonpolitical, was the first to actually succeed in shutting down a prestigious institution.

In addition to the civil rights and free speech movements, the Vietnam war was a major catalyst for the protest movements of that era. While the 1960s are often blamed for fostering lax attitudes toward education and courses devoid of academic rigour in the name of "relevance," radicals were actually attacking the universities for their increasing reliance on corporate and military funding and for the invasion of capitalist ideology into the educational system. Statements such as those put forth by Clark Kerr, then-president of the University of California, describing the university as a "knowledge factory," were challenged and critiqued by progressive students and faculty members alike.

Kerr had maintained that the university's principal function was to serve the needs of industry, government, and the military. In addition, Kerr minimized undergraduate education and boasted instead of the university's service to corporations and the state.[31] In other words, he championed the fact that educational institutions had become appendages to, and transformed by, corporate capitalism. Indeed, the universities had become corporations whose purpose was to produce a trained workforce and ideas which were convenient to the status quo. To a great extent, it was this type of mentality which served as the inspiration for protest movements and unabashed challenges to the established order.

Reacting to Kerr's views on the university, FSM leaders developed an ideology that linked student dissatisfaction to the larger political and economic forces changing the university and American society. In 1964, Mario Savio, a key figure in the Free Speech Movement at Berkeley, responded to Kerr's conception of the university as a "knowledge factory." At a mass rally Savio delivered what is now often remembered as one of the most powerful orations of the student movement. In it he denounced the university as a factory for processing students—its raw material—into standardized personnel. Resistance to bureaucracy and the capitalist apparatus spread as many students cringed at the thought of being relegated to the status of cogs in a machine, or nameless, faceless members of an inhumane technological society. The university was cri-

tiqued by many as a factory-like abyss, which served to manu-
facture vassals for the vicissitudes of corporate capitalism and
whose professors and spokespersons imparted a kind of "one-
dimensional" misanthropic world view to students.

Reflecting on the FSM in *Roll Over Beethoven: The Return of
Cultural Strife*, Stanley Aronowitz argues that it

> condemned not only Chancellor Clark Kerr's idea of the university as
> a rationalized, corporate, and military-dominated institution, but
> offered the rudiments of a critique of curriculum, the academic divi-
> sion of labor, and authoritarian styles of pedagogy . . . Whatever their
> specific critiques, the new radicals agreed that they wanted, and ex-
> pected, that universities would meet their need for an education that
> prepared them to participate in the struggle for social change . . .
> Instead of education, they were offered training. (Aronowitz, 1993:49)

Aronowitz also discusses the activities of many Black and working class students, who became acutely aware of how dominant
academic discourses systematically excluded their cultures and
histories—a recognition which resulted in the struggles by Black
and ethnic minorities to get universities to establish programs
that would address such exclusions. In retrospect, the origi-
nality of the Free Speech Movement was its challenge to the
role of universities as repositories of "legitimate" intellectual
knowledge. Aronowitz claims that with this challenge came a
fundamental questioning of the role of the intellectual as students began to ask whether the professors were agents or opponents of the establishment and, equally important, in whose
interest the curriculum was formed (Aronowitz, 1993).

Sixties radicals disputed the university's leading positions—
impartiality, objectivity and value-neutrality—claiming that
these positions were inconceivable in a society where knowledge was always connected to issues of power. As Benjamin
Barber points out:

> What rebellious students as well as critics of the university were in-
> sisting on in the sixties was that the "objectivity" of the academy and
> the "impartiality" of the social sciences were a sham. The university
> was no less politically committed than its "politicized" critics, but it
> was prudently committed, covertly committed, committed to estab-
> lishment rather than to reformist values and ends. Because they
> blended in with the backdrop premises of the dominant social order
> and were not thrown into sharp relief in the manner that challengers'

values were, establishment values tended to be invisible. (Barber, 1992:88)

Research in the 1960s and 1970s directed attention to the cultural context of the dominant curriculum and began to illustrate the ideological foundations of knowledge. Revelations about how educational practices reflected the ideologies of governing social groups came to the fore. Inquiries into the subcultures of the oppressed and marginalized demonstrated how the educational system failed to value their specific experiences, histories, and voices. Moreover, the 1960s gave birth to a number of intellectual advances which questioned the prevailing quantitative, empiricist, and positivist notions of social theory and research. These approaches developed as a result of the increasing dissatisfaction with mainstream theories and methodologies, which seemed unable to adequately grasp the nature of social reality. The influences of continental theory and French philosophy were also being felt within the academy, mainly in the humanities. In addition, the critical theory of the Frankfurt School, especially that of Herbert Marcuse, grew in popularity.[32] In retrospect, one can recognize the political relevance that Marcuse's ideas held for 1960s radicals for his unyielding and caustic critiques of advanced capitalism, the oppression of Blacks and other minorities, and the hellish realities of war spoke eloquently and explicitly to a generation disenchanted with and disillusioned by the barbarism of "Western civilization." *An Essay On Liberation*, written by Marcuse at the apex of 1960s radicalism, captured the essence of the revolutionary spirit that had been flourishing and at once invigorated radicals and infuriated the stolid academic establishment, as did the writings of renegade sociologist, C. Wright Mills and others. Thus, there was both a social and an intellectual revolution in the 1960s, and to a certain extent, given the popularity of radical intellectuals like Marcuse and Mills, theory played an integral role in radicalizing students. Aronowitz and Giroux (1985:14) remind us that in the 1960s, many progressive cultural critics became instant "organic" intellectuals:

The new left succeeded in exerting considerable influence among intellectuals, even if something short of hegemony in the Gramscian

sense. Its work in all countries might well be described as pedagogical . . . Ideas such as grassroots democracy to replace the oppressive
structures of representative government, the critique of consumer
society, the demands for community control and individual freedom
in major institutions such as schools became commonplace public
issues.

Undoubtedly, the events of the 1960s illuminated the democratizing and radicalizing potential of educational institutions,
while at the same time illustrating their limits in the larger
project of social transformation. From the free speech movement at Berkeley to the civil rights movement and the Vietnam protests, university teach-ins and campus activism played
an indispensable role in changing the course of events. It is
therefore imperative to recognize that the campus politics of
the 1960s cannot be "disassociated from books, ideas or intellectuals" (Jacoby, 1987:114).

Naturally, these developments did not bode well with conservatives who felt threatened by the growing influence of Left
intellectuals and unruly student radicals. As a result of this
uneasiness, beginning in the late 1960s and continuing into
the 1970s and 1980s, conservatives set out on a journey to ex-
orcise the ghost of Sixties radicalism and to erase from collective consciousness the "dangerous memories" of that decade.
Leading the way were a number of Old Left-liberals who had
grown disillusioned with the social movements of the 1960s.

The Sixties Under Siege: The Rise of Neoconservatism

"A neoconservative is a liberal who has been mugged by reality."
                                            —Irving Kristol [33]

While the New Left and the counterculture were capturing the
attention of the media and the nation as a whole, the YAF
continued to flourish and Buckley's Old Right proceeded to
develop an institutional infrastructure on campuses, largely in
an effort to combat the influence of the SDS and other groups.
Between 1968 and 1972, the *National Review* published a bi-
weekly bulletin called *Combat* which provided hyperbolic reports about campus activists while the YAF's "Tell It To Hanoi"
campaign was busily attempting to undermine the work of anti-

war protestors. Other conservatives, appalled by the activities of campus radicals, began to speak out against federal funding for higher education while others concerned themselves with the legal implications of the "politicization" of the academy, which had, in their minds, created a new brand of "conformity" and radical orthodoxy.[34] At the same time, events, namely the Vietnam war and the growth of protest movements, began to fracture the Old Left-liberal anticommunist alliance. For the most part, the "reality mugging" (alluded to by Kristol) which ultimately transformed anticommunist liberals into neoconservative ideologues, took place on university campuses. The campus unrest and the alleged "barbarism" which it produced led anticommunist diehards like Irving Kristol, Sidney Hook, Daniel Bell, and others to denounce the young student protesters. Subsequently, their politics turned sharply to the Right thereby earning them the neoconservative designation.

Neoconservatism, however, cannot be described as a "movement" in the conventional sense of the term. Unlike the Old Right conservatives whose explicit intent had been to further the cause of conservative philosophy, prior to the 1970s, neoconservatives expressly identified themselves as liberals and were sympathetic, for the most part, with the aims of the Democratic Party. But the events of the 1960s eventually changed that, and they began to forge alliances with those on the political Right.[35]

Blumenthal (1988:125) maintains that two decades were of special significance for the neoconservatives: the 1930s, when they were student radicals, and the 1960s when they reacted against the student radicals. Many of the forefathers of neoconservatism were student radicals attending the City College of New York during the 1930s; hence they are often referred to as the New York intellectuals.[36] Perhaps the most defining characteristic of this group was its Trotskyist slant which was highlighted in the bitter battles between them and the more Stalinist oriented members of the American Communist Party (Blumenthal, 1988; Dorrien, 1993). Eventually, it was the Old Left's rigid anticommunism which led the new generation of leftists to disassociate themselves from the ideological proclivities of the elder generation.

Furthermore, the Old Leftist-turned neoconservatives resented the fact that the New Left rejected their philosophy and agenda. Indeed, while members of the SDS were clearly opposed to the communist system, they eschewed the anticommunist atmosphere in the United States, claiming that an unreasonable form of anti-communism had "become a major social problem for those who want to construct a more democratic America" (SDS, 1962:39). The position of the New Left was that the daunting mood fuelled by anticommunism often served as an obstacle for those people who would otherwise "join political organizations, sign petitions," and "speak out on serious issues" (SDS, 1962:39). In essence, the New Left, and more specifically, SDS, claimed that the tactics and ideology of the anticommunist Old Left actually prevented activism and precluded democratic, political struggle. This stance, of course, infuriated the Old Left-liberals who "at the moment of their arrival at their properly tenured stations" and at a time when "they believed they had earned deference for their accumulated wisdom," were faced with "hordes of longhairs" claiming that they "belonged in the dustbin of history" (Blumenthal, 1988:125). Eventually, the generational chasm, coupled with the cultural disparities between the two constituencies, contributed to the sense of alienation among Old Leftists and drove them to conservatism. While there were a number of obvious differences between the old conservatives and the neoconservatives, they both shared an avid hatred of Soviet Communism and a distrust of student radicalism.[37]

In the late 1960s, a number of neoconservatives writing in the pages of publications such as Norman Podhoretz's *Commentary* used McCarthyite tactics and red-baiting slurs against the student radicals. Podhoretz himself loathed the New Left's apparent attack on "academic standards and the principle of merit" and the "preferential treatment of Blacks and women" (Gottfried and Fleming, 1988:60). Not surprisingly, his views were shared by a number of other prominent neoconservatives. In an article entitled "The Agony of the Campus," Irving Howe (himself a democratic socialist and life-long opponent of Stalinism) condemned the New Left and saw in every protester the face of a budding Stalinist. Howe (1969:387-394) complained of "left authoritarianism," accused the "desperado-totalitarian left" of "irrationalism and anti-intellectualism," bemoaned the "cultural revolt against the modernist tradition" and issued a dire warning about the "romantic primitivism" that had engulfed campuses. Howe's tirade against the student protest movements of the 1960s, not unlike Senator Joseph McCarthy's infamous list and most of the jeremiads against P.C., lacked any evidence which would have substantiated the claims made. Indeed, Howe's essay was completely devoid of evidence to support his preposterous accusations, yet, without citing a single example, Howe managed to equate the entire New Left with the vagaries of Stalinism. In addition to his hostility toward the New Left, Howe was also in the habit of launching literary attacks against "angry black and feminist writers" (M.J. Buhle, 1992:336).

Paradoxically, then, as now, McCarthyite rhetoric was being used to malign progressives—but this is not surprising for anticommunism has been a defining feature of the American political landscape for decades. The ideology of anticommunism has become so deeply ingrained in the collective American psyche that its persistence no longer depends on the actual existence of communism (Kovel,1994). Indeed, stand-ins for the "evil empire" are constantly being invoked, as the recent attacks on P.C. clearly demonstrate.

While Howe busied himself with concocting unsupported attacks on the student Left, another paragon of neo-conservatism, Irving Kristol, writing in *New York Times Magazine* set out to develop the foundations for a plan to quash student revolt. Kristol (1968) argued that a small but vocal minority of "rebels without a cause" had no interest in higher education or intellectual pursuits. He claimed that the disruptive rebels' passions had been inflamed by a "debased popular culture," which prevailed unchallenged by the leftists in charge of college campuses. Kristol also maintained that the public (who paid taxes for public higher education) had the unassailable right to demand that funding be channelled in ways that would help to "overcome" rather than "deepen" the crisis which the universities were allegedly experiencing. Kristol advocated an end to public funding for the universities, with the exception of student loans, and maintained that students, obliged to use loans rather than financial aid to fund their education, would be less likely to engage in subversive campus activities against the U.S. government. In another forum, Kristol (1965) belittled the "adolescent" immaturity of the New Left and claimed that the student movement was motivated, in part, by American youth who had grown bored with their parents' aspirations for material success and suburban utopia.

In addition to denouncing the activism which had characterized the campuses of the 1960s, conservatives attacked higher education for its waning "standards." The conservative indictment against higher education was sweeping. Several points were made repeatedly: standards—of instruction and civility—had been lowered; the university had lost all sense of its original purposes; conservative ideas were excluded from most departments, and so on (Gottfried and Fleming, 1988:40). The standards rhetoric has re-emerged again in contemporary bromides about the "crisis" of the universities, as has the charge that conservative voices are ritually excluded from academic discourse. As students in the 1960s, the New Left had been the target of the Right. In the recent invectives against P.C., alleged descendants of the student movement who have since assumed the status of "tenured radicals" have once again become the targets of right-wing wrath. While the times have changed, the strategies remain the same.

The Conservative Counter-revolution

The 1960s had taken their toll on the conservative Right. The values and concerns of Sixties activists and protest movements appeared as threats to corporate capitalist ideology and the establishment in academe. Shor writes that

> the 1960s was a tough medium limiting the advance of conservative politics . . . An autonomous discourse invented from below put the establishment on the defensive. At the grass roots, there was a subversive emergence of action and communication. This new vocabulary validated the demands and the language modes of historically dominated groups—minorities, women, the young, senior citizens, natives, gays, the handicapped . . . Something had to be done fast to silence the daily talk, the rally speeches, the many teach-ins, the underground publications . . . The voice of authority had to move from the defensive to the offensive. (Shor, 1992:5-6)

The student movements of the 1960s, the activities of the New Left, Black activism and feminism, resulted in some efforts at augmenting accepted forms of expression, furthering the democratization of the university and challenging the corporate ideology of higher education. However, by the early 1970s a conservative restoration was well on its way to re-establishing the ideological controls in the universities (Chomsky, 1988). The intensity of the restoration efforts coupled with a number of other factors including the covert activities of COINTELPRO,[38] the rightward shift of the mainstream media,[39] the professionalization of the intellectual,[40] and the lack of a long-term political vision contributed to the ultimate demise of the New Left. In their failure to consolidate a new "radical" democratic politics, one with consensual aspirations, the social movements of the 1960s "provided the political space in which right-wing reaction could incubate and develop its political agenda," while the reforms won by minority groups in that decade provided a "formidable range of targets for the counter-reformers of the 1970s" (Apple, 1989:43).

Between the mid-to-late 1960s and the mid-1970s, the neoconservatives aligned themselves more closely with ideological positions of the old conservative Right (namely on issues of social welfare programs and the virtues of capitalism),[41] and together they initiated a fervent period of conservative organizing with the intent of pushing back the democratic reform movements of the 1960s and restoring conservative hegemony.

Referring to attempts by the Right to re-establish their power after the Sixties upheavals as the "counterrevolution," Herbert Marcuse remarked that

> the defence of the capitalist system requires the organization of counterrevolution at home . . . the counterrevolution is largely preventive and, in the Western world, altogether preventive. Here, there is no recent revolution to be undone, and there is none in the offing. And yet, fear of revolution which creates the common interest links the various stages and forms the counterrevolution. (Marcuse, 1972:1-2)

Indeed, it was largely fear among conservatives and neoconservatives that inspired the development of a counterrevolution which had been simmering for a number of years prior to Nixon's landslide victory in 1972. While Nixon's subsequent fall from grace threw conservatives into a tailspin and opened the way for liberal democrats, the recession which took place in the early 1970s eventually heralded a dramatic rightward turn in the political climate of the country. Ferguson and Rogers (1986:78) claim that the drastic recession which began in November of 1973 and lasted until March of 1975 was the "longest and deepest economic downturn the United States had experienced since the Great Depression." The roots of the recession were to be found in the declining position of the United States within the global economy, and its dire consequences caused the American business community to begin doubting the whole of New Deal liberalism and convinced them to mobilize.

> Big business . . . mobilized in the mid-1970s in response to a crisis it
> saw as political and ideological as much as economic . . . Big business
> did not just see an economic crisis . . . It saw instead a political system
> veering out of its control, and more important, it construed this po-
> litical crisis in the broadest terms possible—not just as a matter of one
> or two bad policies . . . but as a deeper crisis of how politics and the
> role of the state were understood . . . It saw a broad crisis requiring a
> broad response. (Himmelstein, 1990:137)

Part of the business community's response was to initiate ideological warfare through an unprecedented funding blitz of conservative policy think-tanks in the hopes of influencing public opinion and the media. Together with various conservative foundations, they launched an all-out effort to promote free-market ideology. In addition, they contributed large sums of money to research institutes, such as *Accuracy in Media*, to counter what they perceived to be an anti-business bias in the mainstream media, and also helped to fund dozens of campus newspapers with like-minded students at the helm (Saloma, 1984).

The increased involvement of the business community gave birth to what is now commonly referred to as the "New Right," as conservatives themselves began to use the designation to describe aspects of their movement. While there was nothing particularly new about the ideology undergirding the conservative movement, what was new was the greatly enlarged resource base which conservative leaders were enjoying. In addition to the financial support of corporations, the direct-mail appeals perfected by Richard Viguerie provided the New Right with an unprecedented amount of cash flow to be used to expound their ideological agenda. By the late 1970s, what had begun as a "remnant" of conservatism had been transformed into a broad-based coalition comprised of members of the Old Right, neoconservatives, and free-market ideologues, with a vast network of think-tanks and policy institutes sponsoring their efforts to restore conservative hegemony in all public spheres.

Undoubtedly, this had an enormous impact on education as the 1960s cry for the democratization of education was systematically being swept under the rug and replaced with the language of business. Whereas 1960s radicals contested the university administration and called attention to the necessity for universities to "become *less* like a *corporation* and more like a *community*" (Menand, 1991:54), during the 1970s an inordinate emphasis was placed on career motivation and school/business partnerships in an effort to align education goals with those of corporate capitalism. In addition, the Right created a series of moral "panics" and "crises" about "literacy" and "American jobs." Throughout the 1970s, America's economic problems, especially unemployment, were blamed on the schools' failure to educate students to meet the country's needs. The schools were blamed for unemployment while it was argued that revising curriculum might help to ameliorate certain economic problems. Conservatives emphasized vocationalism and "skills" competence and words like "career," "excellence," and "high tech" dominated public discourse on education in an attempt to re-establish the function of schools (at all levels) as purveyors of ideological assumptions conducive to the free-market world view which the business establishment was seeking to advance.

While some left and liberal economic arguments attributed the shift in educational priorities solely to the recession, others maintained that the conservative attacks were motivated by their "horror of the 1960s generation that made colleges the bases for political and cultural opposition" (Aronowitz and Giroux, 1985:172).[12] Indeed, the anti-war movement and protests against military-university partnerships threatened the very ideology undergirding the military-industrial complex. Therefore, big business intervention into education and the funding blitz which engendered the shift to careerism was, to some degree, an attempt to curb political and cultural activism. By equating democracy not with freedom but with material "success," New Right mandarins were able to align the business of education with the business of American capitalism.

By the late 1970s, the corporate-sponsored ideological rally was gearing up for action and its intensity barometer skyrocketed. In 1978, William Simon (former Secretary of the Treasury under presidents Nixon and Ford) proclaimed that the country was going to hell in a hand basket because of an "assault on America's culture and its historic identity," and he called for

> nothing less than a massive and unprecedented mobilization of the moral, intellectual and financial resources which reside in those . . . who are concerned that our traditional free enterprise system . . . is in dire and perhaps ultimate peril . . . [and] those who see a successful United States as the real "last best hope of mankind."(Simon, 1978:229-30)

To rectify the deplorable malaise, Simon suggested the following three-point remedy:

> 1) Funds generated by business . . . must rush by multimillions to the aid of liberty . . . [and] funnel desperately needed funds to scholars, social scientists, writers and journalists who . . . [would] dissent from a dominant socialist-statist-collectivist orthodoxy which prevails in much of the media, in most of our large universities, among many of our politicians and, tragically, among not a few of our top business executives; 2) Business must cease the mindless subsidizing of colleges and universities whose departments of economics, government, politics and history are hostile to capitalism; 3) Finally, business money must flow away from the media which serve as megaphones for anticapitalist opinion and to media which are . . . at least professionally capable of a fair and accurate treatment of procapitalist ideas, values and arguments. (Simon, 1978:230-232)

For Simon then, nothing less than the creation of a "counter intelligentsia" would suffice to further the right-wing agenda.

The crowning moment of the conservative movement's efforts occurred when Ronald Reagan assumed the presidential throne in 1980. The exigency of the "culture wars" became a top priority and Reagan and his cronies were quick to enter the fray of educational politics. By the early-to-mid 1980s, the goal of inculcating education with a corporate mentality was augmented with at least two other agendas—undermining educational equity and ridding educational institutions of their "liberal-humanist" bias. The first agenda was most explicitly expressed by an amalgamation of neoconservatives and policy analysts working out of the American Enterprise Institute (see below), who held that excellence in education was being subverted by the drive for educational equity. They sought to reduce both the amount of money being spent on equity initiatives and the federal government's intervention in promoting them. According to Pincus (1984) the AEI clique wanted to rearrange the priorities of public education so that its aims would be to (i) promote economic growth for the country; and (ii) help preserve a "common culture" by instilling in students the values upon which American capitalism had been based. Only after these two criteria were met should education concern itself with the messy issues of equity.

The second project, expunging traces of secular liberal humanism in education, was vigorously advocated by the Christian Right[13] and policy analysts from the Heritage Foundation (see below), who suggested, among other things, the elimination of federal funding for education and the dismantling of the Department of Education. While they did not succeed in abolishing the Department of Education during the Reagan/Bush years, the Christian Coalition's aim to do so became a central issue in the campaigns of several Republican candidates in the recent election. In addition, the Coalition's suggestions for a voucher system and the need to litigate "reverse discrimination" cases continues to guide the broad conservative agenda today.

In the mid-1980s, Paul Weyrich, William Lind and others associated with the Free Congress Foundation began to map out a project of "cultural conservatism" to combat what they perceived to be a form of cultural drift (i.e. the decline of traditional and moral authority) generated by 1960s radicalism and the forces of liberal largesse. Cultural conservatism, largely a populist strategy, was in effect the brainchild of Weyrich, who, envisioning the denouement of the Evil Empire's red threat, had begun to embrace social issues as a ground to rally the conservative troops back in the 1970s.[44] It was in 1987, however, that Weyrich commissioned a study—*Cultural Conservatism: Toward A New National Agenda*–which outlined the benefits of waging a "culture war" and which found that "antiliberalism" was a far more encompassing theme than was "economic conservatism" for the purposes of advancing conservatism and capitalist ideology. Central to the cultural conservatives platform is the promotion and valorization of "traditional Western culture" and its "values"—a project which they deem necessary for the smooth and successful functioning of American society.[45] It is not surprising, then, that this defence of "Western culture" became the cornerstone of the Right's vigorous assault against the "forces" of P.C. in the early 1990s.

It is important to note, however, that while the current attack in the academy is being waged in the name of defending Western culture and upholding standards and traditions, its ideological intent is also motivated by the need to fashion minds "sufficiently deadened to reason and history to allow the capitalist project to reproduce itself from generation to generation" (Cockburn,1991:691). After all, the "attacks" on Western culture, while not explicitly expressed as attacks on capitalism do represent a formidable foe in the paranoid minds of conservatives and capitalist ideologues. Here Marcuse's words about counterrevolutions being largely preventive ring all too true. Although the "threat" posed by P.C. is relatively minor, for reasons which will be addressed in subsequent chapters, in the overactive imaginations of conservatives it is a threat in need of containment. As one observer has adroitly pointed out:

> PC has been viewed as a potential (if distant) threat to capitalist hegemony because it has recognized the harm caused by Western culture's racism and sexism, and consequently has hinted at America's continuing lack of social justice and its urgent need for an egalitarian politics. (Neilson, 1995:78)

This may partly help to explain why so many corporate-sponsored think-tanks have expended exorbitant sums of money to combat the scourge of P.C. politics. After all, the last thing conservatives want is a repeat of the 1960s.

Funding the New Right Agenda

Complaints about leftists in the academy are not novel, as previous sections have demonstrated. What *is* unprecedented, however, is the amount of corporate funding underwriting contemporary conservative laments. Given these circumstances, one must identify the recent epidemic of newspaper articles and books about the P.C. menace for what it really is—a byproduct of more than two decades of heightened corporate influence in the affairs of academe. It is also important to note that the attack on P.C. and all that it entails is not an assault aimed at combatting liberal or leftist hegemony (although conservatives would have us believe that it is); rather, it is an attempt to dismantle many of the democratic gains for which leftists have fought so vehemently. The New Right, quite simply, wants to turn back the clock and in recent years it has had unopposed success in labelling as blasphemous anything which could be even remotely considered liberal let alone leftist. In addition to these conservative restoration efforts and the network of corporate money underwriting them, there have been within academic circles, groups of neoconservative and New Right spokespersons who have become the organic intellectuals for much of the rightist resurgence.

This "third generation" of young reactionaries, recruited and nurtured by older neoconservatives and well-funded by right-wing think-tanks, have been successful in convincing the public at large that universities have become hotbeds of radicalism. Hegemonic intellectuals like Dinesh D'Souza, Roger Kimball and a host of others have been enlisted in the war against the academic blue-bloods supposedly plotting no less than the demise of Western civilization in their weekly graduate seminars.

For the most part, the debate over P.C. and educational reform has been predictably one-sided, for the moneyed manacles of conservatism have, through tales of "discrimination," been able to silence the voices of progressives. In short, they have been remarkably successful at circumscribing the bounds of the expressible. Since the Right has had an onerous grasp on the debate thus far, democratic considerations have been virtually absent in deliberations about curricular reform. Rather, the imperatives of contributing to economic productivity and

preserving the sanctity of Western "civilization" have served as the parameters of discourse. While one cannot neglect the Left's relative inability to provoke *public* discourse on this issue thus far, one cannot underestimate the strength and scope of right-wing power.[16] In other words, the success of the anti-P.C. backlash seems to lend credence to the old cliche—money talks! Such a situation warrants an examination of those institutions, foundations, corporations, and major players that have helped to orchestrate the assault aimed at undermining progressive change in our institutions of learning, for they have been instrumental in setting the agenda and propelling conservative incendiaries into the limelight of mainstream consciousness.

Prior to the 1960s, the thorn in the sides of old conservatives was New Deal liberalism. In an effort to revitalize free-market ideology in the aftermath of Roosevelt's welfare state, Lewis Brown founded what was then called the American Enterprise Association in 1943, with a budget of $80,000 (Blumenthal, 1988:32). Following Brown's death, William Baroody Sr., assumed the presidency of the AEA, and subsequently renamed it the American Enterprise Institute (AEI). Baroody's decision to rename the AEI was in part due to the fact that he wanted the organization to sound less like a "trade association and more like an intellectual centre,"(Blumenthal, 1988:39) for Baroody clearly understood, in a perversion of Lenin's famous dictum, that without conservative theory there could be no conservative movement. The AEI, however, functioned in relative obscurity until the 1970s, when corporations and conservative foundations began to fund the institute's free-market research. By the late 1970s, more than 200 corporations were helping to bankroll AEI's $5 million budget with the list growing to 600 corporate sponsors by 1981, at which point the institute boasted a budget of $10 million, sponsorship of four journals, and a monthly television show. By 1985, this organization, which had started out as little more than a letterhead, had a budget of $12.6 million, a staff of 176 and ninety adjunct scholars, thanks to corporate benevolence and the fundraising ventures of neoconservatives like Irving Kristol (Blumethal, 1988; Himmelstein, 1990; Peschek, 1987).[17]

A pillar of the establishment, AEI is a self-proclaimed flagship of conservatism dedicated not only to espousing free-market economics but also to promoting an educational agenda geared towards the preservation of a "common culture." In order to further their agenda, AEI was one of the first think-tanks to gain access to the mainstream media by hiring ghost writers for scholars to produce op-ed articles, which were then sent out to newspaper outlets which were willing to comply with the AEI. The AEI regularly supplies editorial articles to more than 100 daily newspapers and it receives financial support from various media sources including the *New York Times,* the Philip L. Graham Fund (*Washington Post*) and Times Mirror, the parent company of the *Los Angeles Times* (Lee and Solomon, 1990:83). In addition, several AEI scholars have connections with all three major mainstream television networks and some serve as paid consultants for the networks. Among those who have served as resident scholars of the AEI are economist Milton Friedman, neoconservative Irving Kristol, and former U.S. Ambassador to the United Nations, Jeanne Kirkpatrick. Dinesh D'Souza, author of *Illiberal Education,* and more recently, *The End Of Racism*, currently serves as AEI's educational pundit.

One philanthropic family which has assisted extensively in building the conservative infrastructure is the Coors family, whose empire began in 1873 when German immigrant, Adolph Coors, set up a brewery in Golden, Colorado (Bellant, 1991). Over the years, the company has remained firmly under the control of the various Coors sons, who have generously contributed to a network of ultra-conservative and far-right organizations and institutions. Among those who have been lucky recipients of the Coors family generosity are persons whose views reflect not only traditional conservatism, but also "nativism, xenophobia, theories of racial superiority, sexism, homophobia, authoritarianism, militarism, reaction, and in some cases out-right neo-fascism" (Berlet, 1991:v).[48]

The Coors family is also linked to a number of right-wing groups which advocate the abolition of publicly funded schooling and the creation of private educational companies. In addition, the family has supported a number of textbook censorship campaigns aimed at ridding schools of books that are unpatriotic or anti-Christian, or which espouse "anti-family sentiment" (Bellant, 1991:95).[49] They are also the proud sponsors of *Accuracy in Academia*, a national education watchdog group established in 1985 to purge college campuses of their alleged Marxist bias. They were also instrumental in helping to establish the Free Congress Foundation (FCF), the key think-tank behind the Christian Coalition.

While the Coors family has been involved with a number of recent right-wing organizations, one of its early enterprises was helping to establish what is regarded by many as the most powerful think-tank in America. In 1973, Joseph Coors provided a $250,000 grant to Edwin Feulner and Paul Weyrich to found the Heritage Foundation as yet another vehicle to propagate right-wing ideology.[50] In addition to establishing the Heritage Foundation, Weyrich, often referred to as the New Right's strategic architect, also helped to start the Moral Majority in 1979 and inspired the formation of the Christian Coalition in 1989. Weyrich is currently president of the FCF[51] which initiated the project known as "cultural conservatism" in the 1980s and which currently runs National Empowerment Television,[52] the right-wing network that carries Newt Gingrich's TV college course, "Renewing American Civilization." The FCF, chaired by none other than Jeffrey Coors, boasts annual revenues in excess of $5 million and has played an instrumental role in advancing a conservative agenda for public elementary and high school education in the country.

According to the Heritage Foundation's 1991 Annual Report, its operating budget exceeded the $19 million mark, with more than 50 percent of that derived from individual contributors via direct-mail solicitation. Among its corporate sponsors are Chase Manhattan Bank, Mobil Oil Corporation, Dow Chemical, and the Reader's Digest Association. In addition to housing dozens of policy analysts, more than fifty adjunct scholars and a 160-member staff in its Washington building overlooking Capitol Hill, Heritage also produces the theoretical journal *Policy Review*.

In order to disseminate their ideological messages and policy recommendations to as wide an audience as possible, the foundation relies upon a four-part delivery system consisting of: (i) a public relations division, largely responsible for the media and the general public; (ii) a government relations division, which targets Congress and various government agencies; (iii) an academic relations division, which supplies information to the university community and other research institutions; and (iv) what is referred to as the Corporate Relations division, through which businesses and corporations are recipients of Heritage propaganda (Messer-Davidow, 1993:52). In addition, the foundation keeps tabs on thousands of journalists,[53] who are arranged by specialty in the Heritage computer databases so that when the foundation completes a study on policy or other related matters, it goes out with a synopsis. "Every study is turned into an op-ed piece" which is then distributed "by the Heritage Features Syndicate to newspapers that publish them" (Blumenthal, 1988:49).

Among the various think-tanks and foundations, the Heritage Foundation is often characterized as the most extreme, and has gained some notoriety for its linkages with the Klu Klux Klan and Reverend Sun Myung Moon's ultra-righist Unification Church.[54] The foundation is best known, however, for its production of tomes aimed at influencing various governmental policies. The foundation was especially influential during Reagan's reign and its *Mandate for Leadership*, published in 1980, was used as a sort of "guidebook" by the Reagan administration. Among the thousands of recommendations made in the document were suggestions to increase Pentagon spending and beef up intelligence operations while reducing spending on social services and education. Many of the recommendations were subsequently implemented by Heritage people who were later hired by the Reagan administration (Bellant, 1991:9). When Reagan was re-elected in 1984, the Foundation produced a sequel to the original document entitled *Mandate for Leadership II*. Among its recommendations were cutbacks or outright elimination of food stamp programs, special educational programs for the handicapped, and child nutrition programs. Heritage's vision and critique of education is epitomized in its 1985 publication, *A New Agenda for Education*. While the document as a whole deals mainly with elementary and high school education, the one section that deals explicitly with universities suggests that they have been corrupted by an excess of liberalism and argues against affirmative action, equity programs, and federal funding for universities.

In 1978, William E. Simon and Irving Kristol created the Institute for Educational Affairs (IEA), with grants of $100,000 each from the Olin Foundation, the JM Foundation, the Scaife Family Trusts (whose largest benefactor is actually the Heritage Foundation), and the Smith-Richardson Foundation—four powerhouses of the conservative establishment. For its part, the New York-based Olin Foundation cites as its purpose the provision of financial support

> for projects that reflect or are intended to strengthen the economic, political and cultural institutions upon which the American heritage of constitutional government and private enterprise is based. The Foundation also seeks to promote a general understanding of these institutions by encouraging the thoughtful study of the connections between economic and political freedoms, and the cultural heritage that sustains them. (*Olin Annual Report* cited in Henson, 1991:8)

In 1990 alone, the Olin Foundation paid approximately $19.8 million in grants to scores of conservative scholars, think-tanks and political organizations. Olin also contributes generously to conservative publications including *Commentary, The American Spectator, The National Review* and *The New Criterion.*

The Scaife Foundation has been a major supporter of the conservative counter-establishment for more than three decades. With its assets (most of them garnered from Gulf Oil Company stock), it began funding the AEI in 1963 and helped to subsidize the Draft Goldwater campaign. In addition, the Scaife Foundation also helped to launch the Heritage Foundation along with Joseph Coors. Although the founding of the Heritage Foundation is often credited to Coors alone, Scaife was, in essence, a silent partner in that enterprise. In fact, Scaife contributed $900,000 to Coor's $250,000, for the establishment of the Foundation. According to Rothmyer's (1981) estimation, the Scaife Foundation donated more than $100 million to building the conservative infrastructure in the 1970s. The Scaife Foundation's president, Richard Mellon Scaife, also owns several media outlets and funds *Accuracy in Media,* the organization founded by Reed Irvine to combat the alleged liberal bias of the mainstream media. In 1990 alone, Scaife contributed $75,000 to the IEA.

Founded in 1935, the Smith-Richardson Foundation (its assets attributable to Vicks Vaporub), began bankrolling conservative causes in 1973 when Randolph Richardson, son of founder H. Smith Richardson became the foundation's president. The Smith-Richardson Foundation made its mark by bankrolling an idea—that of the supply-side revolution (Saloma, 1984:34). Indeed, the appointment of Leslie Lenkowsky as director of research in 1976 paved the way for directing a large portion of Smith-Richardson's budget to the support of supply-side theory, which became central to the Reagan administration's ideology (Himmelstein, 1990).

The foundation has systematically funded right-wing causes in addition to contributing to CIA-linked media projects and training programs for CIA and Defence Department people. The conservative plan to infiltrate campuses was spelled out in a confidential memo written by Roderic R. Richardson for the Smith-Richardson Foundation. The memo outlined two potential anti-left strategies at the university level: deterrence activism and high-ground articulation, also termed idea marketing. According to Richardson, deterrence activism "exists purely in response to the left-wing agenda. It is not very interesting . . . At best it is a form of cheerleading that can focus some attention on stirring media events" (Diamond 1991:48). Rather than deterrence activism, Richardson preferred high-ground activism which he defined as

> the attempt to steal one or another highground away from the left, by . . . doing things like insisting on rigorous discussion and debates, setting up political unions, battling divestiture and other causes . . . by proposing better ways of solving the problem. Student journalism is a highground approach. It is . . . an approach geared to long run success. (Richardson, 1984)

Richardson further recommended that the Right "mimic left-wing organization" by forming "regional resource centers," and faculty networks, aimed at setting up a permanent network "to defuse the left, to grab the highground" and "to change the atmosphere on campuses" (Diamond, 1995[b]:26).

In addition to the support of conservative foundations, IEA's corporate sponsors include Coca-Cola, the Ford Motor Company, Mobil, Dow Chemical, Kmart and General Electric (IEA Annual Report, 1980). IEA's commitment is to both the development of a conservative infrastructure and the recruitment of young conservatives willing to produce scholarship that makes the case for the morality of capitalism. Unlike the Old Right's ISI project which published, and continues to publish, a number of journals and articles with abstract and impenetrable philosophical underpinnings, the strategy of the IEA was to spread conservative ideology as widely as possible—something that demanded that the material produced be accessible to students.

In 1980, the IEA began funding the "alternative" student journalism movement after two students from the University of Chicago approached IEA for a grant to support their journal, *Counterpoint*. The students had convinced IEA that control of campus publications was firmly entrenched in the hands of radicals who systematically excluded conservative points of view.[55] By 1983, IEA was supporting thirty-three so-called "alternative" journals and newspapers on campuses across the country, with the *Dartmouth Review* (Dinesh D'Souza's old haunt), perhaps the most notorious of the lot. Prominent conservatives and neoconservatives, including William F. Buckley and Patrick Buchanan, often sit on the boards of the student publications.

In September 1990, the IEA merged with the Madison Center, which was founded in 1988, by Allan Bloom and former education secretary and drug czar, William Bennett. The hybrid organization is now known as the Madison Center for Educational Affairs (MCEA). The Madison Center's financial supporters run the gamut from private citizens to business corporations and corporate and family foundations. In 1990, some of the more generous donors included the Dow Chemical Company, the W. H. Brady Foundation, the Lynde & Harry Bradley Foundation, the Scaife Foundation, and the Olin Foundation.[56] The MCEA, headquartered in Washington, D.C.,

> works to propagate right-wing ideas on campuses across the country and to transform higher education so as to reflect more closely the values and ideas of conservative business, governmental and cultural elites. (Hager, 1992:58)

At the heart of the Madison Center is its student journalism program, which operates as a support base for a consolidated system of right-wing student newspapers. This system, known as the Collegiate Network, has *no* precedent in the history of campus journalism. In 1990, the MCEA spent $330,617 on its reactionary network of campus newspapers and a total of $1 million on other projects.[57] According to figures in its 1991 Annual Report, MCEA is a major force behind seventy notorious tabloids published on more than sixty campuses, with a combined readership of approximately 600,000. In addition to generously supporting the Collegiate Network, the MCEA provides editorial and technical assistance to its student staffers. Prior to the merger between IEA and the Madison Center, the IEA set up a toll-free hotline back in 1986 to make the organization more accessible to its band of conservative student journalists (Delaney and Lenkowsky, 1988). Today, under the auspices of the MCEA, in addition to the hotline, the organization publishes *Newslink*, a monthly newsletter, distributes conservative publications such as *National Review* and *American Spectator,* and sponsors conferences for its newspaper staffers (MCEA, 1991). Through an intern program, the MCEA helps to support the career aspirations of its student editors, many of whom go on to assume positions within the mainstream professional press. The internships at various publications, including *Academic Questions* (the NAS journal), and the Heritage Foundation's *Policy Review* are also graciously funded by conservative foundations such as the Bradley Foundation. In 1990, the Bradley Foundation donated almost $138,000 to the internship program for student journalists and it also provides regular financial support for academic programs conducted by the Heritage Foundation. According to Messer-Davidow (1993:62), the "Bradley Resident Scholars program" brings young scholars, mainly from the social sciences and humanities, to Heritage for five-to-ten month tenures to "conduct research, teach seminars, deliver public lectures, and learn firsthand about the policy process." The MCEA also spent in excess of $120,000 to produce a guide, aimed at parents, about the state of college campuses and undergraduate education:

> The guide is based on a 36-page questionnaire sent out in 1990 to NAS members, asking questions like: "Are there any groups on campus critical of the core curriculum?" and "Do homosexuals comprise a vocal, active interest group on campus?" . . . The questionnaire also asked whether there were any "minority and/or women's studies on campus?" . . . Yet another question asks: "Are many courses used for indoctrination?" . . . As should be clear from the questions asked and

> the people chosen to answer them, the MCEA had no intention of creating an *apolitical* handbook for choosing universities. Instead, the MCEA will use this "guide" as a means to pressure universities into capitulating to the academic right's agenda by invoking the fear of a parental backlash. (Henson and Philpott, 1992:12)

This vast network has also helped to bankroll the frontrunner in the attack on P.C.—the National Association of Scholars (NAS). The NAS's predecessor was a small New York-area based group called the Campus Coalition for Democracy. The Coalition was founded in 1982 with some help from the IEA and the Committee for the Free World, a right-wing organization directed by Midge Decter (the wife of neoconservative guru Norman Podhoretz and a board member of the Heritage Foundation). The head of the Campus Coalition for Democracy was New York University dean Herbert London, and its president was City University of New York professor of government, Stephen Balch. In the year of its founding, the organization held a conference which included speakers such as convicted Nicaraguan contra supporter Elliott Abrams; contra leader Arturo Cruz; William Doherty of the American Institute for Free Labor Development (the CIA-funded labor organization which specializes in union-busting worldwide); Michael Ledeen (active in defending Nestle Formula phony nurses responsible for poisoning babies in the Third World); and Jeanne Kirkpatrick (Diamond, 1995[b]:25).

Three years later, the organization held another conference at New York University, which was covered extensively in conservative journals and magazines. These articles provided the basis of the ensuing anti-P.C. campaign. The calls to "reclaim the academy" intensified following the 1987 publication of Allan Bloom's *The Closing of the American Mind*, and the CCD eventually changed its name to the National Association of Scholars (NAS), with London as its board chair and Balch as its president.[58] The NAS currently boasts a membership in excess of 3,000 scholars and has chapters in at least thirty-five states. Not surprisingly, the NAS is generously funded by the Coors, Olin, Smith-Richardson, Scaife, and Bradley foundations.

According to its own statement, the NAS is an organization of professors, administrators, and students committed to "rational" discourse in academe; enhancing the quality and content of the curriculum; encouraging intellectual balance and realism in campus debates about current issues; maintaining rigorous standards in teaching and research; resisting the "politicization" of teaching and scholarship; and "recalling higher education to its classic function of grounding students in the rich heritage of their civilization."[59] While the NAS claims that its aim is to defend traditional methods and scholarly standards against "politicization" and ideology, this seems highly unlikely given the corporate funding that underwrites the organization. The NAS also maintains a research center for the study of contemporary issues in higher education. The center allegedly conducts studies and publishes reports and policy statements in a non-partisan matter, but, as Messer-Davidow (1993:64) points out, the center also "assembles the stories of alleged conservative victims" of P.C.'ers and is "rumored to compile data on Left academics." This activity from an organization whose members have charged leftists with the new McCarthyism!

In addition to these nefarious activities, the NAS also publishes the journal, *Academic Questions*, which is edited by Herbert London. The first issue, published in the winter of 1987, was a call to arms for conservatives to reclaim the academy. In the opening salvo of the journal, London proclaimed that:

> Ideological orthodoxy has insinuated itself into the Academy . . . The liberal arts disciplines themselves have been infected . . . Subjectivism is the reigning deity . . . The collaborative search for truth involving faculty members and students has retreated before manipulators shaping the past to serve the present. While the traditional vision of the university promoted the ideals of Western civilization through a broad-minded empiricism and a respect for the world's complexity, the new vision . . . relies on dogmatism, conspiracies, relativism, and notions of society that challenge the pillars of liberty and constitutional democracy. (London, 1987:3)

London then states that the purpose of the NAS and its journal is to restore the "pursuit of truth" to its centrality in academic life and to ask the "right" questions about higher education. Presumably, these "right" questions do not include an examination of the New Right's influence on higher education. In fact, while the NAS suggests that it wants students to ask basic and fundamental questions about education and scholarship, at various conferences and forums it has objected when "the answers derived are not the 'right' ones," or when they do not coincide with their highly partisan agenda (Weisberg, 1992:87). Other gems in the inaugural issue include Carol Iannone's "Feminist Follies" and Peter Shaw's hysterical contribution entitled "The Abandonment of Literature." In virtually every issue, the same discourses are targeted: feminism, ethnic studies, environmental studies, Marxism and deconstruction. Affirmative action initiatives are also regularly attacked. In one article, a critique of affirmative action is offered by none other than Michael Levin, the City College of New York philosophy professor who subsequently made headlines in the early 1990s with his public announcements about the genetic inferiority of Blacks (Miller, 1995:162) and his suggestion that Black students in New York should ride in separate, police-supervised subway cars.[60]

While a variety of themes are regularly attacked, the unifying "master narrative," is a broad-based attack on the 1960s and leftist intellectuals. The assault itself is two-pronged: both intellectual and political. Common to most of the articles is a belief that the radicalism of the 1960s has become ensconced in academia to such an extent that it now constitutes basic, unquestioned elements of campus culture:

> The most remarkable aspect of the transformation of academic culture over the past quarter century has been the thoroughness with which ideas and attitudes that once represented protest, rebellion, iconoclasm, and nonconformity turned into their opposite: widely accepted conventional wisdom, a new form of conformity, values that are taken for granted . . . The main reason these survivals of the sixties often go unnoticed is precisely that they have become absorbed into the climate of opinion, into what has become the prevailing "mainstream" thinking. (Hollander, 1989:31)

Similar sentiments are echoed in Rothman (1989) who also suggests that the rise of New Left intellectuals has led to a decline in "standards," and Wildavsky (1989:55), who maintains that "inequality of condition, both in academic life and outside it, is desirable." Basically the argument is as follows: the drive for equality and democratic reform engendered by the events of the 1960s have led to a significant decline in standards, and the pedagogical initiatives stemming from that decade have failed to adequately educate students. The problem with this explanation, however, and the failure of progressives to respond adequately to such vituperative blather are due, in part, to the fact that progressives have been put in the awkward position of defending the pedagogical policies initiated in the 1960s in a cultural climate hostile to democracy and inclusiveness. Although many of the programs and initiatives spawned during that decade were either improperly implemented or never set in motion (Aronowitz and Giroux 1985, 1991, 1993), the Right has enjoyed considerable success in demonizing the educational vision which supposedly emerged from that decades' movements.

The power of the conservative attempt to redefine education in America partly resides in the Right's ability to link schooling to the ideology of the marketplace and to successfully champion the so-called virtues of "Western civilization" by equating it with a mythical notion of real "Americanness." By capitalizing on popular sentiment and discontent with the educational system, New Right discourse has conveniently argued for educational policies that extol traditional values and the rectitude of corporate capitalism. Their efforts to advance this agenda and their success in launching it into mainstream consciousness were only strengthened when the controversy over P.C. captured the attention of the populace in the early 1990s.

Notes

1. Cited in Shapiro (1991:705).

2. Paul Berman (1992:5) claims that P.C. was originally an "approving phrase on the Leninist left" used to "denote someone who steadfastly toed the party line." He argues that "politically correct" then evolved into P.C., an ironic phrase used among "wised-up leftists to denote someone whose line-toeing fervor was too much to bear." In other words, P.C. was revived among the Left as a gesture of preventive irony, to mock any attempt to assume a holier-than-thou purism. Ruth Perry (1992:72) suggests that P.C. came into the New Left vocabulary "through translation of Mao-Tse-tung's writings." Perry indicates that Mao himself often used the terms to "correct" and "incorrect" in what is now commonly referred to as his "little red book". Perry further suggests that P.C. first gained widespread currency in the United States in the mid to late 1960s within the Black power movement and the New Left.

3. Before P.C. became part of mainstream popular discourse, the crusade against "Leftists" in the academy was being waged in forums such as *Campus Report*, a publication put out by Reed Irvine's extreme right-wing group, *Accuracy in Academia*.

4. See especially Balch and London's (1986) critique of AIA's tactics.

5. Accuracy In Academia Conference Flyer, May, 1991.

6. This promise was made in Peter LaBarbera's January 1995 letter to distributors of *Campus Report*.

7. Silber's campaign against Henry Giroux, a leading critical education and cultural theorist, is but one example. Despite the fact that Giroux had published widely and that several deans and committees had unanimously recommended him for tenure, Silber appointed neo-conservative Nathan Glazer to an ad hoc committee which reviewed the other committee's recommendations. Glazer wrote a scathing attack on Giroux claiming that he belonged to a political "sect" which was then accepted by Silber, who denied Giroux tenure (Jacoby, 1987:137).

8. The survey cited was conducted by the American Council on Education and found that only "three percent" of the nearly 360 public and private institutions surveyed said "battles had erupted on their campuses over textbooks or information presented in the classroom," while only ten percent reported controversies of any kind involving campus speakers (*The Chronicle of Higher Education*, Aug. 7, 1991:A23). Even these statistics, however, cannot be relied upon to determine the num-

ber of P.C. incidents since they include reference to controversies over "leftist" speakers as well.

9. For a comprehensive look at this "myth," see Graff (1992) and Wilson (1995).

10. As previously suggested, it would be inaccurate to suggest that the New Right is a monolithic, cohesive group with a set of homogeneous ideas and values, for in fact, there are differences between various factions of the New Right. However, the "debate" over education appears to be a unifying force in that all sectors of the Right, from free-market capitalists to the Christian Right, have a stake in rolling back the democratic gains won since the 1960s. Hence, when I use the term New Right or Right in these pages, I am referring to that confederacy of loosely related groups ranging from the free market capitalist ideologues to the cultural conservatives and Christian traditionalists. As this chapter attempts to demonstrate, the New Right represents an amalgam of the Old Right, neo-conservatives, Christian fundamentalists, and business interests.

11. In many respects it is useful to think of the attack on P.C. as part of the New Right's larger "war of position." In his *Prison Notebooks*, Antonio Gramsci makes a vital distinction between two power strategies, "war of position" and "war of movement." For Gramsci (1971:238), the war of position in politics *is* the concept of hegemony, which he considers superior to a war of movement, for it is better able to grasp the "proper relation between the State and civil society." Gramsci was, of course, attempting to develop his critique of previous revolutionary strategies, particularly those of Trotsky, and to articulate what he believed to be a more appropriate course of action in the struggle for progressive social change. It is therefore paradoxical that Gramsci's insights have, in recent years, been summoned to better understand the success of the New Right (cf. Hall, 1988), but it has been conservatives who have better understood the affective and emotional dimension of the means by which consent is secured. They more easily employ nostalgic appeals to a mythical history of a Golden yesteryear and emotional cues to help mobilize support for their agendas which, more often than not serve to buttress privilege and simultaneously impede the progress of precisely those constituencies who willingly sanction such agendas. Much of the recent success of the New Right and their campaign against radicals—tenured or otherwise— is best understood in this light given that nostalgia has played a key role in convincing large sectors of the population that P.C. (and all it allegedly encompasses including multiculturalism, affirmative action, feminism, civil rights) poses a serious threat to the "American way of life."

12. The funding of the New Right is subsequently taken up in greater detail.

13.   Shortly after the completion of *God And Man At Yale*, Buckley assumed
       a CIA post in Mexico City to watch over its growing student move-
       ment. His stay there was curtailed due ostensibly to his return to the
       United States to face the controversy which his book had spawned.

14.   On an edition of his PBS show, *Firing Line*, which aired in the midst
       of P.C. fever, Buckley situated himself as a defender of free speech in
       opposition to the alleged presence of left-wing campus vigilantes.
       Buckley's defence of free expression in addition to many other con-
       servatives whose records on free speech are atrocious, would be ludi-
       crously humorous if it were not for the seriousness accorded to their
       assertions.

15.   For a far more nuanced and detailed examination of this fusionism
       and the differences and similarities between libertarianism and tradi-
       tionalism, see Himmelstein (1990:28-62).

16.   These are extracted from "The Magazine's Credenda" *National Re-
       view*, Nov. 19, 1955, p. 6.

17.   Evan Carton (1991:40-47) argues that the hysteria over multi-
       culturalism reflects deep-rooted tensions about the challenges to a
       homogeneous (i.e. white, European) notion of Americanness and
       American identity.

18.   In recent years, ISI has taken to the task of aggressively promoting
       the project of cultural conservatism on university campuses. Consider
       the following remarks delivered at a 1989 lecture to the Heritage Foun-
       dation by ISI president T. Kenneth Cribb:

       We must thus provide resources and guidance to an elite which
       can take up anew the task of enculturation. Through its journals,
       lectures, seminars, books, and fellowships, this is what ISI has
       done successfully for thirty-six years. The coming of age of such
       elites has provided the current leadership of the conservative re-
       vival. But we should add a major new component to our strategy:
       the conservative movement is now mature enough to sustain a
       counteroffensive on that last Leftist redoubt, the college campus
       . . . We are now strong enough to establish a contemporary pres-
       ence for conservatism on campus, and contest the Left on its own
       turf. We plan to do this by greatly expanding the ISI field effort,
       its network of campus-based programming (cited in Messer-
       Davidow, 1993:47).

19.   The Sharon Statement was named as such because Buckley's estate
       was located in Sharon, Connecticut. For the full text of the Sharon
       Statement see the *National Review*, Sept.24, 1960, p. 173.

20.   A YAF rally honoring Republican senators John Tower and Barry
       Goldwater attracted over 18,000 people to Madison Square Garden in
       the winter of 1962 (*National Review*, 1962:190-191).

21. For a discussion of the "new revolt" and the significance of the 1960s for the conservative movement, see Evans (1961) and Gottfried and Fleming (1988).

22. According to information obtained from the Goldwater Page on the Internet, *Conscience of a Conservative* had sold 3.5 million copies by 1964.

23. Sara Diamond (1995[a]:62-63) points out that Goldwater's opposition to civil rights made him especially popular among southern voters who were upset about desegregation policies.

24. According to John Saloma (1984:45), Viguerie started with the names of 12,500 contributors to the Goldwater campaign, from which he systematically built up a "computer data bank containing some 20 million names and 4.5 million contributors."

25. For example, both Echols (1995) and Wallace (1989) have argued that many of the "histories" of the 1960s and the New Left have been written from the perspective of white males, while the experiences of women and minorities have been downplayed.

26. For example, see Davidson (1967).

27. It is important to note that while the SDS was often regarded as synonymous with the "New Left," it was, in fact, only part of the New Left or "the movement" as insiders called it, and the movement itself was part of a larger cultural upheaval that occurred during the decade (Lee and Shlain 1985:133).

28. This, however, is not to suggest that the struggle for civil rights in the African-American community *began* in the Sixties for the civil rights struggle "really began following World War Two, culminated in several important events in the mid-to-late 1950s, then carried over into the 1960s." The sixties "marked a time when whites in the US, especially the young, became involved in social activism as a result of the groundwork laid by the African-American community"(Davis, 1990:29-30).

29. In *The Port Huron Statement*, SDS members articulated several root principles as they related to participatory democracy. In essence, they argued that participatory democracy had to be based upon decision-making carried out by public groupings, and that politics had the purpose of bringing people out of isolation and into community. For an insightful and illuminating re-evaluation of the pertinence of SDS activities and the Port Huron Statement, see Flacks et al., (1987).

30. It is important to point out that the Free Speech Movement was, in part, triggered by the Berkeley authorities' refusal to allow public campus fundraising for the civil rights movement (Buhle, 1987).

31.   For a critique of Kerr's notion of the "multiversity", see Draper (1965).

32.   Kellner (1984:281) reminds us that Marcuse was the only member of the Frankfurt School who openly and enthusiastically supported the student movement and the political activism of the 1960s.

33.   As quoted in Blumenthal (1988:xii-xiii).

34.   For an insightful discussion of conservative reaction to campus radicalism, see Gottfried and Fleming (1988), and for thoughts on the legal implications of academic politics, see Bork et al., (1970).

35.   Of course, not all neoconservatives came from the Old Left; however, it is important to note that the first generation of neoconservatives "became conservatives not by inheritance, but by conversion" (Dorrien,1993:7). Dorrien further notes that the turn to the Right was a surprise to the Old Left-liberals themselves; the social movements of the 1960s and 1970s had driven them to positions they hadn't expected to defend. In recent years a number of former members of the New Left have since joined the ranks of neoconservatives. Consider Peter Collier and David Horowitz, former radicals who have discovered the financial rewards of Sixties-bashing. According to the jacket of their 1989 book *Destructive Generation: Second Thoughts About The Sixties*, Collier and Horowitz are leaders of a movement called Second Thoughts—a movement for former radicals who have re-examined their prior radical commitments and rejected them. Collier and Horowitz also initiated the journal *Heterodoxy*, largely a vehicle used for promulgating anti-Sixties sentiments. In 1993, the duo edited the book, *Surviving the PC University*, which allegedly documents the horrors of P.C. on American campuses. In addition, Horowitz (who used to work for Bob Dole) runs a Los Angeles-based Center for the Study of Popular Culture—an outfit which is funded by the Olin, Scaife, Bradley and other right-wing foundations to "the tune of approximately $700,000 per year" (Diamond, 1995[b]:34). Horowitz is also a regular commentator on CNN.

36.   While neoconservatism had its origins in the New York intellectual tradition, it is important to note, as does Dorrien (1993:8), that neoconservatism is "more heterogeneous" than is suggested in many renditions of its historical trajectory. He points out that many of the movements prominent theorists were neither New Yorkers nor Jewish.

37.   For a discussion of the differences between the Old Right and the neoconservatives, see Gottfried and Fleming (1988) and Diamond (1995[a]).

38.   In *War At Home*, Brian Glick (1989:13-19) describes the covert activities of COINTELPRO (the code name for an FBI Counterintelligence Program) which were aimed at Sixties activists. He maintains that it is

necessary to understand the 1960s context in order to grasp the impact COINTELPRO activities had on dissidents. While the 1960s were characterized by a rejection of dominant culture and ideology, by the mid-1970s the social upheavals had largely subsided, and radicals found themselves on the defensive; meanwhile the Right gained major government positions and was increasingly able to define the contours of accepted political debate. While domestic covert operations were scaled down after the social protests waned, they did not cease. The harassment of former radicals continued into the 1970s and 1980s.

39.   Glick (1989:14) also discusses how the mass media, "owned by big business and cowed by government and right-wing attack, helped to bury radical activism by ceasing to cover it." In a similar vein, Todd Gitlin's *The Whole World Is Watching* (1980) surveys the mass media's treatment of the New Left, specifically the SDS, and argues that the coverage ultimately resulted in the subsequent decline of the movement and the containment of serious political change.

40.   Despite the nostalgic undertones of Russell Jacoby's *The Last Intellectuals*, he correctly points out that the "intellectuals associated with the sixties failed to maintain a public presence; many departed for other careers; others disappeared into the universities" (1987:26).

41.   See for example Kristol's essay "About Equality," originally written in 1972 and reprinted in his *Two Cheers For Capitalism*.

42.   Apparently the "growing" radicalism of professors was important enough that the Carnegie Commission on Higher Education saw fit to commission a study of the phenomenon. See Boland and Boland (1974).

43.   I have not explicitly traced the trajectory of the Christian Right in this book, since most of their efforts at intervening in education have been geared towards the elementary and secondary levels. My choice in doing this, however, is in no way intended to minimize the influence of the Christian Right, for they have successfully moved what was once considered a "radical Right" agenda to the center of American politics. Furthermore, Ralph Reed (1995) has explicitly stated that education will be *the* number one social issue of the decade. The Christian Coalition's legislative priorities include abolishing the Department of Education, or at least downgrading it to an agency level; defederalizing educational policy by bloc granting federal functions back to states, locally elected school boards and parents; and creating scholarship and/or voucher programs so that parents have a choice of where to send their children.

44.   Paul Weyrich is regarded as the "issues man" and major strategist of the New Right. In addition to co-founding the Heritage Foundation, he also helped to start the Moral Majority in 1979, and has been instrumental in garnering financial support for the Christian Coalition.

He was one among other "secular" players who helped to turn the religious right into a major political force during the 1970s and 1980s.

45. For detailed descriptions of cultural conservatism, see *Cultural Conservatism: Toward A New Agenda* (1987), and Lind and Marshner (1991).

46. The current dilemma of the "Left" is taken up in Chapter Four.

47. During the mid-1980s, the AEI suffered a major financial crisis due to overexpansion, stagnant revenues, internal mismanagement and external competition from other more conservative organizations (Himmelstein, 1990:147). This crisis notwithstanding, the AEI continues to sponsor right-wing scholarship, most recently, that of Dinesh D'Souza.

48. In addition to supporting a free enterprise capitalist system and being active in union-busting, the Coors family has helped to fund a number of "pro-family" organizations and has spoken out against women's rights. The family has also been vocal in its opposition to gay right's initiatives claiming that "homosexuals are an abomination" and that "AIDS is God's judgements on homosexuals" (Bellant, 1991:xv). In addition, the Coors family has a lengthy history of racist practices and have lent financial support to overtly racist groups and organizations (Bellant, 1991:66-74).

49. Since the early 1980s, the Coors foundation has contributed in excess of $130,000 to Mel and Norma Gabler's non-profit organization, Educational Research Analysts. The organization, which operates out of the Gabler's Texas home, has, since 1962, searched textbooks for what they perceive to be anti-Christian, anti-family sentiment. Their work has earned them praise from the likes of Richard Viguerie, Jerry Falwell and Phyllis Schlafly (Bellant, 1991:95).

50. Paul Weyrich was also a long-time associate of the extreme right-wing John Birch Society. In 1974, he left Heritage to found the Free Congress Foundation to further the agenda of "cultural conservatism." The FCF and Weyrich still work closely with Heritage and are currently strong supporters of Ralph Reed's Christian Coalition.

51. The FCF evolved out of the Committee for the Survival of a Free Congress. The FCF's lobbying arm is the Coalition for America and it has close ties with the religious Right through the coalition activities, board of directors and staff liaisons. The FCF's operating budget was estimated to be between $6 to $7 million in 1993. Major donors include members of the Coors family, Michael and Helen Valerio of Papa Gino's and Richard and Helen DeVos of the Amway Corporation (Institute for First Amendment Studies, 1995: 369). Among the FCF's "distinguished" associates is convicted Nazi war criminal, Lazlo Pasztor, who works out of FCF's Washington Office.

52. Currently, FCF's National Empowerment Television (NET), has a $2.1 million budget that is expected to double by 1997. Weyrich is president of NET, Ralph Reed of the Christian Coalition is a director and former Secretary of Education, William Bennett, is chairman (Institute for First Amendment Studies, 1995: 369).

53. According to Solomon (1996:10), Heritage is the most widely cited think-tank in the United States. Heritage personnel regularly appear on television and radio, and generate an endless flow of op-ed pieces for newspapers.

54. Reverend Sun Myung Moon is the theocratic authoritarian who considers himself the Son of God and the new Messiah. His many organizations have been used by the Korean CIA as a propaganda vehicle to maintain high levels of U.S. military and economic aid and the continued presence of U.S. armed forces in South Korea. His many organizations have supported the World Anti-Communist League (WACL) and have helped "solidify cooperation between WACL and members of the American political right wing" (Bellant, 1988:65). For further discussion of Moon's organizations and activities, see Boettcher and Freeman (1980) and for a brief account of the Unification Church's links with the academy, see Junas (1991).

55. The history of the "alternative" student journalism movement is discussed in greater detail in Delaney and Lenkowsky (1988). Leslie Lenkowsky was recruited in 1975 by the Smith-Richardson Foundation to serve on its staff and later served as the president of the IEA. He is now president of another right-wing think tank, the Hudson Institute.

56. In 1989, the Bradley Foundation supplied half a million dollars to the Madison Center and when it merged with the IEA in 1990, it granted another $93,000 (Henson and Philpott, 1992).

57. These figures were taken from the MCEA 1990 Annual Report. For a fairly current list of locations and titles see Dodge (1990).

58. Among London's "scholarly" contributions is a piece entitled "Marxism Thriving on American Campuses", which appeared in the monthly publication, the *World and I* in 1987. The *World and I* is published by Reverend Sun Myung Moon's *Washington Times* Company. According to Wiener (1990:167) London is also a columnist for the *New York City Tribune*, a sister paper of Moon's *Washington Times*.

59. Cited from the NAS home page on the World Wide Web.

60. For a detailed discussion of Levin's affiliation with the controversial Pioneer Fund and his eugenics research, see Miller (1995).

Chapter 2

Products of the "Ideas Industry" and Other (Not So) Great Books of the Culture Wars

The New Right Goes to School

Taken together, the various think-tanks, foundations and institutes discussed in the previous chapter have helped further the agenda of cultural conservatism by creating what Smith (1991) has called an "ideas industry." This industry is aimed largely at dismantling and undermining democratic progressive initiatives in both political and educational domains. In the guise of seeking to restore a "lost tradition" to the academy, a stream of corporate-sponsored conservative authors have emerged as the organic intellectuals of the rightist resurgence.

Leading the charge and setting the tone for the contemporary attacks on P.C. was the 1987 publication of Allan Bloom's *The Closing Of The American Mind,* which many agree was the opening salvo in a concerted campaign to sabotage the public's faith in higher education. For his efforts, Bloom received more than $3 million in grants and donations between 1986 and 1989.[1] In *The Closing Of The American Mind*, Bloom conjures up images of decay and chaos in contemporary moral and intellectual life which he attributes to the democratic reforms and critical discourses which emerged during the 1960s. For him, the imperatives of promoting equality and redressing racism, sexism, and elitism, have become the concerns of those who could "define no other interest worthy of defending" (Bloom, 1987:314). In his diatribes against critical scholarship,

he argues that the academic engagement of contemporary social issues is, at best, a distraction from the intellectual's true
vocation and at worst, a total subversion of scholarly integrity.
Bloom's best-selling book created a firestorm of controversy
and incited a number of thoughtful critiques which need not
be recounted here. Nonetheless, it is important to point out
that many of his themes share a great deal of similarity to those
in two books that dominated the "debate" over P.C.—namely,
Illiberal Education and *Tenured Radicals*. It would appear that
Bloom's torch has been passed on to two more youthful lackeys of the New Right's ideas industry—Dinesh D'Souza and
Roger Kimball.[2]

While Bloom's book was more of a "scholarly" harangue
against critical philosophy, the tracts penned by D'Souza and
Kimball are unmistakably unscholarly, transparently idiosyn-
cratic critiques of higher education based on anecdotal evidence and "tourism"—in the case of Kimball, attendance at
academic conferences, and in that of D'Souza, visits to the campuses of elite universities. Cavalier about facts and often dis-
regarding any pretence of intellectual honesty and balance,
these texts purport to describe the P.C. horrors on campuses,
yet their underlying purpose is to denigrate progressive initiatives, negate "difference," and promote a one-dimensional,
monocultural vision of Western society.

Kimball's *Tenured Radicals*[3]—a pastiche of previous essays
that appeared in Hilton Kramer's conservative art journal *The
New Criterion*—was generously supported by both the IEA and
the Olin Foundation.[4] In order to illustrate the contemporary
assault on the academy, Kimball offers his book as a self-proclaimed "report from the front." This use of military slang is
indicative of the hysterical and aggressive tone of Kimball's
book which, far from being a sophisticated critique of
academia, reads more like a log book, in which Kimball provides blow-by-blow descriptions of the "wars" being waged
against Western civilization at academic conferences and in
college classrooms.

The case of D'Souza is far more intriguing. Born in India
and educated at an elite Jesuit school, D'Souza came to the
United States as a teenager and went on to attend Dartmouth
College, where he gained some notoriety while serving as editor of the *Dartmouth Review*.[5] The abominable activities which

he engaged in during his heady days at Dartmouth undoubtedly endeared him to conservatives and he subsequently served
as a domestic policy analyst in the Reagan administration.
D'Souza was catapulted from virtual anonymity to media stardom after the publication of *Illiberal Education,* which instantly
became the right-wing bible of academic condemnation. His
meteoric rise from obscurity to a national best-selling author
is almost as bizarre as it is remarkable, especially for someone
whose first book, an admiring biography of Jerry Falwell published in 1984, remains virtually unknown and unread (Henson,
1991). Yet D'Souza's background provides a prime example of
the way in which a few right-wing institutions can transform
an unsung incendiary into a national public figure.

Blumenthal (1988) provides a detailed description of how
conservative think-tanks recruit youthful lackeys, usually under forty, and launch them into stardom—all it takes is money.
In 1988, as a John Olin fellow at the American Enterprise Institute, D'Souza received, through the IEA, a $30,000 grant
from the Olin Foundation to begin work on a book tentatively
titled *The New Elite,* which was eventually renamed *Illiberal
Education.* When he became a research fellow at the AEI in
1989, the Olin Foundation contributed another $50,000. In
1990, Olin provided yet another $50,000 and the Madison
Center authorized a $20,000 grant for promotion of the book
upon publication.[6] In total, D'Souza received $150,000 for the
writing and promotion of his book from a variety of think-
tanks which have, in popularizing the book, also advanced their
political agenda. Shortly after the text was published, it became a best-seller, and D'Souza began appearing on nationally
syndicated talk shows and news programs as a revered expert
on educational issues—despite the fact that D'Souza is a think-
tank research fellow and not a trained scholar or professor of
education.[7] This is a textbook example of a trend identified by
Messer-Davidow (1993), who claims that think-tanks have been
able to endow an "academicized" aura of authority on research
actually done outside of the academy.[8]

Since much energy has been expended by others to expose
the lies and distortions promulgated by both D'Souza and
Kimball, my intent here is not to recount those criticisms, but
rather to take up the general ideological presuppositions which
undergird their narratives and to address some of the recur-

ring themes, which include the defence of the Western tradition, Western culture and its values; the unrelenting belief in
value-neutral scholarship; the free market liberal usage of the
concept of free speech and academic freedom; and the concerted attack on "special interest" groups and multiculturalism
in general.

The Canon and the Politics of Knowledge

Within academe, the canon generally refers to a range of cultural artifacts and texts which are taken to represent the foun-
dational values or essence of a given culture. It is generally
held that exposure to, and engagement with, canonical texts
provide the basis for a definition of the well-educated person.

In *Tenured Radicals*, Kimball follows Matthew Arnold in describing the canon as tradition which represents "the best that
has been thought and said."[9] For Kimball, the Western canon
is intrinsically worthy of careful study and its awe-inspiring
value is self-evident. It is, in other words, simply the "best,"
and Kimball condemns those who would contend that "the
best" is a socially relative and highly contestable term. He in-
vokes Arnold who "looked to criticism to provide a bulwark
against ideology, against interpretations that are subordinated
to essentially political interests" (Kimball, 1991:74). Despite
Kimball's admonitions, what is considered the best or important is indeed contextual and political for the canon is based
upon a hierarchizing project where cultural objects are ranked.
Some of these objects are granted canonical status and deemed
fundamental, while others are excluded. More often than not,
these decisions are influenced by the regnant practices and
cultural imperatives of a given social formation. What constitutes the canon at any given time, in any given culture,
depends largely on who has access to the story-making apparatuses.

Not surprisingly, Kimball completely dismisses such a formulation and clings to the notion of the canon as a warehouse
of knowledge with an objective existence and, which is allegedly impervious to ideological taint. In this regard, Kimball,
like most canonical conservatives, is guilty of a form of idola-
try which fixes the "classics" in an ahistorical realm where they
are "worshipped for their embodiment of the Western

metaphysic" (Taubman, 1993:36). For Kimball, to merely question the superiority of the Western canon is treasonous.

While Kimball appeals to an Arnoldian notion of the canon, D'Souza simply defines the canon as a set of required great books which he claims are being displaced from university curricula. Minor differences aside, both D'Souza's and Kimball's indictments of P.C. canon-bashers rest on the conviction that the Western tradition is comprised of recognized great works which are of universal human interest and which speak to people across the barriers of race, ethnicity, gender, time, and geography. Both also maintain that Western culture and its values represent the highest standard of achievement and civilization and that they form the bedrock of American society. In these accounts, what is considered Western is constructed as being synonymous with what is American. This conflation of the West with America is intended to create a sense of "Americanness" which is defined in narrow Eurocentric terms.[10] June Jordan (1985) draws attention to the highly disputable definitions of Westernness which permeate contemporary struggles over meaning, representation, and values. She asks, for example, how it is that the histories, cultural narratives, and writings of African-Americans, who have populated the Americas for centuries, are now deemed non-Western. The issue Jordan raises illuminates the powerful ideological implications of the appeal to narrow and mythical notions of Westernness and Americanness.

The laments about the abandonment of the Western canon in both D'Souza's and Kimball's texts have been exposed for the preposterous drivel that they are, yet the championing of a seemingly homogeneous, unproblematic Western tradition as inherently superior, continues unabated in the discourse of educational conservatives.[11] In many respects, conservative critics have sought to "naturalize" the idea of the Western tradition's superiority by emptying it of its history in a process similar to that described by Roland Barthes in his seminal text *Mythologies*. In his discussion of myth, he argues that

> myth is constituted by the loss of the historical quality of things: in it, things lose the memory that they once were made . . . A conjuring trick has taken place; it has turned reality inside out, it has emptied it of history and has filled it with Nature . . . Myth does not deny things, on the contrary, its function is to talk about them; simply, it purifies

them, it makes them innocent, it gives them a natural and eternal
justification, it gives them a clarity which is not that of an explanation but that of a statement of fact. (Barthes, 1972:131-132)

In much the same fashion, conservative myth-makers have
sought to render the Western canon/tradition's historicity
transparent by occluding the fact that it is a socially constructed
entity, an invention, an imagined community of sorts, which is
imbricated in much broader power differentials.[12] Indeed, de-
ciding which texts to include and what counts as "legitimate"
knowledge reflects decisions which have been made out of an
endless array of possibilities, and such decisions inevitably
mirror dominant relations of power and privilege.

The view of knowledge espoused by conservatives suggests
that knowledge is neutral and transparent; however, this view
neglects significant political concerns regarding the creation
of canons and the interests they serve. Although conservatives
maintain that their defence of the canon is "disinterested," Toni
Morrison illuminates the political character of contemporary
debates:

Canon building is Empire building. Canon defence is national defence. Canon debate, whatever the terrain, nature and range . . . is
the clash of cultures. And all of the interests are vested. (Morrison,
1989:8)

Furthermore, in conservative narratives the Western tradition
is reified in a manner which supplants social determinations
and historical struggles and moves the discussion to a terrain
of timeless universal values. Scott argues that

the fetishizing of "tradition" allows the publicists to present a particular version of culture—one that gives priority to the writing and
viewpoints of European White men—as if it were the only true version
without, however, acknowledging its particularity and exclusiveness.
This kind of practice, which discounts and silences the voices and
experiences of others, is profoundly undemocratic. In the guise of
protecting an objectively established "tradition" the publicists can
disavow any association with undemocratic practices while still engaging in them. (Scott, 1995:113-114)

It is therefore imperative to reiterate that the creation of a
tradition is always predicated on the process of selection; that
is, tradition is not simply a matter of a fixed or given set of

practices, beliefs, values, and texts which are passed on. Rather as several observers have noted, the "invention" of a tradition is very much an issue of present-day politics, and of the way in which powerful institutions and interests function to select particular objects, texts and/or memories from the past, and to mobilize them in the interest of furthering contemporary political and cultural agendas (Hobsbawn and Ranger, 1983; Spivak, 1990; Wright, 1985).

Despite D'Souza's and Kimball's attempts to naturalize the superiority and apolitical nature of the Western tradition and pass it off as common sense, common sense as Gramsci (1971) reminds us, always has a structure and a past which are related to particular historical and social imperatives. Indeed, the monoculturalism that underscores the Western tradition

> only emerged in the late nineteenth century to create the impression of an intellectual tradition where there was indeed none . . . by mid-century, this monocultural . . . Eurovision had become cemented in the United States as hegemonic intellectual ideology and institutional practice. (Goldberg, 1994:3-4)

Predictably, both D'Souza and Kimball cast the debate over the canon in typical Manichean fashion—as the West vs. the Rest, as a choice between "culture and barbarism," as a titanic struggle between forms of civilized "high" culture (read: White, Western) and the "primitive," contaminating forces of "other" low-brow cultures (read: non-White, non-Western) thereby reinscribing the rigid binomial opposition of "ours" and "theirs" characteristic of neocolonial discourses (Said, 1978:227-228). From the standpoint of conservative authors, any interrogation of the canon becomes commensurate to threatening the foundation of Western civilization and is branded as an exercise in ideological brainwashing. Thus Kimball suggests that:

> In this war against Western culture, one chief object of attack within the academy is the traditional canon and the pedagogical values it embodies . . . Instead of reading the great works of the past, students watch movies, pronounce on the depredations of patriarchal society, or peruse second or third-rate works . . . after four years they will find that they are ignorant of the tradition and that their college education was largely a form of ideological indoctrination. (Kimball, 1990:xii-xvii)

The trepidation and sanctimonious indignation that typifies this perspective rests on a defensiveness in which all "others" are seen as enemies intent on ravaging "our" civilization and way of life. In this account, the hard-fought changes which multiculturalists have wrought come to epitomize the debasement of all "authentic" Western culture. The "we" and "our" constructed in conservative narratives is highly exclusive. We, as Whites of European descent are civilized; intellectually and morally superior; and represent the highest standards of cultural achievement. The "multicultural" presence is thus constructed as a problem or threat against which "a homogeneous, white, national 'we' could be unified" (Gilroy, 1991:48).

In conservative accounts the West is characterized as intellectually fecund and the rest of the world as intellectually sterile and stagnant. Moreover, Eurocentricity and whiteness represent the normative frame of reference and are the standard of valuation used to judge other works and other cultures. By creating this reductive, binary formulation and positing a vision of cultural entropy and moral decay engendered by multicultural defenders, conservative traditionalists become, by default, the defenders of civilization itself.[13] Indeed, the valorization of Western civilization and its values in these accounts (particularly D'Souza's) is predicated upon representing "other" cultures as barbaric, savage, irrational, uncivilized, and backwards. This posturing becomes all the more apparent when depictions of "Third" world practices are contrasted to those of the West in D'Souza's rather puerile discussions of multiculturalism.[14]

For example, D'Souza (1992:79-80) directs his attention to the fact that non-Western cultures have no "developed tradition of racial equality," that many of these cultures have "deeply ingrained ideas of male superiority," and that non-Western attitudes toward "homosexuality" and other "alternative lifestyles" are harsh to the point that the practice of such lifestyles is most often greeted with severe punishment. He even points out that among some African tribes, homosexuality is regarded as "a sin and a sickness." One is tempted to ask, however, how this differs in any fundamental respect to structural arrangements and "attitudes" which exist in the West. Although "tolerance" is allegedly the cornerstone of Western culture, institutionalized and systemic racism is rampant, even though D'Souza would have us believe that it does not exist; patriarchal relations still structure many of our Western institutions and world views, and homophobia is a constitutive feature of our social fabric. D'Souza need not look to Africa or elsewhere to find those who deem homosexuality a sickness or a sin; he could easily read any of the literature circulated by the Christian Coalition and other far Right religious organizations in the United States. Hence, while D'Souza attempts to paint an auspicious portrait of the West, and the United States specifically, as a paradise which is tolerant, open, and based on the tenet of equality, the grimy realities of everyday life provide a starkly different image.

Furthermore, the West-is-best logic that informs the monoculturalist tirades of D'Souza and Kimball conveniently ignores the legacies of colonialism, imperialism, and oppression which have characterized the enterprise of Western civilization.[15] As Walter Benjamin so cogently reminds us, what traditionalists call "cultural treasures" must be treated with caution, for their origins cannot be contemplated without a profound sense of "horror." There "is no document of civilization which is not at the same time a document of barbarism" (Benjamin, 1968:256).

Cultural conservatives also tend to perpetuate the myth that the West has enjoyed some rare historical advantage, some unique feature of culture, environment, race, or mind, which imparts it with a permanent superiority over all other cultural communities or traditions. Blaut (1993:1) refers to this form of reasoning as diffusionist. "Diffusionism," or more specifically, European diffusionism, is a form of spatial elitism that has been perpetuated for centuries across fields and disciplines. Diffusionists tend to view the world in binary terms. The West is positioned as the core, the center from which all ideas and culture emerge and, the Rest (of the world) as the periphery, which is on the receiving end of Western civilization and culture. Blaut (1993) argues that diffusionism is the foundation of Western thought and that all scholarship is diffusionist insofar as it accepts the Inside-Outside model, or the notion that the world has one fixed center from which all culture-changing ideas originate and a periphery that responds or changes as a result of such diffusion.[16] For Blaut, Eurocentricity and European diffusionism represents the "colonizers model of the world."

Of course, the fact that their diffusionist logic is erroneous hardly ruffles the feathers of conservative ideologues, for their well-funded apologias of the West are merely part of the New Right's larger strategy of cultural conservatism. Consider D'Souza's and Kimball's defence of Western culture in relation to the assertions of Paul Weyrich's advisor, William Lind (1986), who claimed that traditional Western culture must be preserved because it is "functionally true" and "necessary" for the proper maintenance of the "social order." Here, the defence of the canon is used to advance a pedagogy of submission, in which critical and independent thought are subverted in the name of acquiring a body of knowledge which is purportedly transhistorical, pristine, and universal. Conservatives tend to view educational institutions as sites to propagate and sanction the economic and political interests of capitalist elites and the privileged cultural capital of ruling groups. This is made explicit by D'Souza (1992:xx) when he remarks that a new vision of education must integrate the preeminent ideal of excellence, thus "enabling future generations of young people to be more productive workers and harmonious citizens." The underlying logic of capitalist legitimation becomes apparent in this "banking" vision of higher education.

In *Pedagogy of the Oppressed*, Paulo Freire delineates his conceptualization of the banking method of education. Freire claims that in this model, knowledge is a "gift bestowed by those who consider themselves knowledgeable upon those whom they consider to know nothing" (1970:58). That is, students become the passive recipients of a stagnant and unchanging storehouse of knowledge and information rather than the dynamic creators and interpreters of knowledge. The banking method of education regards people as adaptable, manageable, beings and recognizes that the more students work at storing the deposits of knowledge entrusted to them, "the less they develop the critical consciousness which would result from their intervention in the world" (Freire, 1970:60). In the current debate over the canon and in the conservative cry for the preservation of Western tradition, one can identify the banking mentality informing the conservative position. By treating the Western tradition as the highest achievement of human-kind and as something to be revered unequivocally, students are expected to be the passive recipients of a "classic" store-house of information while their lived realities, histories, and voices are silenced. Here, the notions of critical consciousness are subverted by conservative positions intended to legitimate a form of pedagogy that serves as a hegemonic apparatus for maintaining current conditions of inequality and injustice.

It is necessary to point out that part of the New Right's struggle to valorize Western culture emerges from an urgently felt national imperative to

> reimagine cultural and civic identity in the United States in the wake of vast changes produced by the decline of its global hegemony, the rapid internationalization of capital and industry, the immigrant im-plosion of the "third" world onto the "first" and the democratization of American institutions and political processes that occurred in the two decades prior to 1980. (Pratt,1992:14)

This national imperative to redefine American identity and Americanness must be understood contextually—that is, in light of the New Right's larger "war of position." Much as Thatcherism sought to redefine the terrain of common sense by invoking an imaginary vision of England and a mythical definition of Englishness[17] in its bid for hegemony, the New Right in the United States is seeking, through its identifica-tion with Western culture and values to imbue its anti-P.C. stance with a sense of authentic "Americanness," while those advocating greater inclusiveness are characterized as anti-West-ern, anti-American, and by fiat, anti-democratic demagogues.[18]

In many respects, the ideology of nationalism was summoned to distort the discourse of multicultural education by portray-ing proponents of inclusive curricula as destroyers of national identity. Of course, these tactics and Americanist sentiments are not limited to the struggle over curricula. In fact, they are evident in the vocabularies of a number of right-wing politi-cians who are currently attempting to transform common sense by employing populist rhetoric to construct an imaginary "us" which is then pitted against an imaginary "them." Conserva-tive ideologues recognize all too well the deep-rooted need felt by many to belong to a community, whether it is real or imagined and they direct their attention to carving out new identities and new spaces for those who feel displaced.[19] Although conservatives acknowledge that American culture is demographically diverse, they insist that only the values of the Western tradition can provide the cement which binds the country together; in short, these values are said to constitute the "common" culture. The common, however, is itself a contested category whose meaning varies. Quite simply, the "common" is not a transhistorical given but rather a social construction based on arbitrarily agreed upon assumptions. To simply claim that something like a common culture exists, begs obvious questions—common to whom? Defined by whom and for what purpose?

While conservatives concede that diversity is a defining characteristic of contemporary campuses, they nonetheless argue that the common good can only be realized by an unquestioning acceptance of the "common culture." In essence, one is expected to adopt a consensual view of culture and learn to accept the Euro-American, patriarchal, and capitalist norms embedded within traditional academic discourse. McLaren (1995) reminds us that the appeal to an instituted, neutral, universal, common culture not only occludes the structural advantage of those petitioning the discourse of the "common" but also serves to mask the logic of assimilation and the suppression of difference which undergirds such a formulation. In general, conservatives view difference as a problem because it allegedly endangers common culture or what D'Souza prefers to call the "neutral framework" or the "shared community which transcends . . . narrower interests" (1992: 186, 55). Of course, there is *no* one common culture as is claimed by the guardians of the status quo; rather there is a hegemonic culture which is promulgated as though it were common. Furthermore, in accounts which summon the idea of a common culture, it is assumed that the content of that culture is already settled and definitively defined. Thus, culture is viewed as a static, already existing entity—a finished and completed phenomenon, rather than something which is fluid, contested, dynamic, and constantly renegotiated by social actors.

Although the efforts to assert the primacy of Western culture are, no doubt, driven by a highly-charged ideological agenda, New Right mandarins have, predictably, constructed the "debate" in a manner which suggests that only one side

has a political agenda and that they themselves are merely interested in protecting the common good and defending the
virtues of "truth" against the incursions of ideology. Stanley
Fish explains the strategy by which this is accomplished:

> [F]irst detach your agenda from its partisan origins, from its history
> and then present it as a universal imperative, as a call to moral arms
> so perspicuous that only the irrational or the godless . . . could refuse
> it. (Fish, 1994:8)

The Right's success in accomplishing this task is largely due to
the fact that they have seized the high ground by laying claim
to the highly charged terms of "objectivity," "common culture"
and "rights and freedoms" to buttress their own agenda. Their
strategy, therefore, requires further elaboration.

The hallmark of both D'Souza's and Kimball's arguments is
an appeal to a mythical Golden Age in academe. They weave
tales of a lost age of social cohesiveness which has since been
corrupted by the combined forces of P.C. and multiculturalism.
Central to their narratives is the claim that the political neutrality and ideological disinterestedness that once characterized the enterprise of higher education has been ruthlessly
abandoned by today's tenured radicals. Rather than engaging
in the disinterested pursuit of "truth," it is claimed that a new
generation of academics have shed their scholarly robes and
donned the brownshirts of political activists. Arguing that classrooms are now used as laboratories for political indoctrination to leftist agendas, conservatives inveigh against those who
have sought to unmask both the ideological and epistemological presuppositions which undergird the Western tradition they
exalt. For these efforts, critical scholars have been deemed as
"enemies of democracy" and accused of sabotaging the once-
pristine Western canon with forms of multiculturalist tribal-
ism and philosophical chicanery. Given that their views have
been so widely accepted among the public and media at large,
it is necessary to further unpack the premises of conservative
ideology.

Conservative scholars emphasize cultural retrieval and restoration and their expressed mission is to recover and promote appreciation of the Western tradition and its truth and
authenticity, while keeping safely at bay any challenges to the

assumptions undergirding that tradition, or any attempts to locate it in its proper social and historical context. That the value of the Western canon could be reasonably subject to debate is vehemently resisted by traditionalists who reject the idea that reality and interpretation are intrinsically related, and who hold to the belief that something called "pure" knowledge exists.

For the most part, conservatives argue that pure knowledge and truth are arrived at through the use of rigorous methods which are untainted by ideology and whose standards of excellence are objective rather than political. Conservative traditionalists have long contended that social order can only be maintained by the "truths" of the objective moral order. For older conservatives like Meyer (1962) and Kirk (1962) the dissemination of a "common" stock of knowledge, which reflects the "absolute truths" of society and culture, is a necessary prerequisite for the maintenance of social order and social control. It is generally held that through disciplined, disinterested study the fundamental "truths" of society will somehow reveal themselves to the trained mind. However, this view can only be sustained if one subscribes to the logocentrism and positivist rationality which informs conservative philosophy. Its logocentrism is evident in the quest for an authoritative language capable of uncovering moral correctness and Truth while positivism, which adheres most closely to the methodology of the natural sciences, is predicated on the notion of transcendental, universal reason and the belief that it is possible to generate value-free knowledge.

Pierre Bourdieu (1991:38) recently remarked that should a new form of totalitarianism arise, it would stem, in all likelihood, from the valorization of science and the attendant concern for objectivity. Quite simply, the effect would be the valorization of those voices that invoke "science" while undermining those that argue from a politically committed posture—with the former being treated as sacred and the latter, profane. Linda Alcoff explains how this practice is manifest in the current debates over P.C. She is worth quoting at length:

> The tyranny of this subject-less, value-less conception of objectivity has had the effect of authorizing those scientific voices that have uni-

versalist pretensions and disauthorizing personalized voices that argue with emotion, passion, and open political commitment. Most recently, this struggle has been framed as a conflict between the (correctly) apolitical and the "politically correct." Only the latter group . . . is said to have a politics . . . this notion of objective inquiry, then, continues to have significant political effects in censoring certain kinds of voices and obscuring the real political content of others. (Alcoff, 1993:74)

Faith in scientific and positivistic rationality are deeply rooted elements in American culture (Aronowitz, 1988), and part of the Right's strategy has been to unite their political and pedagogical agenda with traditionally received epistemological themes and foundations which are "at the heart of the constitution of social power" (Goldberg, 1993:149). In this regard, it is the widespread acceptance of notions such as objectivity and value-neutrality and the discourse of scientificity that have enabled conservatives to take the lead in the culture wars. Among anti-P.C. enthusiasts, the rallying cries for "disinterestedness," scholarly "detachment" and the defence of truth have been among the most effective rhetorical strategies for disguising the Right's own politically charged perspective. In short, the Right summons the discourse of science and the attendant notion of objectivity while imposing the label of "ideology" and "politics" on all those who dare challenge the established orthodoxy of the Western tradition. At the same time, by identifying themselves as defenders of objectivity, authors like D'Souza and Kimball imbue their own texts with a certain degree of credibility and an aura of authority and authenticity.

Of course, it is precisely these assumptions, like value-neutrality that are being called into question by the philosophy which allegedly informs P.C., left eclecticism.[20] Kimball (1990) argues that this left eclecticism—a seemingly raucous fusion of postmodernism, deconstruction, neo-Marxism, and multiculturalism—has corrupted the academy and transformed it into an arena of ideological warfare. Decrying the rampant nihilism and the dissolution of objectivity and gravely predicting the demise of civilization as we know it, D'Souza and Kimball contend that only the restoration of objectivity and disinterestedness will save us from our current descent into the dark recesses of Hell. For conservative traditionalists, scholarly detachment is necessary for the discovery of truth and facts. It is alleged that the adoption of a rigorous methodological approach devoid of ideological pretensions will result in the acquisition of knowledge and truth. Of course, among the questions that must be asked is whether scholarship can ever be value-free. From a traditionalist perspective, informed by the Cartesian paradigm of objective knowing, value-neutrality is not only desired but possible. However, research is conducted by humans—subjective, embodied, historically located agents—who undoubtedly bring to their work, not the unadulterated perspective of reality which traditionalists claim, but rather a host of ideological, ontological, and epistemological presuppositions. As Edward Said argues:

> No one has ever devised a method for detaching the scholar from the circumstances of life, from the fact of his involvement (conscious or unconscious) with a class, a set of beliefs, a social position, or from the mere activity of being a member of society. These continue to bear on what he does professionally . . . the general . . . consensus that "true" knowledge is fundamentally non-political (and conversely, that overtly political knowledge is not "true" knowledge) obscures the highly if obscurely organized political circumstances obtaining when knowledge is produced. No one is helped in understanding this today when the adjective "political" is used as a label to discredit any work daring to violate the protocol of pretended suprapolitical objectivity. (Said, 1978:10)

Scholarship and education are not nor have they ever been value-neutral enterprises. Because the production of knowledge is mediated by culture, politics, and economics, it is ideologically based. While defenders of the canon often seek to deflect attention away from this, it is necessary to recognize that notions like objectivity are ideological constructs and neutrality often means, as Gramsci (1971:212) cleverly put it, "support for the reactionary side." By making claims to objectivity, conservative accounts seek to obscure the fact that epistemology and knowledge are inherently political entities.

Long before the discourses encapsulated under the rubric "left eclecticism" or postmodernism arrived on the scene, members of the Frankfurt School were among the first to present a radical critique of positivist rationality and the ideological function of objectivity. It is an historical bit of irony that while

traditionalists are now fretting about the new barbarians cor-
rupting the disinterested pursuit of truth and the waning standard of objectivity, more than fifty years ago in the *Dialectic of
Enlightenment,* Horkheimer and Adorno (1993, [orig.1944])
were lamenting a form of barbarism which had emerged out
of the modern faith in notions like objectivity. According to
Horkheimer (1972), positivism presented a view of knowledge
that stripped intellectual pursuits of their critical possibilities.
For the Frankfurt School, the fetishism of facts and belief in
the ideal of value-neutrality represented more than an epistemological error, for they argued that positivist rationality was
often used to buttress the status quo. Furthermore, the lack of
ethical considerations, the separation of facts from values, and
the absence of critical self-reflection within positivist logic
served as impediments to a serious examination of its own
normative structure. In other words, the ideological dimensions and historical genealogies of concepts like objectivity
and value-neutrality remained unquestioned and taken as
givens.[21]

There are, however, a number of ways in which the inherently political nature of knowledge production and epistemology can be identified. First, the *conditions of production* must be
taken into account since knowledge is not produced in a social
and historical vacuum. The cultural and politico-economic
conditions in and of themselves are political in that they often
tend to reflect social hierarchies of power and privilege, which
determine who can participate in epistemological discussions
and whose views on epistemology have the potential to gain
wide influence (Alcoff, 1993).

Second, the *identity* of knowledge producers has a significant impact on the kinds of theories created, since their assumptions and values often frame the terms of the epistemological project. Indeed, in recent years, a number of feminist
and critical scholars have identified the "masculine" and
Eurocentric character of Western thought (Lloyd, 1984;
Goldberg, 1993; Grimshaw, 1986). What is problematic is that
the subject—universal man—assumes that he can unproblematically generalize from his own experience to the experience of all other human beings. Such is the epistemological
error committed by traditionalists who maintain that the West-

ern canon embodies knowledge of a universal human interest that speaks to everyone regardless of race, ethnicity, religion or gender. However, because the "core" canon is often limited to the works of White, mostly European males, the experiences and histories reflected cannot possibly encompass the diversity which characterizes the demographic orientation of the contemporary academy. Furthermore, the story told by the Western canon is highly exclusive; forgotten in such tales are the legacies of colonialism and imperialism and the impoverishment which they wrought. It is therefore intellectually irresponsible to equate the history of civilization with the genealogy of the West. Indeed, to do so is to indulge in a "narcissistic form of self-centred 'egology'—a form of ontological imperialism, in which all of human history is seen from the viewpoint of . . . Europe and the West" (Morley and Robins, 1995:8). Of course, this is not a prescription to purge the curriculum of the works of "Dead White Males," for this suggestion taken to its extreme would be ridiculous. Many of those currently posing challenges to the Western canon are not calling for its wholesale abandonment, but rather are merely attempting to reveal its exclusive character and to debunk the idea that it is "The Story" of human history and civilization.

Epistemologies also have discursive effects in that they ultimately serve to authorize certain discourses and disauthorize others (Alcoff, 1993). The epistemology that structures Western thought is distinguishable by its hierarchical and binary formulations (universal/particular, sameness/difference, white/black, West/the "rest," etc.) where the primary term in each binary set is privileged and posited as the normative frame of reference. Conservative traditionalists valorize and naturalize this hierarchical epistemology while rendering opaque the fact that the universal claims of Western knowledge depend upon the ontological and epistemological erasure of "Other" knowledges.

Say What??: Speech Codes and the Politics of Verbal Hygiene

Another rather successful stratagem deployed by conservatives has been to claim that the forces of P.C. are undermining the right to free speech and the ideal of academic freedom. This, they suggest, has taken place most forcefully through the imposition of speech codes at some universities and, more subtly by faculty and students who police language use and behavior on college campuses.[22] While these activities exist at two very separate and distinct levels—the latter as an informal mode of control and the former as a more institutionalized mechanism of regulation, they are often conflated in conservative rhetoric.

According to most conservative commentators, academic freedom and the right to free speech are being circumscribed by P.C. zealots intent on destroying the First Amendment privilege in the name of protecting the rights of "groups." It is often argued that professors are increasingly subjected to censorship tactics exercised by students. One of the most frequently circulated examples of this was an incident involving Stephen Thernstrom, the Harvard historian and poster boy for conservative anti-P.C.'ers.[23] Thernstrom was allegedly charged with being a "racist" by some students attending his "Peopling of America" course. These charges came after Thernstrom had made objectionable comments, including some that suggested that Jim Crow laws were beneficial; that affirmative action amounted to government-enforced preferential treatment of minorities; and, that the breakup of the Black family was a cause of Black poverty. Upon hearing of the charges, Thernstrom accused the Black students of participating in "McCarthyism of the Left" and claimed that being called a racist in the 1990s was similar to being called a communist in the 1950s.

In an article written for the NAS journal *Academic Questions*, Thernstrom (1990:14) claimed that he had become a target of the "ludicrous," "pathetic," and "outrageous" rants of a few students who showed little respect for the concept of academic freedom. Ironically, the students in question had not charged Thernstrom with being a racist, but merely suggested that some of his comments had been questionable and somewhat insensitive. Equally ironic is the fact that one of the students whom D'Souza claims was involved in filing a complaint with the administration, Wendi Grantham (she was not involved, nor was she ever interviewed by D'Souza) did not charge Thernstrom with being racist, but merely suggested that his perspective on Black life was somewhat simplistic and not reflective of the range of Black experience. In a letter to the *Harvard Crimson*, she wrote:

> I do not charge that Thernstrom is a racist . . . [but] as a black student, I am left to question his sensitivity when affirmative action is incompletely defined . . . I am also left to question his sensitivity when I hear that black men get feelings of inadequacy, beat their wives, and take off . . . I also find it interesting that he never once says in his letter, "I apologize if what I said was misinterpreted." Never does he question himself.[21]

D'Souza takes this to be an example of McCarthyism! Yet upon examining this statement, it is apparent that the student in question was asking for little more than some critical self-reflection on the part of Thernstrom, and the recognition that some of his statements could be reasonably interpreted as stereotypical.

Once other conservatives, the NAS, and the media caught wind of this incident, however, it quickly snowballed and suddenly people everywhere were screaming about Stalinist forms of thought control and censorship. The Thernstrom incident is but one example but others abound, and in virtually every instance what was mere criticism was branded as evidence of censorship. Much of what has been labelled censorship by the Right is actually critique; it is the free speech of students and critics which the Right has no interest in hearing. Activists who fight bigotry and discrimination on campus today are seeking to extend the possibilities for free speech to those whose voices have thus far been marginalized from regnant academic discourse. It is these voices that the Right labels as P.C.—a tactic which enables *them* to stifle discourse and free speech.

This situation tends to lend credence to Fish's (1994) observation that the tenet of free speech is never an absolute or universal, but rather a political prize, a name given to verbal behavior that serves particular agendas at particular moments in history. Indeed, the fact that people such as George Bush (whose censorship tactics during the Gulf war are all too familiar) and William F. Buckley, Jr., whose history of decrying freedom of expression is well documented, could emerge as defenders of these liberties attests to the chameleon-like quality of free speech.

In fact, cultural conservatives and right-wing crusaders against P.C. are for free speech only when it suits their purposes. Howard Zinn illuminates this form of political hypocrisy:

> The right declares their admiration for such freedom in principle, and suggests that radicals are insufficiently grateful for its existence. But when teachers actually use this freedom, introducing new subjects, new readings, outrageous ideas, challenging authority, criticizing "Western civilization," amending the "canon" of great books as listed by certain educational authorities of the past—then the self-appointed guardians of "high culture" become enraged. (Zinn, 1991:148)

There is a curious propensity on the Right to resuscitate issues like free speech and academic freedom at different times to advance specific academic and political agendas. Time after time, the sacred tenet of academic freedom is summoned to divert attention away from the fact that what constitutes acceptable knowledge is often used as a tool to perpetuate domination and marginalization. Herbert Kohl (1991) suggests that today, neoconservatives use the complaint that their intellectual freedom is being restricted as a mask for their attempts to exert control over ideas on university campuses and to rid them of disciplines and areas of study which seek to rethink the curriculum and knowledge from perspectives that differ from those offered by a narrow, Western European viewpoint. Thus, in several respects, it appears that the supposed defenders of free speech and academic freedom are those who are taking a rigid, "correct" stance in an attempt to silence students and educators who raise questions about the way in which universities have traditionally defined what is necessary to know.

In essence, the New Right has attempted to coordinate efforts in conservative political, educational, and cultural circles to define a narrow, exclusive, and monolithic vision of what it means to be an educated citizen. The point of conservative harangues is to harass and intimidate those who interrogate the hegemonic assumptions of the dominant groups in the universities that insist that their views prevail because they are somehow transhistorical or natural. While examples such as those mentioned above point to the bogus nature of most cries of censorship, the issues surrounding speech codes have been far more complex and controversial.

The establishment and implementation of speech codes, used to punish students for using sexist, racist, homophobic and other disparaging remarks to insult other students, received an inordinate amount of attention during the pinnacle of the P.C. firestorm. This may be partly because debates over free speech lend themselves to simplistic and sensationalistic reporting. In addition, free speech issues usually make good copy because they are a perennial bone of contention. Challenges to the constitutionality of speech codes were raised in conservative, liberal, and leftist quarters alike. Recently, many of the universities which had earlier enacted speech codes have revoked them, due in large part to various Supreme Court rulings which deemed such codes unconstitutional. Organizations such as the American Civil Liberties Union have been instrumental in taking universities to court, based on their belief that such codes infringe upon the privileges guaranteed by the First Amendment. The legal complexities and implications of speech codes have been discussed by everyone from Stanley Fish (1994) to Nat Hentoff (1992), and therefore need not be recounted here. Rather, of primary concern are the many fallacies and misconceptions which were peddled by the New Right in their furious campaign to convince the American public that a massive wave of institutionally sanctioned censorship had taken hold on college campuses.

One of the most oft cited articles in the P.C. debate has been Chester Finn's "The Campus—An Island of Repression In A Sea Of Freedom," which appeared in numerous publications. Among the many preposterous falsehoods reiterated by Finn (1989) is the idea that universities have historically been sanctuaries for "untrammelled freedom of thought" and that their recent repressive character has been the result of various anti-harassment, anti-bias initiatives and speech codes. What is necessary to acknowledge, however, is that university administrations have *always* had the power to sanction students for verbal and behavioral breaches. In fact, some speech codes, while not labelled as such, were enacted in the late 1960s in order to discipline student protesters during the anti-war demonstrations. Universities have, in one form or another, always had mechanisms in place to regulate speech and activity—after all, what was the Berkeley free speech movement of 1964 about, if not a reaction to that university's policy of policing free expression? The claim that speech codes are new negates and obscures the history of institutionalized regulation of speech and political activity. The difference between earlier types of codes and their contemporary manifestations is that in recent years some institutions have attempted to revise older and vaguer policies by clearly identifying that which is deemed offensive (Wilson, 1995).

The initial decision to establish speech codes on some campuses was made in order to combat an increase in abusive language directed towards various minority groups. For example, Wiener (1990:136-137) points to an incident in which Asian-American students were threatened and taunted by White football players at the University of Connecticut and another where a Black student at Arizona State University was verbally degraded with epithets such as "nigger," "coon," and "porch-monkey." Still others have reported on verbal abuse directed at gays and women. The increase in this type of behavior prompted some institutions to establish codes making such behavior punishable by expulsion and suspension in some cases, or by having violators attend special "sensitivity" training sessions in others.

Among the many and varied criticisms about speech codes is that they are discriminatory since they only make derogatory speech directed at minorities punishable. In other words, to give just one example, calling a Black student a "nigger" would be punishable under certain speech codes, while referring to a White student as "white trash" would not. Those who object to such a formulation tend to treat the epithets of "nigger" and "white trash" as equally offensive—as two sides of an imaginary and symmetrical question. This sort of binary logic however, obscures actually existing, hierarchically arranged social relations through the process of "symmetrization."[25] In other words, the phrase "white trash" can never attain the socially coded and *qualitatively* distinct domination and violence expressed by a White yelling out "nigger," especially in a society such as ours where the historical legacies of racism and bigotry have been used to perpetuate relations of subjugation and marginalization.

While Fish does not rely on the concept of symmetrization in his defence of speech codes, he nonetheless justifies the bias of speech codes by pointing out that not all forms of derogatory speech carry with them the same negative impact; nor, for that matter, do they invoke the same historical baggage. He claims that calling a Black student a nigger cannot be equated with referring to a White student as white trash for whiteness, in our society, is the norm, not only "statistically . . . but more importantly in the sense that normative values are understood to be derived from a White Anglo-Saxon history" (Fish, 1994:76). For Fish, then, there are no epithets that can be directed against Whites and other dominant groups that carry the same degrading impact as those aimed at members of minority populations.

However, since it is difficult, if not impossible, to envision how a prohibitive policy will be interpreted, there is the risk that such initiatives will be used against minority students as well. Hence, whether one agrees or disagrees with Fish's assessment in theory is quite beside the point, since there have been a number of incidents where speech codes have been used against those they were originally intended to protect. Russell Jacoby (1994:77-78) explains how a Black woman at the University of Michigan was disciplined for using the term "white trash" in an argument with a fellow White law student and then forced to write a letter of apology. Wilson (1995:101) notes that during the eighteenth-month period that the University of Michigan enforced its speech code, "black students were accused of racist speech in over twenty-one cases." It is therefore important to recognize that speech codes, and more generally, the issue of free speech are tenacious and thorny problems since the concerns raised are often double-edged. Policies that prohibit certain kinds of speech, even odious epithets, establish dangerous precedents since they open the floodgates for university administrations to move to limit speech in other areas. And if history has revealed anything, it is that university authorities tend to regulate the speech and political activities of leftists with far more frequency than right-wing activists (Wald, 1992).

More important than the particulars of any case, however, is the somewhat superficial dimension of speech codes and the ways in which many were established as part of damage-control strategies by administrations whose campuses had been disrupted by demonstrations. Fearing bad publicity, many enacted speech codes as a quick and easy fix to appease dissident protesters. Speech codes, however, have not and will not right the wrongs, nor will they rid campuses of racism, sexism, and other forms of discrimination. Too many supporters of codes spend far more time concerned with the verbal and public expression of disparaging comments than they do with the existence of institutionalized forms of discrimination and bigotry. In other words, making certain utterances punishable through the establishment of speech codes does not ensure that undesirable attitudes will cease to seethe and fester on campuses and elsewhere. Jacoby notes that in exalting language, speech code advocates, slight reality. He writes:

> They risk misplacing their anger, targeting society's idiom, not the idiom's society. This engenders the central paradox of correct language and campus speech codes: language gets better as society gets worse . . . Stymied by vast social ills, academics can at least identify racist and sexist comments. If we cannot reform society, goes the implicit reasoning, we can at least clean up objectionable language.

Jacoby's indictment of speech codes and the policing of language echoes many of the themes raised by Robert Hughes (1993), who has attacked the euphemistic interventions into language which ignore and in some cases serve to mystify actual social and material conditions of existence. Barbara Ehrenreich (1992) has similarly pointed out that verbal uplift is not the revolution, and argues that in many respects, P.C. represents a discursive withdrawal from politics. In general, critics of "language reform" often object to P.C. remedies because they often manifest themselves in a self-indulgent substitute for politics, a holier-than-thou moralism, a vacuous politics of gestures and surfaces.

In *Verbal Hygiene*, sociolinguist Deborah Cameron counters the claims of those who would dismiss linguistic revision as a superficial and meaningless political gesture. She contends that changing language is an important form of cultural intervention. Ostensibly, it is difficult to dispute the relevance of Cameron's assertions about the importance of language and struggles over the "sign," for language does plays an important mediating role in the production of experience. However, the moorings which Cameron uses to anchor her arguments reveal some major limitations. For example, she valorizes the principles of civility and sensitivity which have motivated various efforts aimed at linguistic revision and suggests that:

> How someone treats me publicly matters more, in political terms, than how they feel about me privately; the fact that the boss seethes with inward resentment while addressing women staff respectfully is less damaging to the women than if he addressed them disrespectfully in accordance with his *true {emphasis mine}* feelings . . . There is nothing trivial about trying to institutionalize a public norm of respect rather than disrespect, and one of the most important ways in which respect is made manifest publicly is through linguistic choices . . . (compare "hey bitch!" with "excuse me, madam") . . . Changing what counts as acceptable public behavior is one of the ways you go about changing prevailing attitudes. (Cameron, 1995:143)

I've quoted Cameron at length since her position on this issue seems to foreground many of the problems inherent in the politics (or lack thereof) of P.C. For example, her suggestion that how one is addressed in public matters *more politically* than privately held views raises serious questions, for it seems to sanction a liberal facade of polite decorum while ignoring much more significant issues. A male colleague might very well adopt the appropriate code of linguistic conduct in the workplace and then skip off for a weekend of cavorting with his militia movement allies, or his Ku Klux Klan comrades. In other words, institutionalizing politeness certainly says little about the true feelings or true politics of those doing the addressing. Indeed, efforts at institutionalization may actually contribute to feelings of resentment among those who feel their language is being policed. The popular backlash against P.C. tends to support this assertion. Furthermore, the result of valorizing language seems to lend credence to the notion that "there is nothing as important" as how one speaks—a posturing that has significant political ramifications (Eagleton, 1996:18).

Yet another limitation is evident in Cameron's brief discussion about the emergence and usage of the term African-American. Responding to Robert Hughes's (1993) lament about the euphemistic character of P.C. and his charge that the use of "African-American" bears no advantage over the term "Black," Cameron points to the importance of calling members of a particular group what they asked to be called. Undoubtedly, this is important, and it does not take much insight to recognize that those currently seeking to name themselves, as it were, are those who have been marginalized and labelled in particular ways. They are, to borrow from Eric Wolf, *people without history*, and therefore people without names of their own choosing.[26] Therefore, the struggle to name or, in some cases, to rename a collective subjectivity must be contextualized in much broader terms and understood as an assertion of political agency. In this regard, Cameron is quite right in signalling the importance of such gestures.

In other instances, however, her championing of linguistic reforms tends to occlude more substantive issues, as when she asserts that another advantage of the term African-American over Black is "that it symbolizes the principle of parity among the various ethnic groups that make up the U.S. population" (i.e. Italian-American, Japanese-American) by appropriating the signifier "American" to describe a people who have, until very recently, been "denied the rights of American citizens" (Cameron,1995:144-145). Cameron's championing of the symbolic parity which such gestures signal, however, remains silent on the concrete material circumstances that many African-Americans endure everyday. The weaknesses of Cameron's formulations are best articulated by Chandra Mohanty (1991:11), who points out that while "discursive categories are clearly central sites of political contestation, they must be grounded in and informed by the material politics of everyday life."

While some may delight in the fact that "we" now politely refer to Black citizens as African-Americans thereby "signifying" their parity, this posturing is hollow in that it does not address the insidious effects of racism and the gross structural inequalities and disparities which *actually* exist between various groups. Nor for that matter do terminological alterations guarantee a shift in regnant perceptions. Indeed, (contrary to many poststructuralists who emphasize the absolute primacy of language) even Cameron (1995:142) concedes that most psychologists and linguists are highly sceptical about the "strong version of the Whorfian claim that language determines perceptions." While she acknowledges, perhaps reluctantly, the limits of language reforms in political struggle, too many champions of P.C. politics and discursive uplift have been guilty of clinging to a form of extreme nominalism and its apparent belief that if things are called by a different name, repressive relations will cease to exist (Hall, 1994).

Therefore, while it is necessary to recognize the importance of language, it is equally important to acknowledge the limits of a politics that concerns itself largely with aesthetic changes to language and terminology. Such efforts do not pose serious challenges to hegemonic assumptions, material conditions, and structural arrangements; rather, they are intended to avoid offending individuals in particular contexts according to liberal notions of politeness, sensitivity and tolerance. Nonetheless, even such non-threatening initiatives have raised the ire of conservatives who attribute such demands to the vigilantism of "special interest" groups—a point to which I now turn.

Feminists, "Special Interests" and Other Politically Correct Bogeymen

In large measure, the attack on P.C. in the university is a camouflage for a much broader-based assault on feminism, multiculturalism, and affirmative action. At a time when university and college campuses have begun to reflect the demographic diversity of American culture at large, bashing multiculturalism has become a favorite pasttime for cultural conservatives seeking to advance narrowly delineated notions of American identity. Despite the fact that the United States is clearly multicultural and multiracial, conservatives repeatedly denigrate multicultural education as a threat to literacy, as a poison which has resulted in a decline in academic standards, and as a menace which jeopardizes the presumed cohesiveness of "our" national identity and sense of "community" by creating ethnic enclaves and promoting separatist values. Moreover, D'Souza argues that the current multicultural madness may be a harbinger of America's demise should the country lose its "predominantly white stamp" (1992:13).

For Kimball and D'Souza, multiculturalism represents an amalgamation of special interest groups expounding an assortment of radical ideologies on campuses. Included in this select group are feminists, Blacks, Latinos, gays, lesbians, leftists, and virtually anybody who is not a White, conservative, heterosexual, male of European descent. Kimball (1991:xiii) claims that every special interest has found a "welcome roost in the academy" while D'Souza (1992:2) proclaims that a "new worldview" has consolidated itself in the universities. Within this context, they argue that a host of unworthy academic eccentricities—subaltern studies, womens' studies, cultural studies and the like—are now being used to indoctrinate a whole generation of unsuspecting students into an ideological worldview which is deeply at odds with the values of Western society.

According to these reactionary innuendoes, an abominable atmosphere prevails on college campuses and the monsters responsible for the contemporary descent into dementia are special interest groups. (Not surprisingly, conservative, White males are not viewed as an interest group.) The fact that challenges to the prevailing monocultural vision of America have been launched from a variety of quarters has made conservatives rather tense, and to undermine such challenges they have appropriated the language of "values" and identified the demands made by heretofore excluded groups as wanton attacks on the sanctity of Western culture itself. Yet what the Right has effectively done is subvert and silence the voices of the "others" while promoting the logic of capitalism.

Predictably, neither D'Souza nor Kimball view corporate influence as a special interest in the academy. They think nothing of the millions of dollars which foundations—such as Olin—have spent on university programs in law, history, and economics.[27] These, presumably, are not vested interests. While their silence on this matter is hardly surprising given their sources of funding, it also indicates their failure to contextualize their arguments within the broader framework of capitalist social relations. Like Bloom, D'Souza and Kimball rarely see the sources of educational decline as economic or political. In these conservative invectives there is not a whisper of criticism of capitalism. In fact, the values and ideals needed to maintain capitalist hegemony are never interrogated—they are exalted. For example, Kimball finds nothing objectionable about viewing universities as corporations. He asks what educators find so unacceptable about being an employee of a corporation and suggests that business influence places no constraints on intellectuals or the academy (Kimball, 1990:23).[28] Presumably, when wealthy alumni donate millions of dollars to an institution to promote the study of Western culture or when universities provide appointments to CIA personnel, these are not attempts to exert influence.

To support his claim that championing Western capitalist values does not carry with it any trace of "moral taint," Kimball reiterates the banality of the now well-worn argument that cites the collapse of Communism as incontrovertible evidence of the supremacy of Western capitalism. He claims that countries the world over are rushing to embrace the principles of Western democracies and uses the plight of Eastern Europeans as testament that everything on this side of the iron curtain is beyond reproach. In a sense, Kimball's position intimates that all one need know is how to conform to the existing Western paradise, while D'Souza claims that educational institutions must embrace the responsibility of preparing young people for the "challenges of a globally competitive workforce" by training "generations of young people to be more productive workers"(1992:xx). In valorizing capitalist values and defining academic success almost exclusively in terms of creating compliant, patriotic workers, the conservative educational agenda advanced by D'Souza, Kimball and other right-wing intellectuals has, in effect, brought democratic imperatives to a halt. A vision of society based on individualism, market imperatives, and competition runs deep in the conservative agenda but this vision is not perceived to be part and parcel of any special interest group; rather, these views are promulgated as universally recognized imperatives, while all others are seen as having vested interests.

Among the bogus special interest groups which D'Souza and Kimball find most disconcerting are feminists. Indeed, one of the major themes in the conservative attack has been the indictment of feminism in general and feminist scholarship and women's studies programs in particular.[29] As Faludi (1991) aptly documented in *Backlash*, the success of the vitriolic hate campaign against feminism owes much to the contributions of a number of conservative intellectuals. One such conservative was Allan Bloom who devoted page after page to an indictment of the women's movement and to feminist scholarship. According to Bloom (1987:65), feminists are the "latest enemy of the vitality of the classic texts," and are largely to blame for the destruction of the family, the university, and Western civilization itself. The media blitz which followed the publication of Bloom's jeremiad enabled him to circulate his views on feminism in more public forums like *Time* magazine. In an interview with the magazine published in the Fall of 1988, Bloom warned that the radical feminist agenda in universities was overwhelmingly powerful and dangerous. In a sense, Bloom's tirade against feminism set the stage for a subsequent round of feminist-bashing. Indeed, Bloom's claim that feminists have invaded every academic sanctuary with disastrous results is a view shared by both Kimball and D'Souza.

In the first chapter of *Tenured Radicals*, Kimball (1990:15) argues that the "single biggest challenge to the canon as traditionally conceived" is "radical feminism" which "seeks to subordinate literature to ideology." According to Kimball, proponents of feminist studies have become one of the "dominant" voices in the academy. It appears, however, that Kimball overstates his case, for there is abundant research that suggests that women, feminist or otherwise, are not equally represented in the academy. In fact, women account for a mere ten percent of the tenured faculty at all four-year institutions (and a mere three to four percent at Ivy League colleges)—an increase of only six percent from the 1960s—and "five times more women with Ph.D.'s are unemployed than men" (Faludi, 1991:293).[30] Kimball also dedicates several pages to the "feminist assault," which is supposedly ravaging the presuppositions of traditional humanistic study.

In a similar vein, D'Souza refers to feminists as a tyrannical minority and the institutionalization of women's studies as an exercise in ideological indoctrination. For D'Souza, women's studies is the Trojan horse of radical feminism and should not be allowed to expand as a discipline any more than the teaching of any other "ism" (except capital-ism, of course). D'Souza's intellectual dishonesty and shoddy scholarship are blatantly obvious in his discussion of reading lists for various women's studies courses. Citing Harvard as his example, he claims that the assigned texts which include Friedan's *Feminine Mystique,* deBeauvoir's *The Second Sex,* and bell hooks's *Feminist Theory: From Margin To Centre* and *Talking Back: Thinking Feminist, Thinking Black,* "reflect a similar if not identical understanding of gender difference" (D'Souza, 1992:213). This statement alone reveals the fact that D'Souza had not even read the books he so freely critiques, and further reflects the tourist approach D'Souza used as his main method of data collection. As anyone even remotely familiar with the positions put forth by these various feminist authors can attest, their views are anything but identical. In fact, bell hooks has been one of the most outspoken critics of White bourgeois feminism and she denounces those feminists who reduce their examinations of women's oppression solely to the study of gender to the exclusion of other important variables such as race and class. Indeed, throughout the 1980s, works predominantly by women of color have been transforming feminist analysis, drawing attention to the white-centeredness of mainstream feminism and its false universalizing claims as well as critiquing it for ignoring or downplaying the vital issues of class, sexuality, and race.

One of the many problems with D'Souza's and Kimball's indictments of feminism is that they treat it as if it were a monolithic discourse, when it is, in fact, a diverse phenomenon complete with its own internal disagreements, both theoretical and political. Yet by inventing a generic brand of feminism which they then imbue with a host of attributes (according of course, to their own ideological imperatives), they can easily denigrate it without having to do the real work that a serious engagement with feminist discourse would entail. Undoubtedly, there *are* strands of thought within feminism that warrant critical engagement for a variety of reasons; however, this is not the task that D'Souza or Kimball take up. Their intent is simply to decontextualize issues and make them appear ridiculous for an audience that is, for the most part, unacquainted with the variances within feminism.

In addition to his blatant disregard for accuracy, D'Souza makes the absurd claim that women's studies courses are biased because they do not include any "text that could fairly be described as anti-feminist"; he further states that such a bias is detrimental given that a majority of women "eschew the feminist label" (1992:213). Although D'Souza stops short of sug-

gesting that Phyllis Schlafly's[31] (his AEI colleague) views should
be included in a women's studies curriculum, should he want
anti-feminist material to be made available to students, he could
easily advise them to watch any number of Hollywood films,
turn on the television, or read virtually anything in the popular media against feminism for as Faludi (1991) brilliantly and
exhaustively detailed, these are the terrains where the backlash has manifested itself. And it is precisely this reactionary
context which has led to the rejection of the feminist label
among younger women. It is clear that D'Souza has chosen to
ignore the vast literature which addresses these issues, perhaps due in part to his proclivity for seeing such work as politically motivated rather than, "objective."

While Bloom, D'Souza and Kimball represent the "first wave"
of anti-feminist sentiment, Ginsberg and Lennox (1996:170)
argue that the latest wave of "antifeminism" has cloaked itself
"in the vestments of feminism." Indeed, feminist bashing has
become *au courant* among anti-feminist collaborators like Christina Hoff Sommers, Katie Roiphe, and Camille Paglia (to name
just a few), who are masquerading as a new breed of 1990s
feminists. These women, who claim to be feminists, argue that
they are saving the women's movement from the dogmatism
which has gripped it in recent years. While brandishing their
feminist credentials,

> the new female antifeminists attack the central principles upon which
> almost all feminist scholarship has been built. Again accompanied by
> a great deal of media attention, in many instances gained by gratu-
> itous name-calling, these new antifeminists have been responsible for
> an outpouring of assaults on scholarship across the political spec-
> trum of feminism. (Ginsberg and Lennox, 1996:171)

These women are part of an alarmingly escalating group of
self-serving and self-promoting authors who are inventing a
generic straw-dog type of feminism (composed of euphemisti-
cally dog/matic women), which they then attack under the
guise of feminism.[32] What is particularly disturbing about this
trend is the sheer amount of public exposure accorded to these
authors. Camille Paglia is a case in point; shortly after the publication of her *Sexual Personae*, Paglia appeared on the cover of
virtually every major magazine in the country and she became
a regular guest on the talk-show circuit—quite a remarkable

feat for a woman who has incessantly complained about being a "victim" of P.C. and the feminist establishment.[33] In her typically arrogant manner, Paglia credits herself for inaugurating a "reform" movement in feminism—in many respects she is partially correct. As bell hooks argues:

> Without Paglia as trailblazer and symbolic mentor, there would be no cultural limelight for white girls such as Katie Roiphe and Naomi Wolf. And no matter how hard they work to put that Oedipal distance between their writing and hers, they are singing the same tune on way too many things. And (dare I say it?) that tune always seems to be a jazzed-up version of "The Way We Were"—you know, the good old days before feminism and multiculturalism and the unbiased curriculum fucked everything up. (hooks, 1994:86)

Paglia has positioned herself as an intellectual renegade and feminist provocateur, lifting a taboo here, exposing a shibboleth there, and waving her biological determinist banner everywhere. Of course, the critiques of White, liberal, establishment feminism which Paglia claims as her own have actually been in circulation for quite some time, having emerged from within feminism itself, but that hasn't stopped Paglia from becoming the spokesperson for the "new" feminism.

While Paglia has emphatically repudiated the charges of conservatism launched against her (after all, she claims, she *is* pro-pornography, pro-gay, etc.) she is, by and large, a conservative wrapped in libertarian clothes. Although Paglia points to her libertarianism as proof of her "radicalism,"[34] her antifeminist views, her celebration of capitalism, as well as her views on the superiority of Western civilization are more closely aligned with cultural conservatives than they are with any faction on the Left. Moreover, her championing of all things "American" reeks of a mean-spirited nationalism which is motivated by *ressentiment*—a tendency most apparent in her indictments of contemporary theory, especially French theory.[35] Paglia's bombastic tirades against feminism have catapulted her from academic obscurity to media stardom and her bromides against P.C. were often cited during the acme of the brouhaha.

Paglia's controversial views on date rape helped pave the way for the 1993 publication of Katie Roiphe's *The Morning After: Sex, Fear, and Feminism on Campus.* Like Paglia, Roiphe positions herself as a maverick persona, boldly going where no other feminist has gone before. Yet, like Paglia, Roiphe recycles old feminist arguments and critiques (many of which emerged during the 1970s) and offers them up as a new, fresh alternative to contemporary feminist dogma. Using anecdotal evidence, Roiphe launches an attack on feminists for using scare tactics and misleading statistics to convince young women and the public at large that campus date rape, sexual assault, and sexual harassment are widespread problems. In fact, Roiphe's book provided P.C. bashers with yet another target—sexual correctness—a spin-off from the big bad wolf of P.C. Suddenly, one couldn't open a news magazine or turn on the television without reading or hearing about the evils of sexual correctness and "victim" feminism. *Saturday Night Live* even parodied the rather bizarre sexual code of conduct at Antioch College: the sheer ridiculousness of Antioch's code invited criticism, and deservedly received it. Nonetheless, the disturbing aspects of such swipes against victim feminism are their underlying subtexts, which not only trivialize violence against women but also posit men as a new cohort of victims. This, of course, meshes nicely with the many anecdotal tales, told by conservatives, about White male victims of affirmative action and helps to buttress right-wing positions on equity initiatives.

Another self-proclaimed feminist who has gained public attention by publishing what is, essentially an anti-feminist book, is Christina Hoff Sommers, an associate professor of philosophy at Clark University in Worcester, Massachusetts. Sommers, a member of the NAS's Boston chapter, received generous support for her book, *Who Stole Feminism? How Women Have Betrayed Women*, from the Olin Foundation and the Lynde and Harry Bradley Foundation. The crux of Sommers argument goes something like this: an unruly, strident, angry and dogmatic band of "gender" feminists have stolen feminism from a "mainstream that had never acknowledged their leadership" (Sommers, 1994:18). Contrary to various critics who have suggested that the popular backlash against feminism has led many women to disavow feminism, Sommers contends that a large majority of women have distanced themselves from contemporary "gender" feminism because of the anger and resentment which informs its discourse. Like Paglia and Roiphe,

Sommers is adept at formulating catchy slogans and sound-bites—as in her gender vs. equity feminism—and like Paglia, she manages to promote her anti-feminist rhetoric as a new brand of feminism.[36]

Feminism has undoubtedly been a central target in the campaign against P.C. for a variety of reasons; however, it would appear that racial minorities, affirmative action programs and multiculturalism have borne the brunt of the conservative onslaught. Both Kimball and D'Souza condemn affirmative action initiatives, charging that they weaken intellectual standards, since merit no longer serves as the determining factor in university admissions, academic appointments and promotion and tenure. While cloaked in the garb of defending standards and the principle of meritocracy, conservative tales about affirmative action and multicultural education tend to espouse the most insidious forms of racism. Despite attempts to distance themselves from overtly racist ideologies, they nonetheless

> charge unsuccessful minorities with having "culturally deprived backgrounds" and a "lack of strong family-oriented values." This "environmentalist" position still accepts Black cognitive inferiority to whites as a general premise and provides conservatives . . . with a means of rationalizing why some minority groups are successful while others are not. (McLaren, 1995:121)

D'Souza's racist penchants are apparent in his discussions of affirmative action. After accurately describing one original aim of affirmative action—finding "capable but disadvantaged minority students"—he then proclaims that there is a "desperate shortage of black students" who, by "any measure of academic promise" are able to meet the "demanding work requirements and competition of the nation's best universities" (D'Souza, 1992:40). Nowhere does D'Souza even acknowledge the structural inequalities and institutionalized forms of racism which continue to act as barriers to Black and other students of color. Rather, D'Souza's text is peppered with references to Blacks and Hispanics as "certified" minorities, who are supposedly granted a privileged status in the university. The suggestion that universities are going to hell in a hand basket because of multicultural admissions policies is one of the most pervasive myths promulgated by anti-P.C. spokespersons. Troy Duster (1991:31) demonstrates that SAT scores and GPA's (the measures that critics themselves use) indicate, to use just one example, that the typical student is now far more competent, more eligible and prepared than the average student in the 1950s—that mythical golden age of education that conservatives are so fond of evoking.[37] In addition, by maintaining that minority student admissions are based on less stringent conditions than those applied to Whites, D'Souza and Kimball ignore the long-standing practice (especially at elite universities) of admitting predominantly White legacies (sons and daughters of alumni) regardless of their credentials (Larew, 1991). Furthermore, when he takes Berkeley as a prime example of affirmative action gone awry, D'Souza fails to mention the athletic and special-skills admissions "set asides" at Berkeley. Gitlin (1995:179) points out that in 1989 alone, "24 percent of *white* students were admitted to Berkeley on criteria other than academic scores." Of course, affirmative action at the University of California is now a rather moot point since its Regents decided in July of 1995 to abolish affirmative action policies—the first university in what has become a growing list of institutions to do so. Paradoxically, while UC has barred its campuses from even considering race and gender in its hiring and admissions practices, the 1,000 plus special admits slots, usually reserved for athletes who actually *are* unqualified for admission, were not repealed (Hayden and Rice, 1995:264).

Nonetheless, D'Souza (1992:2) maintains that universities have altered admission rules so that more Blacks and Hispanics are let in while White applicants are refused admission. He claims that this occurs even though Blacks and Hispanics have considerably lower grade-point averages and standardized test scores than Caucasians and Asians. Although Duster (1991) points out that SAT scores and GPA's are higher (at least in his case study of Berkeley) than in years past, what he, D'Souza, and others fail to mention is that the SAT test used for college admission and other tests which purport to measure intelligence and aptitude have been found to be culturally and racially biased in some regards.[38] But more telling perhaps, is that such tests are inherently classist, for within each racial group, "students from wealthy families of all races score higher on the SAT than students from poorer families" (Hacker, 1989:64). Moreover, the "standards" argument is not only narrow but also misleading, since a great deal of excellent research debunks the merits of standardized testing. In addition, standardized tests

> test logical reasoning but not patience, one's dictionary vocabulary but not metaphorical grace, one's dexterity with numbers but not argumentative power or scepticism—they have very little to do, in fact, with how people perform in the real world, and they are an insult to education. (Brennan, 1991:21-22)

Despite the fact that such tests tell us very little, of late there has been a renewed interest in issues surrounding intelligence and achievement—an interest undoubtedly sparked by the recent publication of two rather controversial books.

For Whom the Bell Tolls

The racism that informs the works of Kimball (1990) and D'Souza (1991) is subtle when compared to two more recent tracts of the culture wars, Herrnstein and Murray's *The Bell Curve* and D'Souza's latest gem, *The End of Racism*. Indeed, the hype surrounding the publication of these texts and their popularity (*The Bell Curve* spent some time on the best-seller list and became a hot topic of conversation on everything from ABC's *Nightline* to CNN's *Larry King Live*) seem to suggest that these days, "white racism can let it all hang out" (hooks, 1995[a]:3).

The Bell Curve represents a return to eugenics and biological determinism, while *The End of Racism* proffers a "culturalist" or "environmentalist" explanation for Black "inferiority"and "underachievement." In short, Herrnstein and Murray say "nature" and D'Souza cries "nurture." Regardless of differences in approach, both books must be understood as part of a major, malevolent anti-Black backlash which is being generously supported and promulgated by conservative forces. The theses proposed by Herrnstein and Murray and D'Souza are not novel (although to listen to the media, you'd think they represent great intellectual breakthroughs) in any fundamental sense; rather, they merely rehash tired arguments which have circulated in various forms for decades, even centuries. The broader questions that must then be posed are: Why now? Why the resurgence of eugenics? Why the interest in explaining away the plight of Black America by pointing to *their* biological and cultural deficiencies? Quite simply, such views tend to provide justification for the New Right's broader political and economic agenda.

While I would generally eschew an appeal to some overarching conspiratorial explanation, the temptation to do so is nonetheless attractive when one considers the curious links behind both these publications—namely the American Enterprise Institute—where both Murray and D'Souza are research fellows. Indeed, the arguments presented in both books mesh quite conveniently with the free-market ideology that has been the cornerstone of the AEI since its establishment in 1943. In addition, the institute has recently played an instrumental role in successfully marketing and legitimizing as "scholarship" overtly racist views which were, until recently, regarded as "outside the mainstream of academic respectability" (Kamin, 1995:100).

But this has been part of their appeal. By positioning themselves as marginalized pariahs outside the P.C. intellectual Beltway, these authors can claim that they are going where no men have gone before. Murray has repeatedly assumed the pose of a risk-taking outlaw, an intellectual Jesse James fearlessly pursuing the Truth regardless of the omnipotent forces of P.C. He was even quoted in a *New York Times Magazine* article as saying that the subject matter of *The Bell Curve*—intelligence—had all the allure of the forbidden (Kennedy, 1995:182). It must be noted, however, that the re-emergence of such ideas has been made easier by "the crumbling of taboos that has accompanied the popular backlash against political correctness" (Lind, 1995:173). The reception they have garnered is also indicative of a general social milieu that is increasingly receptive to racist rants. With the bludgeon of anti-P.C. in hand, Murray, D'Souza, and others are now free to invoke this shibboleth to answer any criticism directed at them. But a brief survey of the authors' backgrounds and their arguments seems to suggest that far from being intellectual pariahs, they are nothing more than conservative lackeys whose pseudo-scholarship is intended to reignite race fires.[39]

Charles Murray and Richard Herrnstein (who passed away in September of 1994) were certainly no strangers to the bourgeois parlours of right-wing policy makers and think-tank gurus. Murray, in fact, first entered American public life more than a decade ago when his book, *Losing Ground: American Social Policy, 1950-1980* made him the Reagan administration's social scientist of choice and earned him a seat on the standing committee of the social policy industry (Reed, 1994:654). A fellow at the AEI, Murray has made a career of attacking welfare, remedial education initiatives, and virtually all social programs aimed at assisting the disadvantaged. Similarly, Herrnstein, a prominent Harvard psychologist, led a more than twenty-year campaign aimed at rationalizing inequality by attributing it to innate differentials in intelligence. Interestingly, Herrnstein's work attracted the attention of Patrick Buchanan back in 1971 while Buchanan was working as an advisor to Richard Nixon. So intrigued was Buchanan by Herrnstein's declarations about the lower intelligence quotients of Blacks that he sent a memo to Nixon proclaiming that Herrnstein's research provided an "intellectual basis" for cutting funding to government social programs (Feagin and Vera, 1995:112).[10]

Given their histories and predilections, it is not surprising that their book was released just months before the Republicans took over Congress and in the midst of a media hoopla which was, no doubt, engineered by the public relations branches of both their publisher (The Free Press—also the publisher of D'Souza's latest book) and the AEI. While Murray has vehemently denied any political motive for writing *The Bell Curve*, it is obvious that its publication was timely, for it provides a respectable cover of science (however bogus) for a political agenda intent on dismantling welfare and affirmative action and curbing immigration. Moreover, the book's obsession with public policy seems to suggest that it is much more than an innocent piece of scholarship whose sole intent is to further knowledge. The endless policy recommendations provided by the authors would seem to indicate that the text is intended as a sort of guide to policy makers, present and future. And given the current drive to tear down whatever remains of the social safety net, it appears as though someone has been listening.

It is necessary at this juncture, however, to point out that the racism that undergirds contemporary policy discussions has a long history in the conservative movement discussed in the previous chapter. Indeed, the emergence of neo-conservatism in the 1960s tapped into the deep resentment felt by many White Americans in the aftermath of the civil rights era, many of whom, by the late 1960s, could accept the demise of legal segregation, but who feared the repercussions of social programs devised to overcome or at least lessen, racial inequality (Hudson, 1995:8). Winant (1994) points out that most conservatives denied that racism was a determining factor of racial inequality, and instead chose to believe that the root of inequality was inherent in the people (meaning Blacks) rather than in the society.

The genetic explanations of racial inferiority were central aspects of conservative ideology during the 1960s. Racial enmity played a pivotal role in the 1968 presidential campaign of George Wallace[41] who, despite losing his bid for the presidency, nonetheless amassed almost ten million votes, many cast by disgruntled Whites from the Beltway and others by members of the racist "Americanist Movement."[42] The expression of overt racism in the conservative movement eventually ebbed, although one would be foolish to believe that it ever fully dissipated. In fact, it lurked beneath the surface for several years, only to re-emerge recently within certain factions of the New Right. More to the point, however, the resurgence of flagrant racism and the acceptance of it among many "mainstream" conservatives can be attributed to "culture war" rhetoric and its obsession with immigration and race (Lind, 1995). The issues raised by *The Bell Curve* authors must therefore be understood within this context.

The ideas espoused in *The Bell Curve* are by no means innovative or original; they represent a revival of decades-old claims about intelligence and its genetic foundations. In one full swoop, Herrnstein and Murray provide an explanation for all of the nation's social pathologies: low intelligence quotients among large sectors of the population. Basically, the book advances eugenic formulations and dresses them up in a thick statistical armature. Indeed, the sheer volume of *The Bell Curve* (845 pages and thousands of references) and its high-profile in the media imbue the text with an aura of scientificity and credibility which it clearly does not warrant. Contrary to its defenders, this is not a work of serious scientific scholarship despite its multitude of graphs, charts, and other embellishments; it is, rather, a work intended to foster a particular social agenda while masquerading under the guise of scientific objectivity.

The intellectual roots of *The Bell Curve* can be traced back to the scientific racism of Thomas Robert Malthus, the English economist whose "Essay on the Principle of Population Control," first published in 1798, was a precursor to what later became known as the eugenics movement. Malthus viewed any form of social welfare as immoral, unpatriotic, and "against the laws of God and nature" (Ridgeway, 1994:15). This view was succoured by the subsequent work of Herbert Spencer (who, of course, coined the phrase "survival of the fittest") and other social Darwinists. It was, however, Sir Francis Galton (who began to write about the possibility of humans directing their own evolution as early as 1869), cousin of Charles Darwin, who first coined the term "eugenics" in 1883. By 1904, Galton had formulated his classic definition of eugenics as the "study of agencies under social control that may improve or impair the racial qualities of future generations, either physically or mentally" (cited in Quigley, 1995:213).

The earliest supporters of eugenics sought to change the human race through artificial selection, or the controlled breeding of people who had certain physical characteristics or mental abilities. From the late nineteenth century through to the end of WWII, eugenics became part of a broad movement to "improve" the human race. Actions taken by Hitler and the Nazi Party, for example, were profoundly influenced by eugenic theories. Indeed, Hitler's sterilization program managed to sterilize an estimated 225,000 people in less than three years.

The American eugenics movement came into being primarily through the efforts of Harvard biologist Charles Benedict Davenport, who in the 1890s, had discovered the works of Galton and his protégé Karl Pearson. From its inception, the movement had racist and elitist underpinnings and was aimed at controlling classes that were deemed socially inferior. The organized eugenics movement evolved, for the most part, from work being done at Davenport's Station for Experimental Genetics located in Long Island, New York. In 1910, Davenport became director of the Eugenics Record Office, and in subsequent years he and fellow eugenicist Henry Laughlin became key members of the Eugenics Research Association and the American Eugenics Society (AES). Quigley (1995:214) points out that the Eugenics Research Association "described itself as a scientific rather than political group and the AES . . . was visualized as the propaganda or popular education arm of the eugenics movement." By the late 1920s, many eugenicists in the United States supported the sterilization of people deemed "defective," some even supported castration, and by 1931 sterilization laws had been enacted by 27 states. In 1936, when medical panels finally rebuked compulsory sterilization, more than 20,000 forced sterilizations had been performed, mainly on poor people and disproportionately on Blacks (Quigley, 1995).

While Herrnstein and Murray (1994) stop short of advocating sterilization, they suggest that the problem of "dysgenesis" or the "dumbing down" of American society, seemingly caused by the higher fertility rates of the "cognitive underclass," could be alleviated by changes in immigration laws, welfare reforms targeted specifically at single mothers, and encouraging rich women to have more babies. This, in short, is "smelly old eugenics, scented with the statistical bouquet of dark-side social science" (Ross, 1994:95).

The principal argument of *The Bell Curve*, however, is that we have become a hierarchical society, polarized into two broad-based constituencies—an empowered cognitive elite at the top and a sociopathic cognitive underclass at the bottom, and the authors set out to provide irrefutable "biological" evidence for the vast differences in intelligence quotients. The idea that the sources for discrepancies between the cognitive classes may be social in nature—that is, in terms of class position, discriminatory practices, etc.—escapes the authors. The sources they use to support their views, however, are dubious. While neither Murray nor Herrnstein received financial support for their research from the Pioneer Fund, the bulk of their data is derived from researchers who have been direct beneficiaries of money supplied by the Pioneer Fund.

Established in 1937 by two American scientists (Harry Laughlin, who received an honorary doctorate from the University of Heidelberg for contributions to Nazi eugenics, and Frederic Osborn, who once declared that the Nazi sterilization law was the most exciting experiment ever tried), the Pioneer Fund, currently under the directorship of Harry F. Weyher, controls $5 million of an endowment left by Massachusetts textile heir Wickliffe Draper. The Fund, run on a volunteer basis by Weyher (out of his New York law office) maintains no formal office and pays no employees, thereby enabling its resources to be directly channelled to research projects which advocate the cause of hereditarianism (Sedgewick, 1995).

The Fund also publishes *Mankind Quarterly*,[13] a journal devoted to "race" science. The journal is edited by psychologist Roger Pearson,[14] who penned a book entitled *Eugenics and Race*, founded the neo-Nazi Northern League[15] in 1958, served as president of the World Anti-Communist League, worked as an aide to United States Senator Jesse Helms, and who has claimed to have had a hand in hiding Josef Mengele (a.k.a. the "Angel of Death"), the Third Reich doctor who "performed brutal experiments on live concentration camp prisoners" (Miller, 1995:174). In addition to funding academic research, the Fund also provides assistance to a variety of political organizations. One of its major beneficiaries in recent years has been the Federation of American Immigration Reform (FAIR) which advocates reducing the number of immigrants allowed into the United States.[16] It should therefore come as no shock to hear that California Governor Pete Wilson has regularly called upon FAIR for advice on immigration policy (Sautman, 1995: 209).

The Fund's overarching philosophy is that intelligence is largely inherited and that one's class position is the inevitable result of an intelligence quotient which is passed on at birth. Sedgewick (1995:146) points out that the "fund's directors maintain that African-Americans" are found at the lowest rungs of the socio-economic ladder not because of invidious forms of racism and systemic discrimination, but because they "are genetically deficient." It is not surprising that the Fund has supported, among others, scholars like Arthur Jensen, one of the most prominent proponents of eugenics in the United States; Philippe Rushton (whose book *Race, Evolution and Be-*

havior was released at approximately the same time as was Herrnstein and Murray's); and Michael Levin, the notorious City College of New York philosophy professor who has openly professed his penchant for resegregation.

For the most part, Herrnstein and Murray rely on data collected by Pioneer-funded scholars, a fact which undoubtedly casts serious doubts upon the veracity of their declarations. However, that in and of itself does not invalidate their findings, as many social scientists, liberals included, have been quick to point out. Nonetheless, those who *have* assumed the task of assessing Herrnstein and Murray's findings on their scholarly merits by closely examining the "data" have found glaring oversights, selective interpretation of data, and numerous, erroneous conclusions based on those flawed interpretations.[17] Far from being dismissed solely because of its alleged "political incorrectness," *The Bell Curve* has been exposed for its shoddy research and questionable methodologies.[18]

The Bell Curve therefore is not a particularly powerful or convincing book in and of itself, but it *has* ridden a powerful wave of emotion, characterized most expressly by the growing frustration of a large middle class who, seeing their opportunities diminishing, are more apt to scapegoat the "underclass" and the "reverse discrimination" allegedly engendered by affirmative action, minority set-asides and the like. More interesting, however, is the firestorm which the book's publication incited, for research of its ilk goes on everyday in universities across the country usually without much fanfare. The difference was that *The Bell Curve* crossed the line into policy and found a niche, an audience willing to accept their ludicrous policy recommendations. What is new about *The Bell Curve* is not its methodologies, its genetics, or its findings, but its audience. Troy Duster offers some insight into this phenomena and is worth quoting at length:

> What is new is not the genetics. What is new is the audience. In 1960 when Jensen published his article "IQ, Race and Intelligence" in the *Harvard Educational Review*, it was the sixties. In the sixties, there was already an audience which would look at Jensen's ideas and conclusions with skepticism ... It is twenty-five years later and what has happened that is new? Nothing is new since Jensen. More compilations of statistical aggregates, behavioral genetics, theorizing back from phenotype to genotype, more data collection on heritability,

about IQ and genetics. That is 110 years old methodology, enhanced
by computer technology . . . What is new is the receptive climate for
this formula. (Duster, 1995:29-30)

Let us not forget that public discontent with various social
policies—discontent no doubt fuelled by right-wing populist
rhetoric—has been steadily on the rise in recent years, and what
Herrnstein and Murray's research offers is a biological, allegedly scientific basis for dismantling such programs. This form
of "essentialist" racism conceives of race differences in hierarchical terms of essential biological inequality with the assertion of White biological superiority used to "justify economic
and political inequities" (Frankenberg, 1993:13). After all, if
biology is destiny, no amount of government intervention will
ever make a difference.

For those unable to stomach the biological determinist fare
served up by Herrnstein and Murray, the AEI's resident education "expert," Dinesh D'Souza, has recently provided what
some may consider a more palatable "dish," an alternative of
sorts, to the eugenicist excrement of Herrnstein and Murray.
In fact, D'Souza has explicitly stated that Herrnstein and
Murray are wrong about genes and instead provides a "culturalist" explanation for Black "inferiority"—an explanation
which is, arguably, more racist than the views expounded in
The Bell Curve. The opinions encapsulated in D'Souza's 736-
page manifesto, *The End of Racism,* enraged two of his colleagues at the AEI—Glenn Loury and Robert Woodson, two
Black Reaganites—to such an extent that they ended their affiliation with the Institute. Like Herrnstein and Murray, however, D'Souza positions himself as a brave intellectual coura-
geously willing to speak the unspeakable and unafraid of
ruffling the feathers of liberals and the "politically correct."
But, as we shall see, D'Souza, like Herrnstein and Murray, simply reinvokes old conservative bromides and dresses them up
in 1990s lingo.

The End of Racism is, without a doubt, an ambitious book,
which attempts to: (i) reveal the folly and futility of liberal
policies (i.e. welfare, affirmative action, etc.); (ii) rewrite American history by arguing that slavery (which D'Souza argues
brought Blacks into the orbit of modern civilization) and segregation weren't as racist as is generally held; and (iii) chal-

lenge the relativism of multiculturalism by demonstrating that
cultures can in fact be classified within a fixed and rigid hierarchy that ranges from the savage to the civilized, with Western civilization occupying the pinnacle of the cultural hierarchy. The main thrust of the text, however, is to demonstrate
that the "real" obstacles facing the African-American community stem from its collective unwillingness to acknowledge its
own cultural "deficiencies"—deficiencies which, among others,
include an excessive reliance on government funding; the nor-
malization of illegitimacy; paranoia about racism; and a resistance to academic achievement which is supposedly perceived
among Black Americans to be tantamount to "acting white."

The basic premise of D'Souza's book is that racism, which
he defines as the belief in the innate, natural, biological inferiority of certain racially defined groups, no longer exists.
D'Souza maintains that those who argue for the relationship
between race, intelligence and biology, or what he refers to as
the "old racism" have long been discredited—something which
D'Souza in turn, interprets as proof that racism no longer exists in American society.[18] In fact, D'Souza makes the outrageous claim that the belief in the persistence of racism is a
myth concocted by the Black civil rights establishment!
D'Souza's denial of the existence of racism should come as no
surprise given his former ties to the Reagan administration.
During that regime civil rights programs were weakened significantly and the political denial of racism became fashionable in media and intellectual circles (Feagin and Vera,
1995:187).

D'Souza's limited and self-serving definition of racism is,
however, the real problem, since as Goldberg (1993:94) reminds
us

> those who insist, by way of the imperative of definition, that biologi-
> cal presupposition is conceptually central to racism will ignore those
> racisms predicated upon nonbiologically defined racial constructions.

D'Souza's narrative is a case in point, for his is a form of the
"new" cultural racism which is predicated on non-biological
notions. In defining racism so narrowly, D'Souza provides himself with an ideological alibi that enables him to spew the most
perfidious, mean-spirited of racist sentiments while claiming

he is not racist because he does not subscribe to biological explanations of inferiority. Throughout his tirade, D'Souza refers to racism as nothing more than an "opinion" or "point of view" which some individuals may hold. In fact, D'Souza maintains that the discrimination that exists today, is not a symptom of racism, but rather a "rational" response to Black "group" traits including criminality and illegitimacy. Racism or, for that matter, classism and sexism, are not matters of individual preference as D'Souza's predominantly psychological interpretation would have us believe. Rather, they are systematic properties of our present socio-economic system. Indeed, racism has been a constitutive feature of modern society; it arose not only to explain difference but also to identify exploitable individuals and populations and to justify conquest, subjugation, enslavement, and in some cases, even extermination. D'Souza, however, attempts to occlude the structural foundations of racism and the way in which it is embedded in the broader matrices of power.[19]

Since racism as defined by D'Souza has allegedly disappeared, he resorts to a culturalist explanation of Black inferiority which he traces back to their experience as slaves. D'Souza's account of American slavery is so absurd and distorted that it does not warrant repeating here. Suffice it to say, in keeping with the Western civilization-cheerleading mode which has become D'Souza's stock and trade, he claims that White America ended slavery on its own initiative. His selective historical memory, of course, ignores the messy details of the Civil War, the Abolitionist movement, and the struggle for freedom which Blacks so vehemently fought. D'Souza contends that the culture that Blacks developed under slavery—a culture which allegedly scorned hard work, denigrated education, and was sympathetic to criminals—lies at the heart of their current "pathology." He contends that their contemporary, excessive reliance on the government dates back to the Civil War, when Blacks first looked to the federal government for protection and assistance. For D'Souza, it is the moral bankruptcy of Black culture (and more specifically Black family life) that is largely responsible for the impoverished conditions of many African-Americans.

According to D'Souza, it is time to acknowledge that the real enemy of progress in the Black community is not racism, but liberalism and anti-racism, and after several hundred pages of rebarbative nonsense, he offers his *pièce de résistance*. The solution, he suggests, to correct the malaise which afflicts Black Americans is for them simply to "act white."

Tales about the intellectual and moral shortcomings of Blacks are nothing new and D'Souza's arguments belong to a genre which has had a long and established history in American culture. Foner (1996:105) points out that during the 1890s, prominent White reformers and educators who took up the "Negro Question" appealed to the deficient personal conduct and character of Blacks as an explanation for their "problems," and argued that self-help, not national assistance, offered the most appropriate route to racial progress. Some seventy years later, in *The Negro Family: The Case for National Action* (a.k.a. "The Moynihan Report"), neoconservative Daniel Patrick Moynihan blamed Black illegitimacy, promiscuity, and the instability of the Black family for the "tangle of pathology" which ensnared many Black citizens. Other examples of blaming victimized Black families for their own plights abound in the rhetoric of the Right. D'Souza has simply drawn on this legacy and repackaged it for the 1990s.

Perhaps the most disturbing aspect of both Herrnstein and Murray's and D'Souza's texts has been their popularity, which, as Willis (1994:31) argues, has served to "release sensitive white people from their pesky inhibitions about calling Blacks violent and hypersexual [and] . . . dumb." Indeed, any such inhibitions have all but dissipated as was strikingly apparent in the aftermath of the O.J. Simpson trial and the White reaction to the verdict. In the endless commentary about the verdict and the jury's "integrity," media commentators, legal pundits (both liberal and conservative), and high-ranking public officials repeatedly claimed that the jury had reached its verdict based on "emotion" rather than "reason" thereby invoking and reinscribing many of the racist assumptions which are deeply ingrained in "our" collective "common sense"—assumptions which include the notion that Blacks are somehow less capable of "reason" and complex thought processes than are Whites. Although addressing the plethora of issues raised by the

Simpson matter is beyond the scope of this text, it appears as though O.J. Simpson has become the "whipping boy" and a target for growing racial hostilities which have been simmering in recent years. In many respects, the contemporary social climate has made racism not only respectable, but popular as well.

As I have sought to demonstrate in this chapter, the views promulgated by various right-wing authors have enjoyed a degree of popularity precisely because they summon traditionally received notions, familiar epistemological themes, culturally "acceptable" ideas, and convincing rhetorical strategies. Their success, however, must also be attributed in large measure to the complicity of the mainstream media and their willingness to publicize conservative viewpoints as though they were accurate and factual representations of the contemporary social, political, and economic reality. This was particularly evident during the apex of the P.C. debate, and so an investigation of the media's role in manufacturing and perpetuating the alleged threat of P.C. is warranted.

Notes

1. See Gottfried (1991/92:186).

2. Indeed, Kimball's book received a glowing cover endorsement from Allan Bloom, who claimed that "all persons serious about education should see it." Not surprisingly, Kimball's assessment of Bloom's book (which was published in *The New York Times Book Review*), graces the front cover of Bloom's book and credits it with being "an unparalleled reflection on today's intellectual and moral climate . . . that rarest of documents, a genuinely profound book."

3. Kimball undoubtedly derived the title of his book from an oft-quoted article penned by Stephen Balch and Herbert London entitled "The Tenured Left," which appeared in the conservative journal *Commentary* in 1986. In that article, Balch (the president of the NAS) and London sought to emphasize the influence and peril of Marxist, Black, feminist, and peace studies in the American academy. Their arguments subsequently provided the backdrop for a whole slew of attacks on academic feminism, cultural studies, and various other seemingly "Left" discourses which appeared in the NAS journal *Academic Questions* and other conservative and mainstream forums.

4. Kimball is the managing editor of *The New Criterion*.

5. While at the *Dartmouth Review*, D'Souza ran an interview with a former KKK leader and included an illustration of a man hanging from a tree (*New Yorker*, 1991). In another incident, he published an article attacking affirmative action written in a parody of Black vernacular (*Village Voice*, 1991), and under his editorship the newspaper also decided to commemorate Hitler's birthday and emblazoned the front page with a picture of the Nazi leader. In yet another piece, written for the Heritage Foundation's *Policy Review*, D'Souza, commenting on gender issues, claimed that: "The question is not whether women should be educated at Dartmouth. The question is whether women should be educated at all" (cited in Henson, 1991:6). In another instance, D'Souza and others working at the *Dartmouth Review* illegally obtained confidential files from a gay and lesbian organization and published excerpts from them in the newspaper.

6. For a more detailed discussion of the funding of D'Souza's book, see Henson, 1991.

7. Within the span of a few months, D'Souza appeared on *Face The Nation*, *Crossfire*, *Good Morning America*, the *David Brinkley Show*, the *MacNeil-Lehrer News Hour*, William F. Buckley's *Firing Line* and a number of other radio and television programs in local markets.

8. Despite the fact that D'Souza and Kimball are not "academic" intel-
    lectuals, they are undoubtedly "public intellectuals" or what Antonio
    Gramsci (1971) called "organic intellectuals." The pivotal role which
    intellectuals played in the production and reproduction of social life
    was one of Gramsci's most important formulations regarding the po-
    litical nature of culture. Gramsci defined intellectuals according to
    their functions in dominance and strove to locate the political and
    social function of intellectuals through his examination of the role of
    conservative and radical organic intellectuals. Conservative organic
    intellectuals supply the dominant class with forms of moral and intel-
    lectual leadership. They are what Chomsky (1987) refers to as the "in-
    telligentsia," those agents of the status quo who identify with the domi-
    nant relations of power and who propagate the dominant ideology
    and its values. D'Souza and Kimball are, in every respect, members of
    the intelligentsia. More specifically, however, they are members of a
    new regressive intelligentsia, seeking not necessarily to maintain the
    status quo but to redefine its very constitution by rolling back what-
    ever semblance of democracy remains in our educational, political,
    and cultural institutions. For an insightful treatment of New Right
    ideologues as the new, emergent class of "public intellectuals", see
    Giroux (1996).

9. There is a certain degree of irony in the New Right's appropriation of
    Matthew Arnold, for Arnold described himself as a Liberal "tempered
    by experience" (Arnold, 1993:56), and much of his life work involved
    efforts to extend popular education. Arnold was also an astute critic
    of the inequality which plagued Britain in the late 1800s and tirelessly
    advocated a more egalitarian form of social life. Paradoxically,
    Raymond Williams anticipated the New Right's appropriation of
    Arnold when he wrote:

    > Arnold is a source for this group, though it is significant that
    > many of them have dropped much of his actual social criticism
    > and especially his untiring advocacy of extended popular educa-
    > tion. That part of Arnold, indeed, is now seen as a main symptom
    > of the 'disease' they believe they are fighting. But that is often
    > how names and reputations are invoked from the past. (Williams,
    > 1980:7)

    Although Williams had made a similar point in *Culture and Society*, the
    context of Britain in the late 1970s led him to make the point much
    sharper in subsequent writings. Of course, certain tendencies in
    Arnold's work, mainly his support of state repression of Hyde Park
    protesters, have attracted charges of authoritarianism.

10. This is particularly interesting given that Europe often defines America
    as its "other" (Morley and Robins, 1995:5).

11. Both D'Souza and Kimball dedicate a great deal of space and time to
    examine the Stanford "debacle" as a clear indication that the malaise

of multiculturalism has infested the universities and displaced the core Western curriculum. As an example of the outright distortions in D'Souza and Kimball, it is worth briefly reviewing. In the fall of 1989, Stanford University, after a long debate among faculty and adminis-tration, decided to change the name of its Western civilization course to "Cultures, Ideas and Values." Shortly after this change was made, a melee initiated by the cultural right-wing ensued, for they viewed the mild reform as an opportunity to bash so-called leftists. D'Souza (1992:59-93) and Kimball (1991:27-32) both argued that the switch to "CIV" no longer required students to take a course on Western civili-zation or to read the "great" books; however, this claim was patently false. Prior to "CIV," new Stanford students were offered the choice of enrolling in one of eight year-long sequences or tracks, each hav-ing a slightly different emphasis. Since the institution of "CIV," seven of these tracks continue to be taught essentially as they were, while the change to "CIV" led to the creation of one new track entitled "Europe And The Americas," which highlights intellectual develop-ments that resulted from the discovery of the New World. D'Souza's and Kimball's claims that the great books weren't being read obvi-ously ignored the fact that *all* eight tracks at Stanford include selec-tions from the Bible, Shakespeare, Aristotle, and St. Augustine (Mowatt, 1992:129-132).

12.   As Pratt (1992) and Graff (1992) have both shown, far from being ahistorical and apolitical, the earliest courses in Western civilization were established as propagandistic interventions sponsored by the United States War Department during World War I. The expressly ideological task of these courses was to reinforce the notion of a "West-ern cultural heritage" and to "educate recently conscripted American soldiers about to fight in France . . . to introduce [them] to the Euro-pean heritage in whose defence they were soon to risk their lives" (Pratt, 1992:14).

13.   In making this point, I do not advocate the extreme relativism or hyper-pluralization characteristic of some versions of multiculturalism and postmodernism for such posturing often leads to a relativization of all values and has significant political ramifications as several recent commentators have aptly demonstrated. See, for example, Hoggart (1996) and Norris (1996).

14.   It must be stated here that in using the terms "other" and "the West" I do not want to lapse into an essentialist form of logic which sees non-Western cultures as homogenous and undifferentiated or a view of the West that constructs it as a monolithic entity. Such a perspec-tive, as several critics (Ahmad, 1992; Lowe, 1991; Thomas,1994) have pointed out, is deeply problematic. However, it is important to note that in his text, D'Souza both implicitly and explicitly succumbs to a form of reductionism which constructs a dichotomy between a homo-geneous West and the rest.

15. One is reminded here of Mahatma Gandhi's response to a British jour-
    nalist when asked what he thought of Western civilization: Gandhi
    replied that it would be a good idea.

16. Paradoxically, some of the scholarship done under the rubric of
    postcolonialism, while critical of the West, nonetheless adopts this
    inside-outside model, thus positing non-Western cultures as passive
    recipients of Western ideas. There has also been a tendency in some
    of this literature to treat the West as a monolithic entity and to ignore
    the "internal" colonization which occurs within Western countries.
    For an elaboration on this theme, see deLauretis (1988).

17. For an examination of Thatcherism, see Hall (1988).

18. Of course, there are significant differences between what transpired
    in Britain and what has occurred in the United States as Grossberg
    (1992:250-255) and others have noted.

19. The issue of identity is discussed in Chapter Four.

20. The phrase "left eclecticism" was coined by Frederick Crews (1986).

21. It is necessary to note, however, that there are at least two critiques of
    objectivity, one derived from the Marxist tradition and developed by
    the Frankfurt School and others, and those later rejections of objec-
    tivity derived largely from postmodernism/poststructuralism. While
    these two critiques overlap in some respects, there are significant dif-
    ferences, not least of which is that Marxist discourse tends to reject
    the radical relativism of contemporary postmodernism, a point which
    will be elaborated on more fully in Chapter Four.

22. Wilson (1995:91) aptly points out that despite the media fanfare, there
    was no "crisis of censorship on American campuses" and no "prolif-
    eration of speech codes restricting student and faculty opinions."

23. For an in-depth look at the Thernstrom fiasco at Harvard, see Wiener
    (1992).

24. Cited in D'Souza (1991:195).

25. For a comprehensive and trenchant theoretical analysis of symmetri-
    zation, see Wilden (1972; 1980; 1987[a]; 1987[b]).

26. See Wolf (1982).

27. For a more detailed account of Olin's many and varied university pro-
    grams, see Wiener (1990).

28. For an insightful, but disturbing, account of the prostitution of aca-
    deme by corporate interests, see Suzuki (1989).

29. Prior the publication of D'Souza's *Illiberal Education* and Kimball's
    Tenured Radicals, attacks on feminism and feminist scholarship ap-

peared aplenty in conservative journals and magazines ranging from *New Criterion* to *American Scholar*. See for example, Hayward (1988); Iannone (1985; 1987[a]; 1987[b]; 1988) and Shaw (1988).

30.   As for minority groups, the situation is even worse. As of 1991, most college and university faculties in the United States still had less than 5 per cent of people of color. For Blacks the percentage was 2.5 percent and for Hispanics 2.3 percent (Anderson, 1991:454).

31.   In addition to helping engineer Barry Goldwater's nomination in 1964, Schlafly, of course, founded the far-right Eagle Forum which vigorously fought the Equal Rights Amendment. Like D'Souza she maintains a position at the AEI and continues to be active in a variety of right-wing projects. She is frequently seen on CNN as a representative of the "moderate" right!

32.   A theoretical discussion of the one-dimensional, reductive premises informing the new antifeminism is presented in Rhonda Hammer's "On Colonization", forthcoming Ph.D. dissertation, York University.

33.   It is somewhat ironic that Paglia, who vehemently denounces so-called "victim" feminism, has repeatedly used the rhetoric of victimhood to explain the difficulties she encountered in getting *Sexual Personae* published. Before her meteoric rise to media stardom, Paglia labored in relative academic obscurity for almost 20 years.

34.   Libertarianism is not, as Paglia would have us believe, a "radical" discourse in and of itself. Indeed, among many factions of the Right, the ideals of libertarianism are deeply rooted.

35.   See for example Paglia (1991[b]) and her long essay entitled "Junk Bonds and Corporate Raiders: Academe in the Hour of the Wolf" that appears in her second book, *Sex, Art and American Culture*. Roger Kimball (1992:A14) approvingly called the latter essay a "full blown assault on the intellectual and moral corruption of contemporary academia." Of course, many tendencies in French theory are disturbing, as I suggest in Chapter Four. The problem with Paglia's dismissal is that she does not explain why she finds French theory lacking, choosing instead to denounce it out of hand.

36.   Sommers (1994) attempts to divide feminists into two delineable camps: gender feminists and equity feminists. Sommers defines herself as an equity feminist who, unlike the strident gender feminists she attacks, are more in tune with the majority of women in America. The creation of such a simplistic binary opposition, however, tends to flatten out the many and varied contradictions, contestations and differences which define the feminist terrain.

37.   D'Souza's attack on admission policies is part of his broader assault on affirmative action. Graff (1992:88), however, maintains that "conservatives who accuse affirmative action programs of lowering aca-

demic standards never mention the notorious standard for ignorance that was set by White male college students before women and minorities were permitted in large numbers on campus." In fact, Graff argues that it has been the "steady pressure for reform from below that has raised academic standards by challenging the laziness and anti-intellectualism of the privileged classes" (1992:88).

38.   For a discussion of the politics of such testing, see Hudson (1995). In addition, Fish (1992:85-86) reminds us that one of the authors of the SAT was Carl Campbell Brigham who, in his *A Study Of American Intelligence*, championed a classification of races which identified the Nordic as the superior race and identifies the least superior race as "Negro."

39.   It is worth noting, however, that *The Bell Curve* is basically about class. In fact, race is not introduced until Chapter 13; nonetheless, as Fraser (1995:4) points out the book "colors the class structure in unmistakable shades of black and white," thus "neutralizing simmering tensions over economic inequality with highly charged notions of race phobia and inferiority."

40.   Herrnstein has a long history in stirring controversy and inviting criticism of his work. Several years ago, after *Atlantic* published one of this articles on the genetic basis for I.Q., members of the SDS (Students For A Democratic Society) launched a critique of his research methodology and findings.

41.   Wallace, the former Governor of Alabama became a national symbol for white supremacy in the mid-to-late Sixties when he declared his preference for segregation policies. In 1965, during the Selma-to-Montgomery civil rights march, he ordered Alabama state troopers to use violence—billy clubs and tear gas—to intimidate the peaceful marchers (Hayes, 1996:11).

42.   For a discussion of the Americanist Movement, see Diamond (1995[a]).

43.   *Mankind Quarterly* was founded in 1960 by British anthropologist Robert Gayre—a long-time associate of Nazis (Sautman, 1995:209).

44.   A rather obscure British eugenicist anthropologist, Pearson's first visit to the United States was sponsored by *Right* magazine, a passionate endorser of the American Nazi Party. Pearson subsequently moved to the United States in 1965, and in 1966 published *Eugenics And Race*, a vitriolic hate-mongering text in which he stated that should "a nation with a more advanced, more specialized, or in any way superior set of genes mingle with," instead of exterminate, "an inferior tribe," it would be committing "racial suicide" (Pearson, 1966:26). By 1975, Pearson had moved to Washington, where he began cozying up to people like Edwin Fuelner (then president of the Heritage Foundation) and others who subsequently assumed top positions in the Reagan adminis-

tration. In fact, Pearson became an editorial board member of *Policy Review* (the Heritage Foundation journal) and eventually headed up his own *Journal of Social and Economic Studies*, which Heritage scholars regularly contributed to. Pearson himself had close ties to the Reagan administration and even received a letter of praise from President Reagan (Sautman, 1995:209).

45. Pearson was the London-based organizer of The Northern League, a white supremist, European organization that included former Nazi SS officials (Bellant, 1988).

46. As of 1993, FAIR had received $1 million from the Pioneer Fund.

47. See, for example, a number of articles in Jacoby and Glauberman (1995); Fraser (1995); and the Winter 1995 issue of *The Black Scholar*.

48. See, for example, the collection entitled *Measured Lies: The Bell Curve Examined*, 1996.

49. In making such an assertion, D'Souza obviously chose to neglect the fact that *The Bell Curve* achieved best-seller status.

50. Contemporary U.S. society is marked by an unequal distribution of wealth and power, in which Blacks and people of color tend to suffer disproportionately from systemic racial and class oppression. This is something which D'Souza refuses to acknowledge for he neglects to situate race within the broader matrices of capitalism—a system of oppression, which especially exploits and oppresses its underclass, particularly people of color (Kellner, 1995:163).

Chapter 3

P.C. in the Media

Media Culture

A terrorist is not just someone with a gun or a bomb, but also someone who spreads ideas that are contrary to Western and Christian
civilizations.[1]

Conservatives of all stripes delight in telling harrowing tales
about the so-called *liberal* bias of the media.[2] From the pages
of William F. Buckley, Jr.'s *National Review* to the vitriolic vitu-
perations of Rush Limbaugh, complaints of the media's liberal slant and its concomitant suppression of conservative viewpoints abound. This assertion, however, is not supported by
the evidence garnered through various studies which have
shown that most journalists consider themselves "conservative"
or "middle-of-the-road" (Lee and Solomon, 1990). Beyond personal political preferences, when the very structures of the
media and the many and varied factors which impinge upon
the *creation* of the news are considered, the idea of a liberal
media reveals itself to be little more than a myth-a *myth* necessary for what Chomsky (1991:48) refers to as "thought control" in "democratic" societies.

Of all the institutions of everyday life, the media, now perhaps more than ever, specialize in orchestrating collective common sense and manufacturing consent to regnant forms of
social organization. Every day, by inclusion or omission,
through emphasis or dismissal, in words, images, and deeds,
the mass media produce spheres of definition, the limits of
meaning, and *reality* itself. The sounds, spectacles, and images
produced by the media exert a formidable influence on how

we view the world and how our perceptions of both ourselves and others are constituted. Our judgments about what is good or bad, just or unjust are influenced, to a large degree, by the media culture in which we are all embedded (Kellner, 1995).

Given the salience of the media in producing the very fabric of everyday life, understanding and interpreting the meanings and messages conveyed is a necessary prerequisite for deciphering the ideological propensities inherent in mass media. The ultimate aim of such an exercise is to lay bare the hegemonic function of the media and the manner in which they induce individuals to identify with and accept dominant social and political ideologies, positions, and representations.

Critical media scholars have illustrated the central role which the media play in setting the public agenda. Because the media are often the primary, if not the only, source of information about events and issues that occur outside the direct orbit of most people's experience, they have an enormous amount of influence on public opinion. While media institutions may not tell us exactly how to think, they undoubtedly tell us what to think *about* for they define what significant events are taking place and which issues are of import. For many people, an issue does not exist until it appears in the media. What issues are defined and how they are viewed is profoundly influenced not only by those who control communication systems and the organizations that have formidable power over them, but also by journalistic conventions.

The media undoubtedly played a significant role in advancing the campaign against P.C. within the larger public sphere and helped to popularize the backlash even beyond the New Right's expectations. Until the mainstream media began to promote the anti-P.C. crusade, attempts to quell progressive pedagogical and political initiatives on campuses had generally been the concern of conservative ideologues. With the support of the mainstream media, however, P.C. became an issue of national importance. Suddenly, reports of P.C. were everywhere. Scoop-hungry journalists, fed mainly by New Right spokespersons, collectively brought P.C. to national attention. In the late 1980s and early 1990s P.C. began garnering headlines, editorials, articles, and commentary in major publications, newspapers, and television shows.

It appears as though the first newspaper article about P.C. was penned in 1988 by Richard Bernstein writing in the *New York Times*.[3] In that article, Bernstein likened a conference on liberal education held at Duke University to the totalitarian "minute of hatred" described in George Orwell's classic *1984*. Then, in 1990, Bernstein wrote another article entitled "The Rising Hegemony of the Politically Correct: Academia's Fashionable Orthodoxy" which set the stage for the flood of subsequent media attacks on P.C. Indeed, the conservative agenda was thrust into the spotlight in late 1990 when a number of mainstream publications began repeating the P.C. tales that the New Right had been circulating for years. P.C. bashers received another boost and began to command even greater media attention after the White House jumped on the bandwagon with George Bush's now-infamous commencement address at the University of Michigan in May of 1991. Basking in his increased popularity after "kicking butt" in the Persian Gulf, then-president Bush, hardly a paragon of civil liberties and freedom of speech, took up the battle cry and joined the chorus condemning the alleged Left-wing plot to take over the universities. That Bush emerged as a great defender of free speech only months after he and the Pentagon had staged one of the most abominable campaigns against freedom of information in U.S. history would be laughable if it were not a sad testament to the historical amnesia of the mainstream media.

Although accounts of P.C. excesses had been circulating within the media since at least the late 1980s, Bush's denunciation of P.C. visigoths as the newest enemies of the American way opened the floodgates for another and more intensified round of P.C. bashing, and provided the presidential stamp of approval for the New Right's political crusade against the forces of P.C. The P.C. "movement" quickly replaced Saddam Hussein's troops as the enemy, and Operation Desert Storm gave way to Operation Campus Storm.[4]

Shortly after Bush's Ann Arbor oration, the media rushed to his side and leapt to defend the "fair-minded," rational, anti-P.C. spokespersons who were characterized as heroes in the war against the terrorists endangering free speech. Of course, media organizations have a special stake in defending the sanctity of free speech since they themselves are allegedly embodi-

ments of the First Amendment. In defining P.C. as the enemy
of free expression, media organizations were, at the same time,
able to portray themselves as guardians of those freedoms,
committed to identifying those in violation of constitutional
privileges. An analysis of the various tactics utilized during
the zenith of the P.C. brouhaha illustrates how, in addition to
fostering the hysteria of a nascent P.C. crisis on American campuses, the mainstream media lent an aura of credibility to the
anti-P.C. agenda. In the few months in which tales of the P.C.
"crisis" were being circulated en masse, the media were used
to rally support against the alleged hegemony of the Left on
campuses. At the same time, the media helped to establish a
hegemonic consensus around the conservative agenda by invoking highly charged and ideologically loaded terms.

The purpose of this chapter is, therefore, to illuminate the
unarticulated presuppositions that informed the media's coverage of P.C. Far from providing an objective account of campus politics, the media figured significantly in expounding the
myth of a P.C. invasion on university campuses. Indeed, the
media were instrumental in making the "plague" of P.C. a
household term, for it was primarily they who launched the
issue into popular consciousness. It is therefore necessary to
engage in a decoding of the media tales about P.C. and to
reveal their tacit ideological assumptions.

Manufacturing the Crisis: The P.C. Menace

The menace of P.C. may have remained confined to the paranoid minds of right-wingers had it not been for the media explosion in the early 1990s. Aside from some scattered rum-
blings penned by ultra- conservative columnists, the Right's
custodial project of preserving the Western canon and its values, was, for the most part, ignored by the media during the
1980s. Then suddenly, a flood of headlines, columns, and editorials washed over the entire country as journalists scurried
about trying to find yet another example of P.C. excess no
matter how crass. The question, of course, is why the media so
zealously began to pursue the issue of P.C. in the early 1990s?

One could proffer any number of explanations, ranging from
the conspiratorial to the mundane, but what is crucially important to note is the general social climate at the time when

P.C. was first catapulted into national consciousness. The crisis in the Gulf had been escalating steadily since July of 1990, and the media, at the disposal of George Bush and the Pentagon, were engaged in a frontal assault against Saddam Hussein, the "crazed" Iraqi dictator who had been, only a few months earlier, an ally of the United States. The characterization of Hussein, and the Middle East in general, reinscribed the most vulgar of "Orientalist" stereotypes. Hussein was repeatedly referred to as a "beast," a "savage," and the Iraqi people as "backwards," "uncivilized," religious "fanatics" capable of mobilizing terrorist attacks on the United States and its allies.

Clearly the defence of all things "good" and "Western," including the canon and its "values," couldn't have come at a more opportune time, given the patriotic zeal that had enveloped the nation. Pointing out this temporal conjunction in no way implies that some grand master plot was operative. However, given the range of critical work demonstrating the manufacturing of consent during the Gulf War, it would seem rather credulous to dismiss this temporal convergence of Operation Desert Shield (and subsequently Operation Desert Storm) and Operation Campus Storm as merely coincidental.[5] In fact, several scholarly observers have suggested that the timing of the campaign against P.C. was related to efforts aimed at creating a monocultural national identity in light of opposition to a unidimensional vision (Carton, 1991; Gitlin, 1992). Furthermore, in light of the popular support for the war in the Gulf, the "war at home" found an even more hospitable social climate for its anti-multiculturalism and pro-West rhetoric, and the media were more than happy to oblige the New Right's agenda with equally patriotic fervor. After all, crises of any sort, be they abroad or in our nation's universities, make for good copy.

Another plausible (and not unrelated) explanation for the media's heightened interest in P.C. in the early 1990s may stem from the way in which the issue was recast, in a sense, by the Right. As Newfield explains:

> Why, in 1990, did the media start to care . . . Because the right suddenly discovered its clear and present danger. In the 1980s they had offered a . . . project of conserving the traditional canon and values free of "political" challenges to their authority. In the 1990s . . . the new danger was described as a threat to freedom of thought and

speech. The media had largely ignored the conservative 1980s canon
police . . . [however] when told that this censorship menace had appeared on the centre-left, it expressed a patriotic ire. (Newfield,
1995:118)

In many respects, the mainstream media may have also been
particularly apt to take up the cause of freedom of speech given
the climate of suppression during the Gulf crisis. During that
time, the media were roundly criticized in the alternative press
for pandering to the Pentagon. Obviously they couldn't speak
of the censorship being imposed on them by the Pentagon and
the Bush administration, so what better way to vent their frustration than to redirect their wrath at those they could openly
attack—the P.C. thought police.

Furthermore, the simple pro-free speech versus anti-free
speech motif provided the media with a perfect frame within
which to cast the "debate." The media lean towards the sensa-
tional and the simple and the "free speech" frame provided
both elements. After all, tales of thought police and Stalinist
censors are more likely to sell newspapers and magazines than
complex accounts about how the humanities are seeking to
broaden the curriculum by making it more inclusive of cultural diversity.

Indeed, part of the journalist's task is to identify or create a
story within frames of meanings that are familiar to the audience. An issue or event only makes sense if it can be located
within a "range of known social and cultural identifications";
hence, the identification, contextualization and classification
of issues in terms of "maps of meaning" or "background frames
of reference" is the "fundamental process by which the media" make the world and issues they report "intelligible to readers" (Hall et al., 1978:54-55). In the case of P.C., the theme of
pro-free speech versus anti-free speech, or in some cases pro-
West versus anti-West, provided journalists with a frame of
reference to make complex issues intelligible to an audience,
the majority of whom probably knew little about academic
theories and campus politics.

While these explanations are speculative at best, they may
help in contextualizing the media's crusade against P.C. Equally
important to consider, however, is the enormous amount of
influence that think-tanks and various conservative foundations

have in purveying their wares to the media and the general public. The aggressive marketing of conservative accounts of the "P.C. threat" and the "crisis" in higher education undoubtedly played a pivotal role in projecting these accounts into the mainstream. Crises and threats of this sort, however, do not simply "appear"; they are "made," and the media, more often than not, are among the principal protagonists in the social construction of crises and moral panics. The definition of a "moral panic" derived from Stan Cohen's study of "mods" and "rockers," is insightful and worth quoting at length:

> Societies appear to be subject, every now and then, to periods of moral panic. A condition, episode, person or group of persons emerges to become defined as a threat to societal values and interests . . . [and] is presented in a stylized and stereotypical fashion by the mass media; the moral barricades are manned by editors, bishops, politicians and other right-thinking people; socially accredited experts pronounce their diagnoses and solutions; ways of coping are evolved or (more often) resorted to . . . Sometimes the object of the panic is quite novel and at other times it is something which has been in existence long enough, but suddenly appears in the limelight. Sometimes the panic is passed over and is forgotten . . . at other times it has more serious and long-lasting repercussions and might produce such changes as those in legal and social policy or even in the way society conceives itself. (Cohen, 1972:28)

A moral panic or crisis is therefore a product of imaginative intensity, a heightened sense of a collapse of boundaries; a breakdown in logic, rationality, and reasonableness; and a perceived imagining of shifting or disintegrating boundaries in the meanings, codes, and values that constitute our cultural world. In the case of P.C., New Right spokespersons were effective in conjuring up nostalgic images of the good old days, as well as images of moral putrefaction and cultural anarchy, which they blamed on a cabal of Leftist agitators. In most cases, the media dutifully reiterated the New Right's rhetoric, often reporting blatant distortions and misrepresentations as though they were established facts. But once a trend is reported in one publication—in this case, the threat of P.C.—it often sets off a chain reaction. The actual existence of the alleged trend has nothing to do with the accuracy of the reportage but rather is the result of journalists' propensities to repeat and copy one another.

Part of the explanation for the media's obsession with P.C. is that it was, in conventional journalistic terms, a good story. Contrary to the notion that "news" somehow represents the "real," the media do not simply and transparently report events which are somehow intrinsically newsworthy in and of themselves. The production of news is a complex process, which begins with a systematic sorting and selecting of events and issues according to a socially constructed set of categories and codes (Hall et al., 1978). Moreover, the media narrativize events and social issues and turn them into "stories" with characters, plots, and issues at stake. P.C. provided journalists with identifiable good (rational, pro-West advocates) and bad (censorship-minded proponents of multiculturalism and irrational deconstructionists) protagonists; a dramatic plot—the demise of Western civilization; a favorite theme of the media—free speech; and an abundance of theatrical and often ridiculous examples of P.C. excess, which could easily be caricatured and sensationalized.

Media also help to mobilize public opinion according to the frames through which they present events, issues, and individuals. Framing involves bending the truth rather than resorting to mere falsehoods. By using innuendo, authorized "knowers," emphasis, and other factors, the media can foster a desired reaction to particular issues and events without resorting to "explicit advocacy and without departing too far from the appearance of objectivity" (Parenti, 1986:220). Framing is achieved in the way the news is packaged, the amount of attention accorded to particular issues, the tone of presentation, the imagery used, and the labelling and vocabulary invoked.

From the onset, P.C.'ers were maligned by the phrases used to describe them—"Hitler youth," "fascists of the Left," "new McCarthyites—and their actions, which were allegedly reminiscent of "Stalin's reign of terror."[6] Consequently, these sound bites offered by conservative critics began to constitute the reservoir of language used to describe campus unrest and helped to establish a frame of reference through which the actual content of media reports was then filtered.

Once the frame of P.C. had been created by the New Right and circulated in the media, the social relations that gave rise to its construction as a pejorative phrase were obfuscated. Most mainstream accounts failed to explain the genealogy of the term. Once a term of self-mockery among Leftists, P.C. was turned on its proverbial head by the Right, stripped of its original ironic subtext, denuded of its historical specificity and then transformed into a term of derision. P.C. thus emerged as a frame whose very construction was unremarked upon and unacknowledged; the role that the corporate-sponsored Right had played in the term's transformation was obscured.

The media often employ the Manichean frame of popular culture, which portrays conflicts as simple battles between good and evil.[7] In the media coverage of campus incidents, leftists were quickly labelled P.C. and cast as anti-Western, anti-democratic propagandists. This, of course, reflects the practice of *demonizing the dissidents*; in a clever manipulation of rhetoric and terminology, critics, advocates and spokespersons for marginalized groups were depicted with disdain as the "new inquisitors." Indeed, one of the most effective tactics deployed by the media was to make an argument, issue, or event *sound* scandalous by nothing more than the scornful tone in which it was described.

Framed by a foreboding cover, *Newsweek*'s December 24, 1990 issue cautioned its readers to "Watch What You Say," intimating that Big Brother was lurking about monitoring speech. The *Newsweek* cover also asked whether P.C. was the "new McCarthyism," and headlines of major newspapers proclaimed the "return of the storm troopers" and the rise of the "new fundamentalists";[8] other reports maintained that an Orwellian-like virus was attacking the values of Western civilization. The imagery used in the articles, as well as the loaded political phrases used to describe the controversies imbued P.C. with negative overtones. Clearly, the use of epithets like "thought police" and "McCarthyism" influence, at least to some degree, the ways in which the reader could interpret the issues. The use of oppositions (Western/anti-Western, democratic/anti-democratic) in structuring the P.C. "controversy" served to decontextualize and dehistoricize the circumstances involved, and effectively *symmetrized* actual existing hierarchical relations of power and privilege in the academy. In other words, intellectual spokespersons of marginalized groups, from whom traditional academic awards and perks are often withheld (hooks and West, 1991), do not have the institutional power of conservative academics. Furthermore, student activists (who were often charged with promulgating P.C.) are situated even lower on the institutional totem pole. Hence, the media characterization that *two* opposing sides were involved in campus controversies disguised both the nature of academic hierarchy and the fact that those conveniently lumped together under the rubric of P.C. did not constitute a monolithic, homogenous "side." As Abbie Hoffman once quipped, the Left couldn't agree on lunch much less a full-scale takeover of the universities. And contrary to what the Right and the media would have us believe, only a small percentage of professors identify themselves as leftists in the first place.

In addition, the invocation of derogatory terms and phrases in media accounts was particularly effective since the major media blitz on the P.C. controversy erupted shortly after the victory in the Gulf.[9] Riding high on the wave of a regained sense of patriotism and nationalism spawned by the military triumph, the New Right's task of demonizing the dissidents was made easier. Indeed, prevailing popular sentiment at the time is significant in explaining how the majority may react to particular messages, symbols, and imagery. Terms such as freedom and democracy pack a powerful punch, especially in a post-war period, and because the defence of free expression and democratic principles were allegedly the foundation of the anti-P.C. stance, conservatives were viewed favourably.

Furthermore, the insinuation that P.C.'ers were anti-Western (and by extension, anti-American) also buttressed the P.C. detractors case, especially given the xenophobic climate in the months following the Gulf War. As Evan Carton (1991:41) has aptly pointed out, "multicultural insurgency on campus" was portrayed as a "threat to the triumph of America's new world order" in much the same way as was the Iraqi invasion of Kuwait. Under those circumstances, viewpoints deemed P.C. were easily dismissed, ignored, or equated with treason. Indeed, one would never have guessed from the overheated and misleading accounts offered by the media that the issues raised in the "battle over education" were ones that could legitimately be debated. Steamrolling over differences and flattening out contradictions, the mainstream media characterized the P.C. "debate" as a simple choice between pro-Westerners and anti-Westerners, and in the climate of frantic allegation and condemnation created by the media framing of issues, merely to raise questions for debate almost guaranteed that one would be charged with the heinous crime of P.C.

Although many of the issues sparked by the hailstorm of controversy over P.C. implied that dominant ideological presuppositions and power arrangements were being contested on campuses, mainstream media coverage of the "debate" was mostly one-sided, as dissident voices were rarely accorded equal, if any, time and space. Indeed, Herman (1992:11) points out that one of the most important and greatly underrated constraints on freedom of speech is dissenters' lack of access to the mass media and hence to the general public. The framing of P.C. in media discourse seems to affirm his assertions, for radical voices of opposition were conspicuously absent in mainstream media coverage. This chapter attempts to illustrate how the Right achieved almost complete hegemonic control of the media during the P.C. fracas, and how few of the reports bothered to investigate complex issues, or for that matter, to check "facts." In order to accomplish this, an analysis of *Newsweek*'s coverage of the issue is provided. Despite the limited focus on this one publication, the same strategies were identifiable in other narratives which attempted to explain P.C. to the public.

Dispelling the Myths

In its December 24, 1990, issue, *Newsweek* dedicated much of the publication to an "investigation" of P.C.[10] The cover was emblazoned with the dire warning "Watch What You Say," while the subtitle proclaimed that "There's a 'Politically Correct' Way To Talk About Race, Sex and Ideas." The cover also posed the vexing question, "Is This the New Enlightenment—Or the New McCarthyism?" Splashed across the middle of the cover design in large block letters was the phrase "THOUGHT POLICE." Although *Newsweek* posed the question as to whether P.C. was the New Enlightenment or the New McCarthyism, the cover design itself and its dominating "THOUGHT POLICE" motif set the tone. Through innuendo and intonation, the existence of thought police and a P.C. code of conduct were, at the outset, established as givens rather than phenomena to be debated.

Prior to examining the articles which constituted *Newsweek*'s coverage of P.C., a few preliminary remarks must be made about their use of McCarthyite rhetoric. *Newsweek*, of course, was not alone in summoning the ghost of McCarthy; in fact much of the commentary on P.C. used the spectre of McCarthyism (in some form or another) to contextualize recent campus events.[11] However, none of them bothered to explain what the "real" McCarthyism was all about. By stripping McCarthyism of its historicity, media pundits were able to summon this politically charged label while obscuring the fact that during that era, Senator McCarthy's witch hunts were largely supported by right-wingers, many of whom are now among the most outspoken critics of P.C. Moreover, the alleged "new" McCarthyism doesn't carry the debilitating force of the original; nowhere has there been the state-sponsored tribunals and off-handed dismissals and black-listings which characterized the real McCarthyism. During the 1950s, many universities worked with the FBI, trading information about faculty members' political activities and ideas, while others collaborated with the House Un-American Activities Committee (HUAC). As a result, hundreds of academics who were identified as communists by their colleagues were fired by acquiescent administrations during McCarthy's reign of terror (Caute, 1978). While Schrecker (1986:10) maintains that exact figures are difficult to ascertain, almost "20 percent of the witnesses called before the congressional and state investigating committees were college teachers or graduate students," and those witnesses called to testify by McCarthy, HUAC, and the FBI who "did not clear themselves with the committees lost their jobs." The situation continued to a certain degree in the early 1960s, when professors of various sorts were often fired outright or denied tenure for their ideological tendencies and activism—mainly their opposition to the Vietnam war or their stands on racism, sexism, classism, as well as their demands for the inclusion of women's, Black, and ethnic studies in the curriculum. Unlike the alleged victims of today's "thought police," they were not allowed the opportunity to simply decide not to teach a particular course. This bit of history, however, is conveniently neglected by media pundits who recognize a good soundbite when they hear one.

Newsweek's coverage of the P.C. "debate" was comprised of one major article by Jerry Adler et al. entitled "Taking Offense," and two shorter pieces, "Learning to Love the PC Canon" by Peter Prescott, and "He Wants to Pull the Plug on the PC" by Patrick Houston. For the purposes of clarity, I will deal first with the Adler et al. article and then briefly with those by Prescott and Houston.

Beginning with the first paragraph, which describes the experience of Nina Wu, a student disciplined by the University of Connecticut for displaying a homophobic poster, to the descriptions of Sixties radicals taking over campuses, Adler et al. obviously saved a great deal of time by reiterating many of the same erroneous arguments made by conservative commentators and reporters. In addition to recycling many of the same examples cited in conservative tracts and journals, the authors haphazardly link together everything from literary theory and academic revision to university administration speech codes. In a sweeping overgeneralized statement, it is suggested that the P.C. agenda is

> broadly shared by most organizations of minority students, feminists and gays. It is also a program of a generation of campus radicals who grew up in the 60s and are now achieving positions of academic influence. If they no longer talk of taking to the streets, it is because they are now gaining access to the conventional weapons of campus politics: social pressure, academic perks (including tenure) and—when they have the administration on their side—outright coercion.

No evidence is provided, no statistic cited—just a blanket declaration claiming that there is a new movement or "program" on campuses. In this sense, *Newsweek's* account sounds strikingly similar to Balch and London's (1986) essay on "The Tenured Left" and Kimball's introductory remarks in *Tenured Radicals* when he writes that:

> Proponents of deconstruction, feminist studies and other politically motivated challenges . . . have by now become the dominant voice in . . . many of our best colleges and universities and . . . exhibit a remarkable unity of purpose . . . the men and women who are paid to introduce students to the great works and ideas of our civilization have by and large remained true to the ideology of the sixties . . . the radical vision of the sixties has not so much been abandoned as internalized by many . . . who now teach at and administer our institutions of higher education . . . the university is now supplying many of those erstwhile radicals with handsome paychecks, a pleasant working environment, and lifetime job security (Kimball, 1991:xi, xiv).[12]

From the outset then, Adler et al. affirm, without question, the New Right's rhetoric about the presence of a P.C. movement on campuses. Given the theatrical preamble used by Adler et al., one would expect a far more engrossing tale of "thought control" than the one they subsequently provide.

The authors then assert that "opponents of P.C. see themselves as a beleaguered minority among barbarians who would ban Shakespeare because he didn't speak or write in Swahili" (Adler et al. 1990:49-50). Now the very use of the word barbarians in the same sentence making reference to an African dialect is a thinly veiled racist comment which reinscribes the West=civilized, Other=uncivilized dichotomy which lies at the root of Western epistemology. But, perhaps more importantly, the authors trivialize the serious intellectual challenges launched against the Western canon and all it represents. Those scrutinizing Shakespeare and other canonical writers do not suggest they be banned; nor, for that matter, do they condemn them for not speaking Swahili. Rather, what is being explored is the relationship between canon building and empire building and the intricacies of imperialism and colonialism—complex issues which are trivialized by Adler and his co-authors. Furthermore, the suggestion that opponents of P.C. constitute a victimized minority reinforces the "white male as victim" ideology which has gained currency in recent years. The absurdity of this stance is aptly explicated by Goldstein:

> What's so wacky about this role reversal is that white men clearly hold the lion's share of political and corporate power . . . But they have lost something less tangible, without which they cannot continue to rule: their legitimacy . . . Once they were 'mankind,' now they're just another niche . . . PC is the official expletive of the Angry White Male . . . [it] has become a term of derision for all things multicultural, feminist or gay . . . The only group it's not hip to dis these days is straight white men. (Goldstein, 1995:25)

A P.C. person is then described in a caricature as someone in a

> tie-dyed T-shirt, with open-toed sandals and a grubby knapsack dangling a student-union-issue, environmentally sound, reusable cup. (Adler et al., 1990:49)

This description embodies the archetypical image of the "hippie"—an image at odds with the much valorized all-American person-next-door-type so integral to our mythical landscape. Without a doubt, cartoonists and satirists had a field day during the P.C. ballyhoo by concocting such images and then passing them off as accurate depictions of P.C. people. Moreover, in the context of a culture that is endlessly seeking to disavow the 1960s, the use of "hippie" imagery assists in characterizing critics as a radical "fringe" whose views are more easily disqualified. Within the realm of mediaspeak, "radical" is almost always invoked in a pejorative sense, and usually evokes the clumsy image of comic-book communism, thereby equating activists with the "vulgarities" of communism.

Indeed, one of the most effective strategies for framing an issue and infusing it with negative connotations is the use of anti-communist rhetoric. Anti-communist ideology is, according to Herman and Chomsky (1988:29), a powerful filter which helps to "mobilize the populace against an enemy," and since the concept is unclear it can be used "against anybody advocating policies that threaten property interests or support . . . radicalism." Thus, liberals or leftists often accused of being anti-American or anti-democratic are immediately put on the defensive in a cultural milieu where anti-communism is a powerful rhetorical strategy.

Despite the fact that Adler et al. describe P.C. as a "movement," which seems to suggest some degree of organization, the authors were apparently unable to uncover any central organization of P.C. activists and strategists to quote. As with communists during the McCarthy era, people who actually profess the extreme P.C. views attributed to them are not so easy to find. They were able, however, to locate members of the NAS to cite. Predictably, the *Newsweek* article suggests that the NAS, an organization which is "committed to rational discourse as the foundation of academic life," was formed to challenge the "march of PC across American campuses." This characterization of the NAS as a "reactive" organization obscures the fact that its existence dates back to 1982, as was illustrated in Chapter One. However, by positing the organization as something that suddenly sprang up, the *Newsweek* article reinscribes two myths, the first being the notion that a P.C. movement exists and is powerful enough to warrant a counter-attack by the NAS and second, that the NAS simply came to be because of the presence of P.C. forces. Here, the agenda of the NAS is rendered invisible; the fact that it helped to *create* the largely mythical threat of P.C. is occluded.

In their attempts to convince readers that P.C. is a new form of McCarthyism, a variety of examples of professors "who have been left in doubt" as to whether or not they will be "allowed" teach specific courses are cited. One case in point is Professor Vincent Sarich, a Berkeley anthropologist who was subjected to student protest after he had suggested in the alumni magazine that the university's affirmative action program discriminated against White and Asian students. Adler et al. (1990:50) claim that his department launched an investigation while the chancellor invited complaints from students about his lectures. Sarich was then left in doubt about whether he would teach the introductory anthropology course he had taught for twenty-three years. But the authors of the *Newsweek* article blatantly misrepresented Sarich's views for he had actually claimed that Asians "had been treated 'fairly' with respect to their academic achievements" while whites were "underrepresented" and the victims of "systematic" discrimination (Sarich cited in Wilson, 1995:145).

Adler and his comrades did concede, however, that Sarich holds "scientifically" controversial views about the relationship of brain size and intelligence, but they contend that he does not espouse these views in his teachings. However, Easterbrook (1995:32) points out that in 1990, Sarich began to suggest that Black success in basketball "proved the inherited basis of talent, which in turn supported the view that whites could inherit superior mental faculties." In fact, Sarich would tell his classes that the fact that there was no "white Michael Jordan" provided evidence in support of his outlandish contentions (Easterbrook, 1995:32). Apparently the long list of successful White basketball players had escaped the dear professor's mind!

Another example of P.C. repression, deemed by Adler and company to be one of the most controversial, took place at the University of Texas at Austin. The case of English 306 at Austin has, in fact, been one of the most-cited examples of the evils of P.C. Indeed, the mainstream media in general and the enemies of P.C. in particular, have scored their points by repeating and recycling a handful of supposedly shocking anecdotes which are passed off as the "truth." In the case of English 306, however, *Newsweek*'s coverage was based on blatant misinformation and brazen lies. Adler et al. (1990:51-52) claim that:

> One of the most controversial PC initiatives took place at the University of Texas at Austin, where the English faculty recently chose a new text for the freshmen composition course, which is required for about half the entering undergraduates. Up till now, instructors had been free to assign essays on a range of topics . . . Henceforth, all readings will be from an anthology called "Racism and Sexism: An Integrated Study," by Paula S. Rothenberg . . . The selections . . . comprise a primer of PC thought.

As it turns out, the scenario painted by the authors was completely erroneous. Proposed changes to the syllabus for a required writing course in the English department at Austin incited an imbroglio which drew the attention of both *Newsweek* and the *Houston Chronicle*, which dubbed the incident an indication of "a new fascism of the left"and described the English department as being under the control of "latter-day versions of the Hitler Youth or Mao Tse-Tung's Red Guards." Ultraconservative *Washington Post* columnist George Will deemed the course proposal an example of "political indoctrination" seeking to "supplant education."

What the *Newsweek* article fails to report, due largely to their negligence and their dependence on unreliable sources, is that Rothenberg's anthology had been dropped by the syllabus-writing committee at Austin in June—six months prior to *Newsweek*'s December expose (Brodkey and Fowler, 1991). Also neglected was the fact that the proposed changes to the syllabus and the course entitled "Writing About Difference" *never* made it to the classroom, for they were targeted and became casualties of a disinformation campaign initiated by the NAS. After Prof. Alan Gribben (who according to Adler et al. was "one of the minority who objected to the course") went public in chastizing the course proposal, the Texas branch of the NAS placed an advertisement, signed by fifty-six professors, in the campus newspaper, which expressed their fears about "standards" being subverted by "politics." The apparent influence of the NAS disinformation campaign coupled with the fact that no substantive changes were made in the faculty of English at Austin therefore begs the question of who the *real* thought police are.[13]

Paula Rothenberg (1992:267), author of the anthology that was subjected to a barrage of anti-P.C. condemnation and media distortion, argues that the real repression and policing of thought is emanating not from the Left but from the Right, whose efforts are undoubtedly being nourished by the media's one-sided coverage of issues. The fact that *Newsweek's* description of what actually happened to English 306 was so completely incorrect not only demonstrates its shoddy research but is reflective of its underlying ideological commitments.

The issue of multiculturalism, condemned in the narratives of various conservative commentators, resurfaces in Adler et al.'s article, which claims that it is a key tenet of the P.C. agenda. However, what Adler et al. manage to do is paint multiculturalism as an invidious trend, a "fad" seeking to brush tradition aside. Rather than probing the issues raised by multiculturalists, *Newsweek* chose to peddle the anti-P.C. rhetoric and portray multiculturalism as an enormous threat to tradition and Western civilization. Similar to the narratives offered in previous conservative tracts, multiculturalism is described as an attack on the "primacy of the Western intellectual tradition, as handed down through centuries of great books" (Adler et al., 1990:54). This multicultural attack, we are told, is also being generously funded. The authors point out that in 1990, the Ford Foundation gave "grants totalling $1.6 million to 19 colleges and universities for diversity" (Adler et al., 1990:53), yet they remain conspicuously silent about the millions that have been spent in financing the backlash against multiculturalism and the conservative networks supporting the anti-P.C. crusade.

Rather than providing an explanation of multiculturalism and its relation to pedagogical practices, the article focuses on the arguments of African-American professor Molefi Asante, which the authors then decontextualize and distort. We are informed, for example, that what Asante and other advocates of multiculturalism want to do is replace the Eurocentric view of the world with an Afrocentric curriculum which would be "one of many such ethnic-specific curricula" (Adler et al., 1990:54). To insinuate, however, that what is being posited is the abandonment of the Eurocentric curriculum obscures Asante's pedagogical project. Had the authors bothered to read

any of Asante's works rather than regurgitating the misinformed opinions of conservative academics, they would have
discovered that Asante does *not* advocate forsaking the
Eurocentric perspective, but rather, suggests that it must not
be regarded as superior to other perspectives. He writes:

> There is space for Eurocentrism in a multicultural enterprise so long
> as it does not parade as universal. No one wants to banish the
> Eurocentric view. It is a valid view of reality where it does not force
> its way. Afrocentricity does not seek to replace Eurocentricity in its
> arrogant disregard for other cultures. (Asante, 1992:303)

In some sense, Asante seeks to transcend the hierarchical relations established by the Western tradition and its accompanying dualisms, which relegate knowledge of and by the "other"
to a subservient status. Asante advocates cultural pluralism
without hierarchy—something quite different than what the
Newsweek article suggests. Paradoxically, while Asante's championing of cultural pluralism is regarded as radical and extreme by Adler et al., it is precisely the sort of liberal pluralism which undergirds Asante's formulation that has been
critiqued by *critical* multicultural scholars (Goldberg, 1994;
McLaren, 1995; Mohanty, 1994; Wallace, 1994). Hence, what
is in essence a liberal position is transformed by Adler et al.
into a radical stance. The spectrum of debate is thus conveniently circumscribed.

Adler et al. also employ what has now become a familiar
strategy to discredit P.C. proponents. By focusing on extreme
examples where instances of "ageism" and "lookism" have been
defined as identifiable crimes, many of the more substantive
issues invoked by progressives are undermined by the reporters' foregrounding of trivial ones. In addition, the authors
proclaim that P.C. "represents the subordination of the right
to free speech" thereby reinscribing the image of Orwellian
thought police. In vilifying P.C.'ers as agents of thought control, however, the reporters in this instance (and the media in
general) effectively conceal the part they play in patrolling the
boundaries of allowable discourse.

The *Newsweek* piece also makes a number of unsubstanti-
ated claims about P.C. by claiming that politically it is "Marxist" in origin and that it is a "totalitarian" philosophy which is

"intellectually" informed by Derridean "deconstructionism." Given the confidence with which these statements were made, a brief evaluation of them is necessary. First, the use of appellations such as Marxist immediately conjure up negative images in the minds of many people (Lee and Solomon, 1990:40). The proclamation that P.C. thinking has Marxist origins also perpetuates the myth that universities are largely populated by Marxist scholars. This is evident when the authors claim that the "failure of Marxist systems throughout the world has not noticeably dimmed the allure of left-wing politics for American academics"(Adler et al., 1990:53). This statement is indicative not only of the rabid anti-communism common in the U.S. media, but also points to the erroneous practice of equating Marxism with the political regimes that existed in the former Soviet Union and other Eastern bloc countries—by no means examples of the classless society Marx envisioned. Furthermore, it would probably surprise many Marxist scholars to find out that P.C. is Marxian in its political origins, especially since Marxists have been among the most vocal critics of P.C. politics (Epstein, 1995; Stabile, 1995).

Raskin (1992) maintains that referring to P.C. as totalitarian is not only an over-dramatization but also reveals a contempt for historical meaning and memory—a contempt, I may add, rampant in mainstream media reporting. The term totalitarianism itself was developed to describe Stalinist and Nazi societies in which the state controlled all aspects of social life, destroyed dissent, and elevated racism, anti-Semitism, and imperialism to official state dogma. To equate totalitarianism with the various attempts by so-called P.C.'ers to increase tolerance is, as Raskin (1992:37) suggests, "a brazen lie." Moreover, to ask whether any of these assertions can even be validated is, according to Berube (1992:139), to miss the point, for what "*Newsweek*'s really saying is that P.C. is bad stuff plus more bad stuff: In Orwell's famous phrase, it's *doubleplusungood.*"

On a theoretical note, it is imperative to point out that conflating Marxism with deconstruction also ignores the fierce debates being waged between these two very different theoretical camps.[14] This, however, is hardly surprising given that Adler et al. do not even offer an explanation of how P.C. is part of the deconstructionist domain, except to say that deconstruction is a famously "obscure" theory which rejects notions of "hierarchy." Since few readers of the popular press are in a position to recognize misrepresentations of complex academic discourses, journalists and critics wishing to debunk them in a column inch or two are freed of the responsibility of doing their homework. Moreover, claiming that P.C. is rooted in an obscure literary theory makes it even less palatable to the average reader, who would in all likelihood dismiss it as academic gobbledygook.

It is also important to note that contemporary critiques of dominant academic discourses are in no way restricted to the goal of textual dehierarchization, nor to deconstructionists' discursive decodings. Indeed, many radicals eschew the "prison house of language" game which has come to constitute much of what passes itself off as critique in the contemporary academy (McLaren, 1994; Zavarzadeh, 1991). This more radical view is, however, not represented in the media. In their attempts to maintain the myth of balanced reporting and to circumscribe what Chomsky (1991) refers to as the "bounds of the expressible," the views of moderate "reformers" are presented as the "other" side. The spectrum of allowable opinion is thus curtailed and radical views are effectively excluded. This becomes particularly clear when one considers the sources.

Unreliable Sources

If the First Amendment remains the banner under which press ideology progresses in the United States, it can be argued that the "code of objectivity" provides the media with its moral artillery. In the most general sense, objectivity in journalism denotes a "set of rhetorical strategies and procedures used in composing a news story" (Sigal, 1986:15). In this regard, objectivity has little if anything to do with the accurateness or validity of a news story. Nor does following the protocols of objective reporting mean that a story is free of bias; rather, objective reporting means only that the reporter has tried not to introject a particular story with his or her own personal views. Hence, media statements are, wherever possible, grounded in "objective" commentaries derived from "accredited" sources. Gaye Tuchman (1978:215) has pointed to the importance of objectivity among journalists as a defence against anyone who would accuse them of bias. The code of objectivity provides a shield so that in the event that a journalist or story is accused of having a slant, they are able to scapegoat their sources while claiming that they were simply reporting the "facts" provided by sources.

Sigal (1986:15) maintains that news is not what happens but rather what someone says happened and since reporters are seldom in a position to witness events firsthand, they rely on the accounts of others. Michael Parenti (1986:10) reminds us that one of the most common tendencies of the mainstream media in terms of sources is to favor the "affluent over the poor . . . whites over blacks, males over females, officialdom over protesters, conventional politics over dissidence." In the case of P.C., most of the commentaries were derived from conservative, traditional academics, many of whom are members of the NAS. Those radicals and "special interests" who had been accused of politicizing the university were either given sparse attention or were not quoted directly in the articles. Indeed, although *Newsweek* claimed that feminists were among the driving forces of P.C., in all three articles together, they saw fit to quote just two women (only one of whom was a feminist), and while they threw in a few citations from some Black intellectuals for good measure, most of their sources were conservative, White, male academics opposed to P.C. More telling, however, is who was quoted as being on the side of P.C.

The semblance of objectivity is achieved in news stories by presenting "both" sides. But this strategy often conceals more than it reveals, for on any issue, there are often "many" sides. The result of this "objectivity" is that radical views tend to get excluded. This was particularly manifest in *Newsweek*'s coverage of P.C. To project the notion of balance, reporters Peter Prescott and Patrick Houston[15] sought out Stanley Fish of Duke University to represent the P.C. side and NAS scholar Theodore Hamerow to represent the anti-P.C. side. For his part in this facade of balance, Hamerow takes the opportunity to bash affirmative action policies and ethnic studies programs, while reporter Patrick Houston (1990:52) again reinforces the myth that the NAS's "reason for existence is mortal combat with the windmills of PC." More interesting, however, is the fact that Stanley Fish emerged as spokesperson par excellance for the P.C. "side." Indeed, Fish became an overnight celebrity and he was widely quoted as the epitome of P.C. thinking. He even went on tour with Dinesh D'Souza (whom he counts among his closest friends) to engage in pseudo-debates about P.C. around the country.

The fact that Fish was selected to be the official P.C. spokesperson is peculiar in several respects. If P.C. is the program of a generation that was nurtured on the ideologies of the 1960s as conservatives repeatedly contend, Fish is hardly an apt candidate to speak for this constituency, since he came to maturity well before the 1960s. Furthermore, Fish's *raison d'etre* is Milton; his work on the canonical poet provides Fish with his six-figure salary at Duke and his posh sports car. Fish, a long-time Republican, is hardly a radical by any stretch of the imagination. Given his predilection to revel in and exalt the professionalization so rampant in the academy, it is unlikely that Fish will ever speak out for the "wretched of the earth," or pursue Left political agendas. In fact, Fish has made a career of "taunting both Left and Right alike with the claim that the real is rhetorical" (Lambrose, 1990:792).

Fish's flamboyance and his apoliticalness, however, made him the perfect choice in a media culture where radical, leftist views are systematically excluded. Moreover, Fish's scholarship, while interesting, is nonetheless limited to deconstructing texts, and does not address the broader social *context* and materially constituted power relations. If deconstruction is the most radical formulation that academic radicals can throw at the Right, they (the Right) need not shiver in their boots. Indeed, much of what passes for radicalism in the bourgeois academy today amounts to nothing more than discourse wars, far removed from the materiality of everyday life. Pseudo-leftists liken the deconstruction of texts to politics, while others equate "resistance" with the politics of pleasure and the excesses of *jouissance*. Under the spell of Parisian provocateurs, the "text" has become the arena for political struggle. If this is radicalism, we might do well to ask ourselves, "Where's the beef ?" It is to this and related matters that I now turn.

Notes

1. Former President and dictator of Argentina, Jorge Rafael Videla, quoted in Nelson (1989:21).

2. The term media is used here in reference to mainstream media publications. Excluded here are *alternative* sources such as *The Village Voice, Mother Jones, Z Magazine,* and other similar publications.

3. Bernstein later received generous funding from conservative foundations to write *Dictatorship of Virtue* (1994), yet another book attacking P.C.

4. I am appropriating the phrase "Operation Campus Storm" from Ferguson (1991).

5. For discussions about media complicity during the Gulf War, see Chomsky (1991); Kellner (1992); and Winter (1992).

6. In his article entitled "Are You Politically Correct?," John Taylor (1991:35) approvingly quotes Camille Paglia's description of P.C. as "fascism of the left," and her suggestion that P.C.'ers "behave like the Hitler youth."

7. For an insightful account of the Manicheanism of popular culture, see Jewett and Lawrence (1988) for their discussion of popular culture's deployment of the metaphysics of the ancient Manichean Christian sect which characterized human existence as a struggle between good and evil. This construction of binary oppositions was also pervasive in the neoconservative critiques of P.C.

8. See for example the *Wall Street Journal*'s editorial of April 10, 1991 entitled "The Return of the Storm Troopers"; John Taylor's "Are You Politically Correct?" and George Will's many and varied diatribes against P.C. including "Poisoning Higher Education," *Washington Post*, April 21, 1991, p. B7; "Literary Politics," *Newsweek*, April 22, 1991, 72; "Curdled Politics on Campus," *Newsweek*, May 6, 1991, 72; "The Cult of Ethnicity," *Washington Post*, July 14, 1991, p. C7; and "Catechism of Correctness," *Washington Post*, October, 1991, p. C7.

9. As indicated previously, articles and editorials about P.C. began appearing in the late 1980s, however, the major media assault on P.C. really began after Bush jumped on the anti-P.C. bandwagon.

10. It is interesting to note that the man responsible for putting the 1990 "Thought Police" story on the magazines cover, Maynard Parker, *Newsweek*'s editor in chief, later became a member of the board of directors of Stanford's (one of the alleged P.C. hotbeds) Alumni Association (Gitlin, 1995:181).

11. For a more detailed discussion of this, see Robbins (1991).

12. While this suggestion of *Newsweek* reiterating Kimball's claims may seem temporally implausible given that I am citing Kimball (1991), while the *Newsweek* article appeared in later 1990, it should be noted that Kimball's book was originally published in hardcover by Harper & Row in 1990. Furthermore, many of the sentiments which Kimball expresses in his book repeat previous statements made in his articles for the *New Criterion*.

13. For a thorough account of what transpired at the University of Texas at Austin regarding English 306, see Brodkey and Fowler (1991). The authors of this article were, incidentally, members of the policy and syllabus committees in the English department at Austin. In their article, they explain the demise of the progressive proposals in greater detail.

14. See for example Zavarzadeh and Morton (1991), and Zavarzadeh (1991).

15. It is interesting to note that in a survey of the media's treatment of P.C., Laura Fraser of Fairness and Accuracy in Reporting (FAIR) found that most of the articles were penned by "none- too-liberal men, usually white, defending the traditional academy" (cited in Smith, 1991:8).

Chapter 4

Theory Wars and Cultural Strife

1968 and After

The high priests of conservatism, right-wing think-tanks, and mainstream media pundits have vastly exaggerated the furor over P.C. and the furtive left-wing takeover of the university. However, the naive abjuration of anti-P.C. rhetoric as a mere symptom of conservative power fails to address *why* this characterization of events has appeared plausible to so many people. Of course, the pervasive anti-intellectualism of American culture has been invoked repeatedly to explain the reception that the P.C. backlash has enjoyed among the public. This is surely part of it. Yet, simply castigating a climate of anti-intellectualism for the bad press leftists have received is counterproductive, hampering a necessary and overdue examination of issues that continue to plague whatever remains of the Left.

When one cuts through the hyperbole of Kimball, D'Souza, and other conservative commentators, many of their observations contain more than a modicum of "truth." As such, they warrant further consideration—not, however, for the reasons they suggest, but because they do, in many respects, illustrate the way in which the academic Left has isolated itself from the broader public sphere. Kimball's account of the "cult of theory" among leftists is rather difficult to deny, as are D'Souza's charges of a burgeoning relativism. Conservatives abhor these developments because they view them as "radical" threats to the established order; yet, I would suggest that progressives be concerned with these developments because they are *not radical enough*. Before grappling with those questions; however, it

is necessary to locate the advent of P.C. within a broader theoretical and political context.

At some level, we can contextualize the emergence of P.C.
in relation to the "linguistic" turn in social theory and the rise
of identity-based politics. For some, this assumption will undoubtedly seem peculiar since, poststructuralist discourse generally rejects the fundamental basis of identity politics: the
role of experience.[1] However, as Barbara Epstein (1995) and
Stuart Hall (1994) have astutely pointed out, identity politics
and the poststructuralist sensibility *do* come together to constitute much of what defines itself as radical today. Hence,
each of these developments warrants further unpacking. In
order to comprehend these phenomena we need to consider
their historical genealogy; both have roots in the 1960s and
both, in varying degrees, represent a repudiation of Marxism,
its attendant concepts, and its political agenda.

It is now old hat to point to 1968 as a watershed in the history of Left politics and Left social theory. In France, student
protesters, joined by workers, staged a massive general strike
which paralyzed the entire country. In Britain, Prague, Berlin,
Italy, and elsewhere in Europe, students seized educational
institutions—the "ideological factories"—and other public
spheres to demonstrate their solidarity with the French Left.
In the United States, campuses across the country were sites of
radical protest; opposition to the Vietnam war was intensify-
ing; the assassination of Martin Luther King, Jr. spawned uprisings; and decolonization efforts abroad were inspiring a number of social movements. The countercultural revolution was
well under way, spreading the seeds of discontent far and wide,
and the "days of rage" were televised for all to see. Of course,
the delirium eventually subsided, and the mass movements were
defeated. Not surprisingly, the political ferment of the 1960s
ultimately had repercussions for academic culture and intellectual endeavors. In fact, Kellner (1995:20) argues that it appeared as if "the tumultuous struggles of the era sought expression and replication in the realm of theory."

In the aftermath of Paris 1968, a number of disillusioned
radicals concluded that "Marxism," especially the version espoused by the French Communist Party, was both too dogmatic and too confining a framework to adequately theorize
contemporary society and its relations of power.[2] For several

reasons, many French intellectuals began to bid adieu to Marxism as both a theory and a political project.[3] In subsequent years, poststructuralism emerged as a revolt against Enlightenment philosophy, the promise of liberal humanism, the materialist underpinnings of Marxism, and structuralism. Of course, the precursor to poststructuralism's rise was the structuralist turn which had flourished in France during the 1950s and 1960s.[4] Largely in reaction to the tradition of humanistic philosophy, especially existentialism and phenomenology and their view of the autonomous, self-directed individual, structuralism sought to move beyond the interests and impulses of the individual by focusing on the underlying rules that organized the basis of knowledge, history, and society. In general, structuralists attempted to reveal the universal structures that organized the thought processes of individuals, and described social phenomena in terms of linguistic rules, codes, and systems (Cherryholmes, 1988; Eagleton, 1983). Moreover, structural analysis attempted to develop a scientific mode through which these deep structures and their functions could be made manifest.

The events of 1968, however, led many to conclude that neither the scientific formalism of structuralism nor traditional forms of Marxist thought could account for the fluid and malleable character of experience and social life. This scepticism in turn led to the ascendency of poststructuralism. While sharing the anti-humanism of structuralism and its valorization of language, poststructuralism did not accept the scientific underpinnings which grounded structuralism and its attempt to foster a scientific foundation for the study of culture and society. Furthermore, whereas structuralists aspired to uncover universal and uniform linguistic patterns, poststructuralists attempted to illustrate the dynamic character of language, the instability of meaning, and the historically contingent nature of various symbolic and linguistic forms. Hence, the uprisings of the late 1960s engendered a seismic shift in French theory and philosophy and a fundamental rethinking of categories and concepts that had dominated French thought throughout the 1950s.

The theory fever which first emerged in 1960s France eventually travelled across the Atlantic to the United States. In addition to the importation of French theory, the experiences of the 1960s and the Vietnam War drove many in the New Left to Marxist theory, which had been driven underground during the Cold War era. The work of the Frankfurt School, particularly their critique of positivist rationality, proved to be a powerful weapon in challenging the theoretical deficiencies and political shortcomings of the then-dominant paradigm which had characterized the academy during the 1950s and early 1960s. Herbert Marcuse's indictment of "one dimensional" thought and his passionate polemics against Western capitalism were especially influential in New Left circles, as were the dissident writings of intellectuals like Noam Chomsky and C. Wright Mills. With the feminist movement and the struggles against colonialism in various Third World countries, a variety of narratives had begun to find their way into the American academy, first taking the form of theory fever and eventually giving way to theory wars between competing discourses (Kellner, 1995:20).

The introduction of these new paradigms helped to enrich an understanding of various social processes and provided more nuanced and complex interpretations of phenomena that had been ignored or marginalized in earlier theoretical frameworks. But the era of theory fever and theory wars also created a particularly peculiar paradox for the Left: ironically in the *aftermath* of the late 1960s, many of the organic intellectuals of the New Right shifted their focus from abstract philosophizing and theorizing to issues of contemporary culture, concrete political organizing, and coalition building. Many Left intellectuals, however, wholeheartedly embraced theory. In fact, theory, "sundered from social movement, took central space" and the agenda of the Left was turned on its proverbial head, "movement took a back seat to ideas" (Davies, 1995:12-13).

While many theories generated *during* the 1960s derived in part from social movement, those that evolved *subsequently* became "institutionalized" to such an extent that their subversive edge was sufficiently dullened. Aijaz Ahmad notes that the dominant strands within theory that unfolded *after* the movements of the 1960s

> have been mobilized to domesticate, in institutional ways, the very forms of political dissent which those movements had sought to foreground, to displace an activist culture with a textual culture . . . with

a new mystique of leftish professionalism, and to reformulate in a postmodernist direction questions which had previously been associated with a broadly Marxist politics. (Ahmad, 1992:1)

In essence, Ahmad is addressing the "linguistic" or "textualist" turn engendered by poststructuralism and its concomitant renunciation of Marx—something which has become fashionable among many self-declared "Left" academics. Given the salience of poststructuralism among radical theorists and the fact that it has permeated virtually every area of inquiry from feminism to cultural studies, one could facilely conclude that poststructuralism emerged as the victorious party in the theory wars. Indeed, poststructuralism has attained the "status of an ironcast orthodoxy among those presumed to know" (Norris, 1993:285). It has, in other words, become virtually hegemonic in many left-leaning constituencies, eclipsing earlier traditions of critical thought, especially Marxism (Ebert, 1996; Epstein, forthcoming; Foley, 1990; Zavarzadeh and Morton, 1994).

The stock phrases and slogans of poststructuralism—textuality, discursivity, antifoundationalism, and the like are so entrenched within the sublime terrain of contemporary "critical" theory that even to question their efficacy is often taken to be a form of "theoretical incorrectness." However, Lazere (1995:351) points out, correctly in my opinion, that the net effect of years of "arcane poststructuralist metacriticism" has been the depoliticization of politics. The speed with which poststructuralism has been accorded academic recognition and the legitimacy it has commanded in Left intellectual circles should tell us something about the "eminently co-optable nature of even the most apparently radical of semiotic enterprises" (Milner, 1994:105). Indeed, Zavarzadeh and Morton (1991;1994) maintain that the dominance of poststructuralism has led to the displacement of more radical modes of social critique and the reinscription of liberal pluralism.

The Cult of Theory

It is a curious fact . . . that the level and quality of theoretical work on the left seems to vary inversely with the fortunes of left-wing politics at large. Then again, one could argue . . . that this should not be any great cause for surprise, since a recourse to theory is typically the response of any marginalised fraction of dissident intellectuals, ex-

cluded from the mainstream of political life . . . Still one might think
it a curious turn of events when this response takes the form of a
deep investment in issues of aesthetics, philosophy of art, and literary theory as the chief areas of concern among a sizeable number of
committed left-wing cultural activists. For it is, to say the least, far
from self-evident that specialised work in these areas could eventually
feed back to exert any influence on the way people live, think, feel,
vote and comport themselves in the public sphere of politically responsible action and choice. The suspicion must be . . . that these
theorists are just whistling in the dark, discovering all manner of
pseudo-radical rhetorics and postures by which to disguise their own
deep sense of political failure or defeat. (Norris, 1990:1)

In the pursuit of theory for its own sake, we have abandoned the
problems of concrete historical analysis. (Hall, 1988:35)

A major theme in the smear campaign against P.C. and Left
intellectuals was the attack on theory. Conservative critics inveighed against new literacies ranging from feminism to
postcolonialism for jeopardizing the political neutrality and
ideological disinterestedness that they claimed once defined
scholarly inquiry. They mocked those who challenged the objective "Truth" contained in the Western canon and ridiculed
those who questioned the sanctity and superiority of Western
values. The content of scholarly work on gender, race, and
ethnicity was cast in the most insipid light, caricatured to such
an extent that critical work in these areas was made to look
ridiculous. Left-leaning academics were portrayed as wild-eyed,
theory-crazed malcontents furiously jumping from one academic fad to the next. Not surprisingly, the mainstream media, with its pastiche coverage, dutifully reiterated these sentiments, all the while reinforcing the lengthy history of
anti-intellectualism in the United States. Given these circumstances, it is no surprise that many Left intellectuals responded
to such charges with a certain degree of recalcitrance. Yet many
of those who attempted to defend contemporary "leftist theory"
from its detractors did so in a somewhat unreflective and self-
aggrandizing manner. As Jacoby (1994:164) notes, it is rather
difficult to ignore the "ease with which the new professors
defend professional reputations and language, sophisticated
theories and distinguished friends," while heaping contempt
on critics as "backward outsiders."

Rather than reflect upon what may be deficient in their own academic and political practices, many "Left" theoreticians resorted instead to a crass form of professional sycophany, choosing to malign their critics and others who questioned the practical political utility of deconstructung texts. In several respects, this logic informs Michael Berube's (1992) otherwise insightful contribution entitled *Public Access*. Berube claims that the Right has succeeded in winning the culture wars thus far because of its simplistic populist approach to explaining complex social issues. Given that context, Berube suggests that intellectuals need to produce new knowledges for and about "ordinary" people in an effort to "popularize" academic professions. His plea to make "left" literacies more accessible and relevant to wider audiences is one that progressives should heed. Yet Berube's desire to "popularize" theory is not, in the final analysis, informed by the desire to effect social change. Rather, he suggests that the academic professions must popularize themselves "because their very existence is being threatened" (1992:176). Otherwise stated, intellectuals have to defend their "turf." Quite simply, the effort to popularize academic discourse becomes a public relations ploy to renew or reinstate a fledgling public respect for intellectuals.[5] The effort, then, to communicate to a broader public is not predicated on the necessity of intervening meaningfully in struggles for social change. Rather, it is advocated by Berube as a strategy to justify intellectual production as an end in and of itself.[6]

Recently, bell hooks (1995:27) has pointed out that Berube's assessments of intellectual works are based not on their significance for, or impact upon, social movements, but rather on whether or not their authors are "popular"—precisely the sort of academic "star" system that hooks and Cornel West (1991) denounce in their collaborative effort, *Breaking Bread*. This "Disneyfication" of the Left lends itself to a situation where current theories, theorists, and academic celebrities create a simulation of social movement, an intellectual pseudopolitics, where the production of theory and deconstruction of texts is deemed politically useful in itself—a posturing that often works in a way that "implicitly empowers

the theorist while explicitly disempowering real cultural subjects" (Turner, 1994:410).

Indeed, both Norris's and Hall's comments quoted above
appear to capture the crux of that which ails much of the academic Left today: the valorization of theory as an end in and
of itself and the production of theory divorced from practical
political considerations. In fact, Stabile (1995:121) points to
the insular nature of most contemporary theorizing, preoccupied as it is with intercine debates, many of which are far removed from the concerns of public life. Norris (1990:44) goes
even further and suggests that theory (especially of the
postmodern variety) has served as an "escape-route from pressing political questions and a pre-text for avoiding any serious
engagement with real-world historical events." The metaphor
of a contemporary "tower of babel" seems appropriate here—
academics perched high above the grimy rooftops of reality,
striking radical poses without ever leaving the confines of their
ivory tower.

Theory has become a hot commodity and many contemporary Leftist scholars have, to "suit their own purposes as phi-
losophers . . . reinvented the meaning of theory" (Christian,
1987:51). Theory is no longer valued for its explanatory power
or its potential to inform social change but rather for how it
can be used to "playfully" decenter, deconstruct, or otherwise
disrupt established meanings and presuppositions. These gestures, while "radical" in the sense that they challenge familiar
ways of thinking, do not necessarily lead to radical mobilization or even to radical social critique (McLaren, 1994[b]; West,
1993). And a considerable amount of "critical" scholarship *has*
been faddish, leaping from theory to theory with little more
than the remotest connection to the multiple struggles against
domination, marginalization, and subordination both inside
and outside of the academy.

Furthermore, many of the developments in contemporary
theory *do*, in their extreme manifestations, invite and deserve
criticism. This was made all the more apparent in the recent
Social Text fiasco, which rocked the academic world and em-
barrassed certain strains of the Left. For those unfamiliar with
the *Social Text* caper, a brief recounting of events is warranted.
Professor Alan Sokal, a physicist at New York University and a

self-described Leftist-feminist who taught math in Nicaragua under the Sandanistas, submitted an article entitled "Transgressing The Boundaries: Toward A Transformative Hermeneutics Of Quantum Gravity," which appeared in *Social Text*'s special issue on science studies. Ostensibly, the essay was about the extent to which postmodernist philosophy had transformed dominant modes of thought in the physical sciences. Sokal dutifully cited the intellectual heavyweights, including Derrida, Lacan and Lyotard; used the fashionable buzzwords and the often impenetrable jargon which defines pomospeak; and proclaimed that "physical reality, no less than social reality, is at bottom a social and linguistic construct" (Sokal, 1996:217). In other words, Sokal claimed that there was no objective material reality.

On the day the publication was released, Sokal revealed in *Lingua Franca* that his submission to *Social Text* was nothing more than a parody of postmodern science studies in particular and postmodern theory in general. Almost immediately, the media caught wind of the scam and major newspapers across the country ran the story. The editors of *Social Text* were left agape and quickly chastized Sokal for intellectual charlatanism and lack of good faith. As expected, right-wing spokespersons like Roger Kimball seized the day and pointed to the Sokal affair as just another example of the excesses of loony Left theorizing. This, of course, was the unfortunate off-shoot of Sokal's prank, for it provided the Right with another excuse for theory-bashing. While the issues raised by Sokal's critique of science studies and postmodern theory are far more complex than I am suggesting here, his parody illustrates much of what is troublesome in those trajectories that take discursivity and social constructivism to their illogical extremes.[7]

In fact, Sokal claimed that his decision to do the parody was motivated by his anger and frustration with scholarship that purported to be left-wing but which actually served to undermine progressive social critique through its sophistry and obscurantism. In exposing the hoax, Sokal's intent was to initiate an intellectual renovation of the Left. Of course, the biggest misconception here is that the postmodernist/post-structuralist/deconstructionist "Left" is really the Left at all (Pollitt, 1996:9), but that is another debate entirely. Suffice it to say, in what follows, I point to some of the politically debilitating aspects of contemporary theory, especially the discursive withdrawal, or what Giddens (1984) calls, the "retreat into the code"—a trend which several commentators attribute to the linguistic turn spawned by poststructuralist theory.

Steven Best and Douglas Kellner (1991:25) point out that poststructuralism "forms part of the matrix of postmodern theory" and is generally regarded as a "subset of a broader range of theoretical, cultural and social tendencies that constitute postmodern discourses."[8] However, Foley (1990) and Epstein (forthcoming) point out that in recent years post-structuralism has been elevated to the status of **Theory**—an assertion which is difficult if not impossible to disregard. Epstein further notes that nowadays the word "theory," unmodified by any adjective, is more likely than not taken to mean poststructuralist theory. That is, rather than being viewed as one among many theoretical discourses, poststructuralism is increasingly equated with theory itself. More ominously, however, is the fact that poststructuralism is now, more often than not, equated with radicalism.

Poststructuralism is, of course, not a monolithic discourse, nor can it be defined or associated exclusively with one or another theorist. In fact, Poster (1989:4) remarks that in the United States, the term poststructuralist "draws a line of affinity around several French theorists who are rarely so grouped in France." Nonetheless, "poststructuralism" is often applied to a range of theoretical discourses including those developed in and from the work of Jacques Lacan, Jacques Derrida, Michel Foucault, Jean Baudrillard, and Jean-Francois Lyotard.[9] It is expected that this characterization of poststructuralism will be charged with reinscribing the Hegelian trope which Judith Butler discusses in her critique of those who dare conflate diverse theorists and "colonize and domesticate" these theories and theorists under "the sign of the same" so as to avoid a close reading of these positions (Butler, 1992:5). However, I am less interested here in the nuances of these various theoretical trajectories and far more concerned with the set of constitutive principles that have come to define the leftist intellectual terrain and their *political* implications.

Despite Butler's observation, the stances articulated by these diverse thinkers *do* converge to some extent in debunking modernist theories of society, history, politics, and subjectivity. While some observers have pointed out that there is little consensus about what modernism itself means (Bernstein, 1987), at the risk of overgeneralization, theories which fall under the rubric of poststructuralism reject modernism's epistemic foundations or master narratives as totalizing (Lyotard, 1984); repudiate modern theory's search for a foundation of knowledge; criticize its apodictic truth claims; and renounce the rational, autonomous Cartesian subject.

Derrida's deconstructive techniques and anti-foundationalism provided a basis for a critique of Western metaphysics and Enlightenment appeals to rationality, reason, and truth.[10] In *Of Grammatology*, and subsequently in *Writing and Difference* and *Positions*, Derrida rejected the very notion of trying to locate an order of truth. His aim was to demonstrate that claims to authority, specifically intellectual authority, could not be justified and that such posturing often concealed a Nietzschean "will to power." The Western philosophical tradition and its strong assertions about truth were, according to Derrida, complicit in the catastrophes and abominations of Western history and civilization. In a somewhat different but not unrelated vein, Foucault's genealogical analyses attempted to reveal the futility of searching for discoverable truths. Foucault (1980) sought to illustrate the historically contingent nature of "truths" and how the articulation of truth was dependent upon dominant discursive regimes. Furthermore, among Foucault's main concerns was to show how historical eras, rather than being regulated by economic laws, were governed instead by discourses and the rules and classifications which enabled some phenomena to be viewed as rational, normal, and truthful, while others were perceived to be deviant, blasphemous, and immoral. Foucault also played a decisive role in shifting the terrain of analysis toward the "local." In particular, his conceptualization of power as diffused throughout society at all levels and as a relational phenomena shifted analysis away from the state and political economy.[11]

The critique of modern theory's conceptualization of sub-jectivity is another shared characteristic of most poststructur-alist theorists.[12] In some of the more overzealous efforts to recant the subject of liberal humanism, some have boldly de-clared the "end" of the subject, while others have suggested that the very concept of the subject implodes in the society of simulations (Baudrillard, 1983). Still others have sought to problematize the subject by producing accounts of an anti-es-sentialist, decentered, and mainly discursive subject. In gen-eral, these approaches dismiss any conception of the subject as a stable entity and argue instead that the parameters of the subject vary according to regnant discursive practices (Fou-cault, 1980, 1982; Lacan, 1977).[13]

In addition to their disdain for humanism,[14] yet another common denominator among poststructuralists is their philo-sophical excoriation of Marx. Many of these theorists had, at some earlier time, adhered in one manner or another to Marxist formulations but subsequently developed an opposition to them. Best (1989:334) wryly comments that within post-struc-turalism "the figurehead of Marx has been burned in effigy and replaced by the new idol of Nietzsche." Given this hostil-ity towards Marxism, it is somewhat ironic that one of the chief architects of deconstructive poststructuralism, Derrida, has recently begun to sing the praises of Marx again.[15]

Undoubtedly, many poststructuralist insights have provided important correctives to some of the blind spots within Marx-ian theory. They have also highlighted the problems of essen-tialism, shed new light on the limitations of the Enlightenment faith in reason, and problematized the privileging of the White Western subject and the hierarchical binarisms of Western epistemology.[16] However, in its "ludic"[17] extremes, post-struc-turalism and its coterminous categories of indeterminability and undecidability as well as its valorization of relativism and its rejection of "meaning" and "truth claims," have left us with-out an ethical leg to stand on and without a normative frame of reference to make political and ethical judgments. More-over, the almost exclusive focus on discourse and texts within poststructuralism as well as its "absolutization of language" has discouraged attention to other levels of analysis, to mate-rial conditions, and to the social agents of history (Eagleton, 1996; Kincheloe, 1994; Stabile, 1995).

How, then, is the linguistic turn imbricated in the politics of political correctness and why must we move beyond such formulations? Terdiman (1995:241) maintains that the one thing that has been

> particularly strange is how much of the conflict about PC has played out in the realm of language. Usually real social conflict has been a struggle over more infrastructural issues and interests . . . The PC wars have been fought in the realm of symbols because our cultural discourses and practices aren't yet at the point of foregrounding the substance behind much of this conflict . . . Consequently we fight about symbols.

Here Terdiman suggests that P.C. has been limited to the realm of language and representation because we have not yet arrived at the point where our theories are capable of fore-grounding more substantive concerns. I would contend, however, that the problem is that while we do in fact have such formulations, they have been largely repressed by the poststructuralist "Left." The emphasis on language and texts within P.C. is, in many respects, a reflection of the emphases found in much poststructuralist theory. In fact, Milner (1994:103-104) points out that poststructuralism has been "far too preoccupied with the high modernist canon" to accord any serious attention to questions that go beyond those of textual representation. Paradoxically, the poststructuralist accentuation on the texts of culture is not very different from conservative traditionalists' preoccupation with the "great" books of the Western canon; their only real point of divergence is the way in which these texts are read—either straightforwardly as in the case of traditionalists or oppositionally in the case of poststructuralists. In this regard, poststructuralism has legitimated a narrow emphasis on texts that "erases the marks of institutional power and concrete social conflicts" (Giroux, 1994:115). Rather than examining and investigating structural arrangements and temporal social relations, the poststructuralist turn has redefined politics as a textual struggle. Quite simply, the analysis of texts has been turned into "a marionette theater of the political" (Gates, 1992:97).

This phenomenon is evident in Michael Berube's (1994) defense of the postmodern sensibility, which has come under attack by the deacons of the New Right. Berube (1994:254) reflects on the "empowering" moment when his students, reading James Weldon Johnson's *The Autobiography of an Ex-colored Man*, discover the "unreadability of race" within the text. Clearly the insights that students Black, white or otherwise could derive from reading Johnson's narrative are undeniable, but revelling in the pleasures of the text and declaring the unreadability of race does little to illuminate the fact that a large majority of African-Americans will never have the opportunity to read Johnson or attend university because of systemic and debilitating forms of racism and classism. Nor, for that matter, can it help to explain that while the unreadability of race may be a factor in textual representations, race is indeed "readable" in American society—increasingly so, if one takes stock of regnant social arrangements and the current virulent backlash aimed at African-Americans. As Gates (1992:97) perceptively notes, it "seems that blacks are doing better in the college curriculum than they are in the streets."

Berube's wresting of *text* from *context* is symptomatic of what Teresa Ebert (1992/93; 1996) refers to as "ludic" theory. For Ebert, ludic postmodern theory has served to undermine progressive political agendas by limiting struggles to those over signs, signification, the textual, and the discursive which she attributes in part to the "theory as play" motif which has come to dominate critical social theory. The distinction she makes between theory-as-play and explanatory theory is an important one:

> Explanatory critique is fundamentally different from theory as play in that the latter addresses itself exclusively to cultural politics, understanding cultural politics as the theater of significations . . . In opposition to theory as play, theory as explanation goes beyond cultural politics and engages the material base of the social formation that in fact conditions cultural politics. For theory as play, culture (as the staging of conflicting chains of signification) is (semi) autonomous, while theory as explanatory critique regards culture to be always articulated by material forces. (Ebert, 1996:15)

Ebert's indictment of ludic theories, however, does not seek to disavow the importance of the cultural arena as a site of contestation and struggle, but rather seeks to contextualize it within the broader matrices of capitalist social relations. Indeed, given the salience of cultural politics on the New Right, it would be detrimental to summarily dismiss the "cultural," for circumventing such questions avoids questions concerning the ways in which we see the world.

It is imperative, however, to reiterate a point made in the introduction to this book—that the Right has successfully understood the *interrelationship* between culture and socio-political and economic relations. Much of the "post-al" Left, however, has failed to articulate the cultural in relation to political, economic, and material considerations and many have fallen prey to an ahistorical and apolitical "culturalism." It is necessary to acknowledge that there exists a marked distinction between underscoring the centrality of culture and the rhetoric of culturalism, which not only reduces everything to questions of culture but also has a reductionist conception of culture (Dirlik, 1987).

Even those who invoke Gramsci to accentuate the relevance of the cultural domain denude his thought of its fundamental concern with the economic constitution of a particular social formation, largely because they uncritically adopt Laclau and Mouffe's (1985) poststructuralist reading of Gramsci.[18] Indeed, many who draw on Gramsci's insights repeatedly take his critiques of economism to mean that analyses of economic and class relations are epiphenomenal or subordinate to cultural considerations. In far too many narratives, the "cultural" is treated as a separate and autonomous sphere severed from its embeddedness within socio-political relations and economic arrangements.

Culturalist assertions about the autonomy of culture, however, represent the most contorted perversions of Gramsci's thought. His attacks on economism were not intended to downplay or neglect the central importance of the economic foundations of a given social formation and their powerful influence in shaping and structuring the whole edifice of social life. What Gramsci was critiquing in his various commentaries on economism was a specific approach (that which had been canonized by the Second International) which tended to read the economic foundations of a society as the *only* determining structure; that is, a view that reduced everything to the economic level, and which tended to see all other dimensions of a particular social formation as merely mirroring the economic or directly corresponding to the economic (Hall, 1996:417-418). Surely, culture is not reducible to the economic, but neither can it be apprehended and understood outside of these relations. What disturbed Gramsci the most were the vulgar economistic renderings of Marx's thought which he saw as forms of theoretical reductionism because they simplified the structure of social formations and the interrelationships between various levels, and reduced their complexity by flattening the *mediations* between those different levels (Gramsci, 1949).

Unfortunately, critiques of political economy and discussions of capitalist social relations have all but disappeared in most "post-al" theorizations that privilege discourse. Ebert (1995:40) notes that at the heart of the "post-alization of politics" is the displacement of "material reality (the nondiscursive) by the discursive" and the abandonment of transformative politics in favor of semiotic play. Most contemporary narratives fail to articulate what Ebert (1991, 1992/93) and Hennessy (1993) refer to as the "materiality" of discourse.[19] That is, the signs of culture are severed from the conditions of their production. Rather than being conceived of as part of an ideological field circumscribed by capitalist social relations, signs are conceived of as historically indeterminate, free-floating chains of signifiers. Moreover, much poststructuralist theorizing of discourse presupposes but leaves unanalyzed the "socially organized practices and relations that objectify, including but not reducible to those visible in discourse itself" (Smith, 1993:3). Otherwise stated, discourse is often treated as inert and static—little attention is paid to the dynamic context in which discourses get produced and the social "actors" who produce them.

Stuart Hall (1994:168) reminds us that P.C. arose in an intellectual culture which had undergone "the linguistic turn," a fact which he credits for the extreme "nominalism" undergirding much of the rhetoric of P.C. In some instances, there has been a tendency to *overstate* the significance of language in *determining* meaning in the world. By practicing a politics that equates language to reality, a certain strain of the Left has reified language to such an extent that P.C. politics has amounted to little more than an academic exercise of nominalism. We have a campaign insisting upon justice at a purely terminological level—a promotion of "verbal and symbolic behaviors far beyond what the material infrastructure or other levels of social practice could authentically sustain or justify" (Terdiman, 1995:246). There is a tendency among some celebrants of P.C. to argue that changes in language or terminology will somehow lend themselves to actual changes in social relations and inequitable power relations. But never hearing a racist or sexist comment, for example, does not mean that racism, sexism, and the like will cease to exist as structural arrangements.[20] This situation is somewhat reminiscent of that described by Marx (1978:149) in his critique of the Young Hegelian ideologists who were, "in spite of their allegedly 'world-shattering' statements," the "staunchest conservatives." Marx goes on to lament that the Young Hegelians were simply fighting against "phrases." He writes:

> They forget, however, that to these phrases they themselves are only opposing other phrases, and that they are in no way combatting the real existing world when they are merely combatting the phrases of this world. (Marx, 1978:149)

Taking a cue from Marx, it could be argued that much of what falls under the rubric of P.C. politics is rather superficial or esoteric. The privileging of language and terminology within the politics of P.C. leads us willy-nilly down a path where politics takes a back seat to aesthetics, where form takes precedence over substance and where pseudo-radicalism replaces genuine political engagement with inequitable arrangements and power relations. In short, we are left with an empty politics, a series of metaphorical gestures which, in the end, have little impact on actual existing relations of power and privilege either inside or outside of the academy. In many respects, then, P.C. could be conceived of as a form of "ludic" politics.

The Ruse of "Truth"?

> It is the responsibility of intellectuals to speak the truth and to expose lies. (Chomsky, 1987:60)

> The purpose of the intellectual's activity is to advance human freedom and knowledge. This is still true, I believe, despite the often

repeated charge that grand narratives of emancipation and enlightenment . . . are pronounced as no longer having any currency in the
era of postmodernism. (Said, 1996:17-18)

. . . the Left continues to be braver in its philosophy than in its politics. (O'Neill, 1995:17)

Michael Berube (1995:50) points out (quite astutely, in my
opinion) that issues related to truth, relativism, and objectivity have enabled "intellectual and political conservatives" to
win "much support among nonacademics." This sentiment is
reiterated by Dasenbrock (1995:173), who claims that the
poststructuralist disavowal of truth has impacted quite significantly on the reception of anti-P.C. rhetoric among the general public. Given the current treatment of truth among some
leftist theorists, it should come as no surprise that the Right
has been far more convincing in its arguments. In fact,
Dasenbrock (1995:174) argues that it is "remarkable how little
disagreement there is about the concept of truth." Theorists
"who agree on little if anything else unite to view the word
and the concept with suspicion." Those who dare to invoke
standards of truth are said to be trapped in the throes of a
nostalgic desire for some definitive truth-telling discourse—be
it Marxist, Platonic, or Kantian. The contemporary post-struc-
turalist doxa suggests that "truth" is simply a product of discourses, signifying systems or language games that happen to
be dominant at a given moment. Truth in any given situation
can only be a matter of "beliefs that happen to prevail among
members of some existing interpretive community" (Norris,
1992:16).

Moreover, appeals to truth are viewed as inevitably authoritarian. The notion of truth is viewed as a form of rhetoric
adopted for no "other purpose than confirming the dominance
of this or that discourse in the endless struggle for mastery
and power" (Norris, 1993:261). Since distinctions between
oppressive and liberating truth claims are buried in the graveyard of modernism, we are left with the residue of a
Nietzschean, relativist creed which holds that all claims to truth
are on equal footing and that there is simply no difference
between competing truth-claims. In the final analysis, however,
this stance merely reinscribes the banality of liberal pluralism

and undercuts the possibility of articulating ethical positions. After all, ethical responsibility cannot be legitimated when truth claims are ensconced in ambiguity and relativism.

Given the suspicion of truth claims among the scions of poststructuralism, it is ironic that, when confronted with the gross and inaccurate misrepresentations of their academic practices by the Right and the media, many of its most ardent proponents began to appropriate the language of "truth." Card-carrying poststructuralists lamented the "imposters" posing as "knowledgeable scholars" and producing reports about academia and leftist theories that were "simply wrong" and rife with "falsehoods." In other words, these accounts were condemned for not being "truthful." But complaints of misrepresentation and distortion require some notion of truth or frame of intelligibility, no matter how partial in order to explore the veracity of the claims being made. That those who have repeatedly undermined the possibility of making truth claims are now criticizing others for being "untruthful" is not only laden with irony but reeks of hypocrisy.

I do not, however, suggest that we embrace the notion of one grand, universal, or transcendental Truth. Rather, the attack on truth within poststructuralism needs to be problematized, especially in light of the attack on P.C. As should be abundantly clear by now, the denial of truth claims may sound fashionable theoretically, but concretely and politically speaking, it raises some rather serious issues. If we abandon the language of truth, we will have abandoned one of the sharpest weapons of critique we possess. Commenting on the political ramifications of postmodernism's suspicion of truth claims and its valorization of relativist doctrines, Norris argues that:

> Talk of 'postmodernism' becomes in the end just a handy pretext for not thinking hard about anything . . . Above all, it does great service to the interests of the state and corporate power in diffusing the idea that there is *really no difference* between things as they seem, things as they are, and things as they might be according to the values of enlightened critique, increased social justice and a genuinely working participatory democracy. For it is only by maintaining a sense of these distinctions—common to every form of emancipatory thought . . . that theory can lay any claim to possessing a transformative or ethico-political force . . . Postmodernism effectively denies such claims through its attitude of out-and-out sceptical mistrust with regard to all truth

claims, normative standards, or efforts to distinguish veridical knowledge. (Norris, 1996:182)

Thus, we need a language or a framework that will enable us to speak of "truths" rather than "Truth," and which will enable distinctions to be drawn between more-or-less accurate truth claims and more-or-less justifiable values; that is, a framework that would allow us to move beyond the Foucauldian or Rortyan articulations about the community-specific nature of "truth."[21] The dilemma posed by a failure to do so is communicated by Dasenbrock:

> . . . as long as we insist on the community-specific nature of truth and stop there, we have no coherent response to any hostile description of our community . . . If we respond to a hostile description by saying "that isn't true" then we must have a theory of truth that allows for the possibility of truth beyond the beliefs and theories of a given community. (Dasenbrock, 1995:182)

While Dasenbrock appeals to a theory of truth, I would contend that a theory or concept of ideology is of particular relevance here.[22]

Of course, the notion of ideology has been deemed "obsolete" in the narratives of many postmodernists and poststructuralists and has, for the most part, been displaced by the concept of discourse.[23] Since the concept has been subjected to a variety of definitions and interpretations a few words of clarification are necessary. The formulation of ideology which I am invoking is not used to refer to political beliefs—that is ideology as an "ism" although certain political beliefs would be one instance of ideology. Nor is ideology being used here to draw boundaries or dichotomies between some mythical notion of impartiality and disinterestedness as opposed to ideology. Rather, following Kellner (1978) and Smith (1987), ideology is understood here as those concepts, categories, and ideas that give experience its social form, ideas and concepts which originate within a specific historical formation. Furthermore, these ideas and concepts must be understood contextually; we must direct our attention to who is producing these ideas for whom, for what purpose and under what material conditions. Ideology, defined in this way, directs us to examine where our social forms of consciousness are derived from. This appropriation of ideology does not rest on the orthodox Marxian formulation of ideology as "false consciousness," rather it points to Marx's use of the concept of ideology as it relates to the material production of knowledges.[24] In addition, it accords attention to the "actual," practical production and organization of ideas, thereby accentuating the ontological dimensions of "the social." In other words, it seeks to illuminate the material conditions undergirding the production of particular knowledges and to reveal the contradictions which enable the articulation of certain ideas to the exclusion of others.

While conservative traditionalists appeal to a transcendental, metaphysical notion of Truth, the critique of such appeals need not be accompanied by a complete and utter abandonment of truth-claims. Rather, what is required is a theory of ideology that makes it possible to explicate the complex ways in which social reality is shaped. I contend that this would enable us to avoid the abstract meanderings and relativism of post-al trajectories and allow us to speak meaningfully about the ideological underpinnings and differences between competing "truth" claims and the *interests* they are intended to serve. The practice of ideology-critique[25] is therefore a necessary element for critical social theory and a progressive political agenda. As Hennessy (1993:15) convincingly argues:

> Ideology critique . . . recognizes the contesting interests at stake in . . . constructions of the social. It does so from a committed position within a social analytic whose legitimacy is argued for not on the grounds of its scientific Truth but on the basis of its explanatory power and its commitment to emancipatory social change.

The ideology critique that Hennessy advances is most closely aligned with what Burbules (1995) refers to as an "alternative reading of Marx"—that is, one which critiques ideology not for its lack of scientific truth (as in the orthodox Marxist conception of ideology) but rather for its function in maintaining or supporting a social system which is itself judged.

As Marx contended in the second thesis on Feuerbach, the issue of truth is a *practical* question. Appraising the veracity of various truths was for Marx not a "quest for necessary and universal forms, essences, substances, categories or grounds, but rather a perennial activity of . . . responding to dilemmas, or overcoming quagmires" (West, 1991:65). The dispute, Marx

(1978:144) argues, about the "reality or non-reality of thinking" (i.e. philosophical discussions about the nature of truth divorced from concrete problems and pressing social issues) "which is isolated from practice is a purely scholastic question." Truths are to be measured in the context of concrete historical struggles, and their efficacy judged in relation to the insights they provide for comprehending the complex and contradictory character of a given field of social practices. Far from seeking some transcendental truth or some measure of metaphysical certainty, Marx sought to further the aims of social transformation (Ebert, 1995; Jay, 1996:64 [orig. 1973]).

This alternative reading of Marx's notion of ideology is, of course, something which a number of postmodernists and poststructuralists fail to consider, for they often base their critique of ideology on its more orthodox manifestations—that is, as something which is defined in opposition to the category of scientificity.[26] The mode of ideology-critique espoused by Hennessy and Ebert (while different in some respects) is not one informed by the discourse of scientificity but rather by a language of ethics and a commitment to social justice. In contrast to ludic attempts at dehierarchization and more traditional appeals to "scientificity," the aim of ideology-critique is to "intervene in the construction of hegemonic cultural meanings that erase social contradictions from the scene of the social" and to go beyond "ludic undecidability" (Zavarzadeh and Morton, 1991:225).

Political ideology critique therefore rejects hegemonic presuppositions and opposes established meanings by revealing the relations of production and the social formation that gives rise to particular meanings. More specifically, it seeks to provide a contextual understanding of the material conditions undergirding the production of knowledge/s. It involves revealing the ideological dimensions of dominant practices and cultural forms. The purpose of such an exercise is to interrupt those formulations which obscure the potential for change by representing themselves as "natural" givens rather than as constructed, historical products. Moreover, this form of investigation does not satisfy itself with simply "interpreting" or "destabilizing" different versions (or subversions) of the world, but rather aspires to produce "revolutionary knowledge" in the interest of transforming oppressive conditions and social relations (Bannerji, 1991; Ebert, 1995).[27]

The poststructuralist critique of truth is undoubtedly related to contemporary critiques of objectivity. As previously stated (Chapter 2), there are at least two critiques of objectivity, one derived from Marx and developed in the work of the Frankfurt School, Gramsci, and others, and the second from postmodernism and poststructuralism. In the former, it is asserted that claims to objectivity are usually invoked to veil power relations. In the latter, the rejection of objectivity stems from the postmodern insistence upon the socially situated character of all perspectives. The two accounts overlap in several fundamental regards, for most critical theorists also acknowledge the socially mediated nature of perspectives or paradigms. The fundamental differences lie in the Marxian rejection of the false dichotomy between absolutism and relativism[28] (Jay, 1996:63) and its disavowal of purely relativist positions which, in their pseudo-radical guises, surrender any possibility of making ethical judgements and negate the basis for a transformative political agenda.

It is also necessary to acknowledge that contemporary critiques of objectivity do not make a clear and necessary distinction between "objective knowledge" and "objective material conditions." To be sure, one cannot claim to know the social world objectively—this "view from nowhere" is precisely what Nagel (1986) and others (Bordo, 1990; Haraway, 1992) have challenged—but neither can one deny the existence of an objective social world.[29] Nonetheless, ludic theorists continue to bury the notion of an objective social reality "beneath the priority of discourse and significations" even as they feel, however indirectly, the pressures of that "objective reality" (Ebert, 1996:24). In her critique of ludic theory's treatment of truth and objectivity and its political implications, Ebert argues for a notion of truth grounded in historical materialism:

> In historical materialism, "truth" is not a universal given nor a metaphysical certainty, but neither is it simply a local effect of language games. Rather, "truth" is an historically struggled over and constructed knowledge-effect. To assert the historical constructedness of truth, however, in no way denies the existence of objective reality nor dissolves it into rhetoric or textual relativity; instead it refers to the way objective reality is made intelligible at any given historical moment. What is validated as "making sense," what is represented as "what is," what is legitimated as "true" . . . these are questions of ideology, for ideology constructs the representations in terms of which we "make

sense of" and live in relation to objective reality—to the material relations of production shaping our lives—and in terms of which we understand and relate to ourselves and each other. (Ebert, 1995:45)

Despite the many and varied (and often misinformed) critiques
of Marx proffered by Parisian prophets and their disciples, I
agree with Ebert that Marx's own writings on questions of
"truth," his concept of ideology, and various other Marxian
formulations remain indispensable for theorizing the current
historical juncture. Furthermore, the revolutionary humanism
that informed Marx's writings on emancipation remains, in
my view, far superior to relativist post-al positions which leave
little if any room for developing ethical stances against the
forms of injustice and inequality which continue to define our
social landscape.[30] I will, however, reserve further commentary on this issue at the moment to turn my attention to the
emergence of identity politics, which has intersected with the
linguistic turn to define the P.C. moment.

Identity Politics and the Politics of Representation

In recent years, there has been a veritable explosion of interest around the concept of "identity." Identity has become a
common word in the lexicon of popular parlance as well as in
our theoretical and political vocabularies where it has taken
on a variety of connotations. This contemporary preoccupation with identity has thrust the notions of experience and
subjectivity to the forefront of political thinking and scholarly
investigations. Whereas poststructuralist theorists like Butler
(1990,1993) and Scott (1992) interrogate notions of consciousness and appeals to lived experience, those sympathetic to identity politics retain the centrality of experience as a reference
point from which peripheralized and marginalized peoples
deconstruct the mystifications of the dominant social order
and the construction of subalterity and "otherness." In this
regard, identity politics is often viewed as a partial corrective
to those "post-al" trajectories which declare the subject's egregious extermination and which relegate issues of agency to
the domain of inconsequentiality. In fact, Ernesto Laclau
(1992:83-84) suggests that the "death of the subject" proclaimed
loudly not so long ago, has been succeeded by a new and wide-

spread interest in the multiple identities proliferating in our social world. While it is important to acknowledge these differences, it is equally important to note that both the poststructuralist turn and the discourse of identity politics converge to the extent that both valorize difference and heterogeneity. Otherwise stated, there is a "fit" of sorts between "poststructuralist theoretical relativism" and the kind of "cultural pluralism which many commentators find distinctive of our contemporary . . . condition" (Milner, 1994:103).

Just as the theoretical fervor detailed in the previous section was spawned, to a large extent, by the political upheavals of the 1960s both here and abroad, so too can some of the earliest formations of identity politics be traced to the late 1960s. As previously indicated, the aftermath of the political upheavals resulted in a volley of challenges to the classical Marxist conception of class struggle. By pointing to the multiplicity of sites and mechanisms of power and domination, a number of diverse constituencies began to challenge the notion of class as an inclusive or exhaustive category for defining the narrative of location and social change (Giroux, 1993). As a result of this, a trend then referred to as "lifestyle" politics began to emerge. The feminist movement, the struggles for Black nationalism, gay and lesbian liberation, and other sundry campaigns that arose in the late 1960s and early 1970s eventually came to be known as "identity politics" (Berman, 992; Kauffman, 1990). In concrete terms, this focus on identity has meant that politics is increasingly based on one's group membership—as a woman, a Jew, a Black, etc. Several commentators have claimed that today's P.C. is a manifestation of a political atmosphere dominated by identity politics and the fragmentation of the political topography into separate constituencies where identity, rather than material interest, class or collective disadvantage, is the mobilizing factor (Ehrenreich, 1992; Gitlin, 1994; Hall, 1994).

Although there is no one text or authority that one can turn to for a systematic account of the central tenets of identity politics, its core presuppositions may be delineated as follows:

> (1) that differences of race, class, ethnicity, gender, sexual orientation, and so on have for too long been obscured by a hegemonic white, upper-class and heterosexual elite which, under the guise of claiming

that there exists a universal human condition, has constructed accounts of reality that serve its own ends; (2) that those groups whose identities were previously subjugated by this elite should now be privileged as sources of both epistemological and moral authority, since their oppression gives them a unique capacity and right to speak about and judge what is true and what is good; (3) that (implicit in the first two claims) access to truth and the authority to make moral and political judgements is not universal, but is always relative to who one is; (4) that to "unmask" or "deconstruct" privileged, universalist readings of reality and to make possible the expression by the previously silenced and subjugated of their own identity and truth are not only valid forms of political action, but *the* most important forms of political action today; (5) that such a politics of unmasking privilege and enabling the subjugated to come to voice needs also to be conducted internally, within groups and movements on the Left. (Kruks, 1996:122-123)

Identity politics, perhaps more than any other issue, has spawned the fiercest of debates in both intellectual and political circles. On the one hand, it has been championed for its affirmation of difference and heterogeneity; its challenges to the "universal" subject of history; its attention to particularities other than class; and for politicizing issues which had previously been viewed as non-political. According to its advocates, the emergence of identity politics opened up the possibilities for a more radical challenge to forms of domination and marginalization such as sexism, homophobia, and racism which had been excluded in more traditional formulations of the political.

Identity politics have also enabled subaltern groups to reconstruct their own histories and give voice to their individual and collective identities. Bannerji (1995:20) points out that the "passion of naming" is at the heart of identity politics, for it has been those who have been marginalized and oppressed, those constructed as "other," who have fought so vehemently to name themselves. But while a number of theorists and cultural critics such as hooks (1992) and Lorde (1984) have pointed to the need of acknowledging the importance of "difference" and "experience" in any project that purports to be committed to social change, in recent years, identity politics has been criticized for a number of reasons, both theoretical and political.

First, the emphasis on experience and feeling within the politics of identity has been charged with *reinstating* a liberal humanist conception of the subject (Bondi 1993:86). Here identity politics is about the (re)discovery of an already existing identity, an essentialized core of being and existence that is founded on a conception of the subject as centered, coherent, and self-authored. In these instances it is assumed that there exists an "authentic" Black, female, Latino, etc., experience or way of being in the world. The discourse of authenticity presumes that one's own "location as an oppressed person" or one's "physical proximity to the oppressed" offers a "special authority from which to speak" (McLaren, 1994[b]:52) and that experience somehow guarantees the authenticity of knowledge. This exclusive emphasis on experience and feeling also reconstitutes a "suspect Cartesian tradition in reverse: I feel, therefore I am" (Jacoby, 1975:104).

Furthermore, the emphasis on the personal and "self-discovery" in some versions of identity politics has often had the effect of replacing critical engagement with institutionalized structures of power with an individualist, introverted form of "cathartic" or "confessional" therapy (Kauffman, 1990; West, 1993). There has also been a tendency to construct a "hierarchy of oppression" which has given rise to the "self-righteous assertion" that one occupying a certain identificatory category has the "moral right to guilt-trip others into particular ways of behaving" (Parmar, 1990:107). Parmar adds that this hierarchization of oppression has been destructive, divisive, and politically immobilizing. It has also ghettoized identity politics to the extent that some people have been unable to move beyond individual and personal experience.

Second, it is necessary to acknowledge that the mere declaration that the personal is political, often ensconced in an "I am, therefore I resist" formulation, is insufficient ground to assume a politicized and oppositional identity (hooks, 1992; Mohanty, 1991). Otherwise stated, occupying a specific experiential realm does not necessitate that one has to adhere to a particular agenda or set of interests. Indeed, Mercer (1992), Wallace (1994), and others have aptly pointed out that marginalized subjects can just as easily be drawn into positions on the Right as they can into positions on the Left.[31]

Third, formulations that presume that only Jews can understand Jewish suffering or that only former colonial subjects can understand colonial experience are flawed because they tend not only to psychologize questions of oppression but also to construct defenses of the experience rather than promote knowledge of it (Said,1986:55). The notion that we can only speak for ourselves based on experience and that others cannot speak out against injustices they have not experienced themselves also raises scepticism about the possibility of ever adequately or justifiably taking advocacy positions (Alcoff, 1991/92:18). Rather than cultivating new political visions, this posturing has stifled productive discourse. Grossberg (1992:367) points out that:

> Every individual and struggle is judged by a standard of linguistic self-righteousness and moral purity. Being morally and politically correct is defined by the constant need to demonstrate the proper deference to the subordinate terms within the systems of differences. Everyone is held accountable to an ever-expanding and unpredictable series of potential exclusions and subordinations.

Hence, despite the trumped up charges of P.C. launched by the Right, there has been a tendency towards a rigidifying orthodoxy and dogmatism among some Left constituencies which promotes not the vigorous intellectual and political openness requisite for social change but rather a "stop-in-your-tracks foreclosure" on discussion and dialogue (Terdiman, 1995:245).

Fourth, the capacity to name oneself in the order of thought, to move, as hooks (1989:12) puts it, from silence to speech, is a revolutionary gesture that is obviously linked to the wider issue of agency—how people either become agents in the process of making history or function as silenced, passive objects buried under the weight of oppression and exploitation. These gestures, however, on their own do not guarantee the conditions and resources, the "material power necessary for social flourishing and living freely" (Goldberg, 1994:13). Identity politics, in this regard, often amounts to little more than a "politics of gesture," to political posturing that fails to interrogate social forms which go beyond the realm of immediate experience and the discursive or textual realm of representation. Much of what is called identity politics, in the end, is little more than a demand for inclusion into the club—a demand for representation. As Bannerji (1991:83-84) astutely points out:

> The politics of "difference" hides in its radical posture a neo-liberal pluralist stance . . . Generally it amounts to advancing a metatheory

of competing interests built on the concept of a free market. The political sphere is modelled on the marketplace and freedom amounts to the liberty of all political vendors to display their goods equally in a competition.

This stance undergirds much of the discourse of P.C. and the drive for multicultural inclusiveness. Many of the groups who have been charged with being P.C. are those who have demanded that curricula reflect the diverse needs of all students, that the works of women, people of color and others be included in the curriculum. Yet, it is imperative to note that a *quantitative* increase in the number of "different" voices "allowed" into the privileged realm of curriculum and knowledge production does not necessarily guarantee a *qualitative* change in the kind of knowledge that is produced. While the aim of inclusive curricula is indeed an important and necessary reform, multicultural add-ons do not, in and of themselves, necessarily accomplish the task of furthering our understanding of the institutional and structural bases of racism, sexism, class oppression, and the like. Nor do multicultural add-ons guarantee changes in the material conditions of peripheralized groups. In fact, a multiculturalist project that is merely "textual" and has no transformative social agenda can be just "another form of accommodation to the larger social order" (McLaren, 1995:126).

Indeed, some critics have pointed out that the focus on the "canon" may be a kind of business-as-usual way of trivializing the issues. Hazel Carby (1989:36) suggests that the "debates about the canon are misleading debates" if all they amount to are questions about what texts to include or exclude in the reading lists of elite universities. Similarly, Russell Jacoby (1994:27) reminds us that while Left academics are pining away about what texts should be taught, the majority of American youth do not even have the opportunity to attend universities due in large part to the "gentrification of higher education—the increasing dominance by the wealthy of the select universities." In many respects, these hotly contested debates over the canon and textual representation obscure more fundamental issues and avoid deeper problems by leading even those people interested in radical change to presume that the inclusion of the texts they favor would take care of structural inequalities (Carby, 1989:36-38).

A pedagogical agenda exclusively concerned with the politics of representation, which focuses solely on questions of canonical inclusion/exclusion and which holds that injustices based on marginalization can be repaired solely at the textual or discursive level, ignores the political and economic roots of marginalization. This, however, is not intended to trivialize the centrality of the issues raised by the politics of representation, for the production and circulation of certain images and representations continues to play an integral role in perpetuating domination. In fact, the texts, paradigms, literature, and frameworks—basically those elements which constitute the curriculum—do not merely supply information and/or knowledge but actually create frames of intelligibility, or what Berger (1972) calls "ways of seeing." Therefore, the concerns with representation are integral; the point is that we should not be straightjacketed by struggles that fail to move beyond the politics of representation, understood here as the critique of omitted and distorted representations. Such struggles should not constitute the be-all and end-all of a progressive political agenda; rather, we need to intervene in the "institutional supports of these representations and their immersion in state and economic rationalities" (Yudice, 1995:273).

Finally, one of the most often heard laments about identity politics is that it has led to the "fragmentation" of the Left. A range of critics have pointed to the "twilight of common dreams," the loss of political vision, and the separatist tendencies inherent in some forms of identity politics. It is imperative to note that this fragmentation has had tangible implications not only for the Left but for the New Right as well.

"Whiteness" and the Politics of Resentment

One of the major aims of identity politics and multiculturalism, aside from their affirmation of difference, has been to unsettle the category of "whiteness" and to challenge its authority as *the* normative frame of reference. Dyer's (1988) observation that whiteness was both "everything" and "nothing" served as a testament to the ubiquitousness of its invisibility and the power which accompanied such transparency. In response, there has been a burgeoning interest in recent years in rethinking whiteness and in exploring whiteness as a set of linked dimensions. For example, whiteness has been interrogated as a location of structural advantage and racial privilege and various efforts have been made to illuminate how whiteness is deployed as a strategy of power which is intrinsically linked to relations of domination. There have also been attempts to locate whiteness, not as the cultural marker against which all "differences" are defined, but rather to see whiteness itself as a form of difference or ethnicity. The purpose of naming whiteness in this way was to displace it from its unmarked, unnamed status and to interrogate the powerful effects of its seeming normativity (Frankenberg, 1993; Fusco, 1988; McLaren, 1995). Clearly, this has been an important exercise for challenging the hegemony of whiteness and its legitimacy and authority, but it has also led to some rather disturbing paradoxes.

In a brilliant essay, George Yudice (1995:261) attempts to foreground some of these paradoxes and contradictions. He argues that there has been a fashionable trend towards "disavowing" whiteness among some liberal and Left constituencies. This, in turn, has created an "explosion" of claims to marginality. He cites examples of Whites from various ethnic groups and gay whites who have declared their "non-whiteness" by appealing to histories of discrimination and oppression, thereby denying any notion of "privilege." Yet donning the badge of oppression and otherness based on what may be "invisible" differences does not negate the real privilege associated with whiteness in our culture. Disavowals of whiteness ignore that privilege is not "wholly voluntaristic," but rather is something which is "accorded" to people. If one is perceived as White, one obtains all "the privileges of membership" (Yudice, 1995:260). Furthermore, repudiating whiteness is a strategy open only to those who have the luxury of "opting out" of White privilege. In several respects, declarations of non-whiteness are opportunistic tactics used to gain entry into what Yudice calls the new value system of multiculturalism.

There has also been a tendency to impugn whiteness. Attempting to build a bridge to the other and to position themselves on the proper side of the "us"-"them" divide (us defined here as those committed to anti-racism and the like), many liberal-left Whites have tried to "share" the pain of non-white "others." Yet this necessary empathy often amounts to little more than patronizing gestures which do little to advance the cause of creating knowledge about the institutional and structural basis of racism and how it is imbricated in much broader power differentials.

For Yudice, the tendencies towards disavowing and impugning whiteness raise serious issues, and are for the most part faulty foundations for progressive politics. He points out that seeking entry into the club of multiculturalism and marginality will not solve the myriad problems (unemployment, poverty, unequal access to education, etc.) plaguing society's dispossessed. Moreover, while whiteness certainly has its privileges in our society, not all Whites are materially privileged. This is not to discount the fact that Whites still occupy the highest echelons of power and privilege in the United States and are as a whole more advantaged than Blacks, Latinos, and others. Nor does it deny the fact that white supremist logic continues to mold our social and political topography. But it *is* important to note as Manning Marable does, that 60 percent of welfare recipients are White; 62 percent of those dependent on food stamps are White; and more than two-thirds of Americans without health insurance are White.[32] Yet the prevailing discourses of multiculturalism have failed to address the concerns of over 70 percent of the population—the White working and middle classes who also have to face diminishing educational, employment, and social resources (Gallagher, 1994; Yudice, 1995).

In their current incarnations, identity politics and multiculturalism have been unable to articulate an agenda for Whites committed to progressive social change. Citing Diane Jeater's (1992) work in the British context, Yudice argues that because the institutionalization of identity politics on the Left meant that everyone had to have an identity to anchor their politics, the problem with being White was that it "did not seem to bestow an identity which could be linked to any kind of oppositional politics" (Jeater, cited in Yudice, 1995:262). In some cases, Whites were viewed with suspicion as "guilt ridden liberals" or "wanna-bes" seeking acceptance by the "other" in order to appease their feelings of guilt and angst. As such, identity politics has been incapable of constructing a social imaginary that does not "call for whites to change on behalf of others or to wanna-be" (Yudice, 1995:261). Nor have identity politics and multiculturalism made themselves particularly appealing to White youth who see themselves as members of a beleaguered, "identitiless" constituency, as victims of a multicultural, P.C. cabal. Such an assertion would be laughable if not for the deep-rooted sense of crisis behind such beliefs, and the reactionary backlash that underpins them (Conran, 1995). This sense of distress is clearly illustrated by Charles Gallagher's (1994) study of youths (mainly Whites) at a large urban university in the United States.

Gallagher's work sets out to challenge the major theoretical supposition undergirding contemporary scholarship on White racial identity: that Whites do not have to think "about being white because white privilege and white standards are so culturally embedded that whiteness has been naturalized" (Gallagher, 1994:167). Gallagher argues that the invisibleness and transparency of whiteness is no longer taken for granted among Whites, given that so much attention has been focused on White privilege in recent years. Furthermore, he contends that the advent of identity politics *has* forced Whites to think about the cultural implications of their whiteness. In many cases, this has resulted in a form of deep resentment among White youth, who are tired of being cast always and everywhere as "the oppressor." This resentment has manifested itself in concrete ways. Indeed, there were a variety of sites where "whiteness" rushed to reconstitute itself and rebuild its defenses. At the cultural level, there have been attempts to reconstruct White histories and an essentialist White identity largely through cultural stereotypes of non-whites. At another level, many of the White students interviewed by Gallagher did not see themselves as privileged based on their skin color. Their own situations of financial insecurity and the prospects of a future of un-and-under employment made them unreceptive to the notion of White privilege. Hence, many of the white youth interviewed by Gallagher (1994:177) sought to construct an identity that "negated white oppressor charges and framed whiteness as a liability."

While some have sought to disavow their whiteness and others to frame it as a liability, still others have injected this "whiteness as liability" with a fierce sense of anger. Indeed, the emergence of White male identity politics is a growing cultural phenomenon, as several commentators have recently pointed out. Feeling threatened and besieged, there has been a tendency among White males to assume identificatory positions which are hyperbolic and in some cases extreme. The combined effects of identity politics which has served to challenge the traditional privileges and status of this group and economic decline engendered by the global restructuring of capital have led many White males to assert their shared "oppression" as a group which is allegedly being victimized by women, minorities, and a "liberal" government which has kowtowed to "special interests" (Goldstein, 1995; Junas, 1995). It is somewhat ironic that conservatives, who routinely condemn people who complain about being victims, are now encouraging victimhood among white males to obtain their votes. Yet, the political ramifications of this posturing were evident in the November 1994 elections when 62 percent of White males voted for the Republican agenda of Gingrichites.[33] As Gitlin (1995:233) pointedly claims, it has been the tilt of White men toward positions on the Right which now constitutes the "most potent form of identity politics in our time." Of course, the economic situation of many white working class males *has* significantly declined in recent decades, and the jobs which had provided them with a sense of dignity have rapidly dissipated.[34] It has been the New Right, however, which has successfully capitalized on this sense of dislocation and tapped into the deep psychological and emotional ramifications that such dispossession spawns. Indeed, talk radio, with its populist imprimatur, has become the forum where disgruntled White males routinely express their anger and frustration.[35] Right-wing pundits like Rush Limbaugh provide a sense of identity and community for, and forge a sense of symbolic solidarity with, White males suffering from a collective loss of authority. By making women and minorities the culprits for the declining material conditions of many White males, right-wing ideologues have successfully deflected attention away from the real culprits in economic decline—shifts in global capitalism, post-Fordist tendencies,[36] and the privileged White men who set wages and who have profited on the backs of their blue-collar brethren. In doing so, these talk-show demagogues have turned up the volume of hate.

In extreme cases, many dispossessed White men have been increasingly attracted to militia movements and right-wing hate groups, which enable them to reconstruct a shared identity (Cohen and Solomon, 1995; Junas, 1995; Mozzochi, 1995). Best and Kellner (forthcoming) maintain that these movements empower disempowered people and provide a sense of meaning and purpose to alienated victims of undereducation and a dramatic restructuring of high-tech capitalist social relations. Less extreme, but no less dangerous in political terms, is the constituency referred to as MARs or Middle American Radicals.[37] This group is comprised of White Buchanan supporters who feel sandwiched between political and economic elites on the one hand, and poor Blacks, Latinos, and Asians on the other (Zeskind, 1996:22). Citing various sources, Zeskind points out that several conservative commentators have identified Middle American Radicalism as a new political identity, ushered in and subsequently nurtured by the Buchanan revolution. Concerned largely with the "economic distress" allegedly engendered by the "multicultural invasion," MARs were drawn to the xenophobic populism of Buchanan (Zeskind, 1996:21-24). While Buchanan was eventually defeated in his bid for the Republican nomination, his followers constitute a formidable force in the spectrum of American politics and have been influential in moving the country even further to the Right.

Unfortunately, Left discourses and political practices organized around difference, multiculturalism, and identity politics have been unable to satisfactorily address the concerns and insecurities of many White working and middle-class people. Insufficient attention has been paid to class-based oppression and the escalating insecurities of the White working class. This is due, in large part, to the fact that many Left theoreticians have downplayed the significance of capitalism. Both Turner (1994) and Yudice (1995) attribute this to the current postmodern romance with the cultural and the discursive and the lack of attention accorded to political economy and other infrastructural issues. They and others contend that this neglect has resulted in a situation where politics has been redefined as a signifying activity, rather than being identified with the mobilization of forces against the sources of political and economic marginalization. Indeed, even though the "Holy

Trinity" of gender, race, and class (Eagleton, 1986:82), is the rubric under which much multicultural scholarship situates itself, more often than not, precious little is said about class and the ways in which it intersects with dynamics such as race and gender.

Nor has multiculturalism succeeded in defining the parameters for a Leftist politics that can stand up to the insurgent Right (Berlant and Warner, 1994:111). In fact, identity politics and multiculturalism have, in several respects, perpetuated the "divide and rule" mentality conducive to the maintenance of the oppressive status quo. As Freire (1970:137) claims, it is in the interest of the oppressor "to weaken the oppressed still further, to isolate them, to create and deepen rifts among them." Yudice (1995:275) maintains that attracting Whites to a progressive agenda will not succeed if they are expected to ignore "their own interests on behalf of those of others." Nor will they be attracted if they are repeatedly bashed as oppressors. What must be effectively demonstrated to them is that their diminishing opportunities are not the result of affirmative action, immigration and the like (as the New Right would have them believe), but to the logic of late capitalism, corporate downsizing, and the greed of the wealthy few.

This realization, however, necessitates two things: that the consideration of capitalism and class be inserted into our theoretical and political equations, and that leftists embark upon the task of exposing what the right-wing vision of society amounts to in all its social and political ugliness. The Right has gained ground and has attracted much White working-class and White youth support not because these citizens are simply racist buffoons, but rather because the Right *has* at least attempted to reach out to this constituency and proffer an explanation, no matter how contorted, for their increasing immiseration. Thus far, the Left hasn't offered an alternative that makes sense to the disgruntled White working and middle classes and disaffected White youth. Unless leftists make a concerted attempt to enlarge the choices on the political menu beyond those proffered by multiculturalism and identity politics, they will continue to cede precious political ground to the forces of the New Right.[38] After all, people can only select from what is offered on the menu, and the list of healthy choices is diminishing at a rapid and disturbing pace.

Beyond the Last "Post"

> In confronting its political antagonists, the left, now more than ever, has need of strong ethical . . . foundations; nothing short of this is likely to furnish us with the political resources we require. And on this score, postmodernism is in the end part of the problem rather than of the solution. (Eagleton, 1996:135)

> What is not possible is to negate the practice for the sake of a theory that, in some fashion, ceases in being theory to become pure verbalism or intellectualism. By the same token, to negate theory for the sake of practice is to run the risk of losing itself in the disconnectedness of practice. I advocate neither theoretical elitism nor a practice ungrounded in theory, but the unity between theory and practice. (Freire, 1993:23)

Paulo Freire's call to emphasize the link between theory and practice resonates with a sense of urgency in light of the rightward turn in American culture and politics. At a time when democracy is being rolled back and the rudiments of fascism being nurtured in our midst, the political soul of the Left must be wrested from the stranglehold of textualism and the seduction of identity politics. Dasenbrock (1995:174) suggests that left-leaning academics who wish to have a meaningful impact in the broader public sphere and who seek to change, in progressive ways, the views of others, must begin by rethinking many of the enervating and self-contradicting theories that have come to constitute the reservoir of leftist critical thought. A host of critical observers have revealed the limits of multiculturalism and identity politics as potential bases for progressive politics, while others have revealed the dangers which identity politics pose for the Left. Moreover, endemic class oppression, racism, sexism, homophobia, joblessness, poverty, homelessness, and other forms of social ugliness that mark regnant social relations will not disappear if leftists limit their social analyses and political struggles to P.C. skirmishes over textual inclusion and terminological purism. As Stuart Hall (1994:177) rightly points out, the agenda of P.C. will, despite any local successes, fail in the long run unless it transcends the dogmatism that has characterized it thus far. Indeed, we've already begun to see the fallout such dogmatism has engendered.

Taken together, these various indictments of contemporary Left theory and political practice reveal the poverty of current formulations. As such, they beg the obvious question: what then, must be done, both theoretically and politically? To these questions there are no easy answers or prescriptions, and I do not purport to offer simple solutions nor to exhaust all possibilities. But if progressive change is the aim the Left must cease in displacing questions about what is to be done with questions about who we are, that is, with questions of identity (Kruks, 1996:122). The first step in discerning what is to be done must entail a re-evaluation of our theoretical proclivities, for as Marcuse (1969:61) reminds us the "groundwork for building the bridge between the *ought* and the *is* is laid within theory itself."

Contemporary post-al theory suffers from some major theoretical and political ailments. First of all, in privileging the discursive and the textual, it has often failed to address concrete material conditions and, in doing so, has forfeited the possibility of making meaningful interventions in the interest of social change. Secondly, in negating the feasibility of making "truth" claims, they lack the "requisite sociology on which to build a new ethical foundation" for a project directed toward possibility (McLaren, 1994c:197). In their relativist extremes, they have actually crippled the very concept of the political by dissolving it in a bubbling vat of indeterminacy. Moreover, the corrosive skepticism found in much postmodernism/poststructuralism has exacerbated the pervasive sense of despair and hopelessness by rendering visions of social transformation as hopelessly obsolete.

The criticisms launched against current trends in leftist social theory in these pages are, as I have attempted to make clear, not an indictment of theory itself, for theory is integral to political praxis. Rather, my concern has been with the kinds of theoretical discourses that have become common within leftist circles. This, however, in no way suggests their mere dismissal, for many recent theoretical developments have deepened our insights and provided a more efficacious understanding of subjectivity, identity, and the many pitfalls of Western epistemology and Enlightenment rationality. But, others, trapped as they are in the prison house of discursivity and textuality, have contributed little to understanding the complexion and complexities of contemporary social life and concrete social forms. Cornel West (1993:241) argues that politically committed leftists must contest "textual leftists" and move, as it were, to the slaughterhouse of history. To this end, he suggests that we seriously examine the enduring relevance of Marx in both our theoretical and political practices. The key for progressive intellectuals is to make theories real, "to ground them in the contextual specificity of real life," to take them out of the "monovalent culture" of the academy in order to get "democracy off the ground." Theories need to help in the mobilization of "material resources and not just describe social life in endless forms of deconstructive textual analysis" (McLaren cited in Borg et al., 1994:11).

In recent years, Marxian theory has been maligned by the prevailing centers of intellectual power which reject it *tout court* as "totalizing," "reductionist," and "repressive." Indeed, in a postmodern climate skeptical about the ideals of revolution, emancipation, and freedom, the heartbeat of Marxism "has been flatlined into a stasis that signifies coma or death" (Best, 1995:269). This has created a situation which has divested "Marxism of much of its explanatory as well as its revolutionary power" (Foley, 1990:17). In these readings, the revolutionary thrust of Marx's work on emancipation, the social agent's role in the making of history, the relationship between consciousness and politics, and discussions about the subjective dimensions of political struggle are often ignored or discounted as outmoded and incapable of grasping the exigencies of our "postmodern" condition. I, however, would contend that Marxist formulations, despite their obvious blindspots, still provide a powerful arsenal of tools to pry open and examine contemporary reality.

Any attempt to apprehend the complexity of contemporary social life necessitates *dialectical* modes of interpretation. In contrast to the fragmented character and one-dimensional, textual foci of post-al theories that often obscure more than they illuminate, dialectical analyses enable us to name and map the general organization of social relations and to make connections between the different domains of social reality. Walter Benjamin's (1968:233) comparison of the magician and the

198 Theory Wars and Cultural Strife

surgeon seems, here, an appropriate metaphor: whereas the
magician acts upon the surface of reality, the surgeon cuts
into it. In much the same way, most theorizing that falls under
the rubric of postmodernism/poststructuralism remains at the
level of surfaces and representations, unable to cut into the
flesh of the social, unable to discern what Best and Kellner
(1991:274) refer to as the "depth dimension." This erasure of
depth, however, flattens out history and experience and undermines the possibility of cultivating conscious resistance to
those oppressive structural and social conditions that give rise
to and shape experience. While a detailed elaboration of the
enduring significance of Marxian formulations is well beyond
the purview of this text, a few observations can be made about
the importance of dialectical social theory.

Dialectical interpretation is not merely a methodology or
mode of analysis governed by "universal" laws; rather, it is
grounded in the specificity and history of human praxis, and
takes as its starting point the concrete socio-historical context
that is its object of study (Bologh and Mell, 1994). Central to
dialectical analysis is the concept of "totality," and in light of
the postmodern hostility towards this concept, a few qualify-
ing remarks are in order. A number of post-al theorists tend to
reject the notion of totality as a remnant of Gulag epistemology. There is a proclivity towards equating totality with totalitarianism—something which is both naive and theoretically simplistic (Jameson, 1990:26-27), as well as politically suspect. On
this point, Terry Eagleton is especially insightful and worth
quoting at length:

> For radicals to discard the idea of totality in a rush of holophobia is
> . . . to furnish themselves with some much-needed consolation. For
> in a period when . . . so-called micropolitics seems the order of the
> day, it is relieving to convert this necessity into a virtue—to persuade
> onself . . . that social totality is in any case a chimera . . . The theo-
> retical discrediting of the idea of totality, then, is to be expected in
> an epoch of political defeat for the left. Much of the scepticism of it,
> after all, hails from intellectuals who have no particularly pressing
> reason to locate their own social existence within a broader political
> framework. There are others, however, who are not quite so fortunate
> . . . Not looking for totality is just a code for not looking at capital-
> ism. (Eagleton 1996:9-12)

Furthermore, while the erasure of totality is done in the name
of subverting metaphysical narratives, we would do well to heed

McLaren's (1994[a]) warning that not all forms of totality are theoretically and politically deficient. Indeed, polemics against the concept of totality rarely distinguish between varying senses and types of totality and the different ways the concept has been taken up by diverse critical theorists (Kellner, 1990).

It is therefore important to point out that the concept is not being deployed here as a subsuming, metaphysical category in the Hegelian sense of an organic, unified, oppressive unity. Nor is totality being defined simply as a structure or system comprised of parts that are constituted by the whole system to which they belong and which are interrelated. That formulation is far too functionalist, and tends to erase the sensuous activities of historically situated agents. Rather, the notion of social totality is used here to refer to the complex, multidimensional, and multi-levelled relations of social organization. The importance of the concept is based on the insight that phenomena must ultimately be understood contextually and relationally within the matrices of a larger social formation. What must be abandoned is not the concept of totality itself, but the reductive use of totality—those formulations that operate with a reified or fetishized concept of totality. Rejecting all notions of totality summarily runs the risk of trapping oneself in particularistic theories which obscure real connections and relationships, and which cannot explain how the diverse relations that constitute large social and political systems interrelate and mutually determine and constrain one another (Giroux, 1992; Lipsitz, 1990).[39]

Central to dialectical formulations is the concept of mediation—a concept which has been sorely lacking in recent postmodern theorizations and forms of identity politics (Kruks, 1996:127). As a constitutive category of the dialectic, mediation deepens and ameliorates the concept of totality and is indispensable for critical analysis since it helps to illuminate the interconnectedness of specific social and political forces, the larger spheres of social organization, and their relationship to self, identity and experience. The purpose of the concept is to capture the "dynamic"—showing how social relations and forms come into being in and through each other. It thereby enables the creation of a knowledge "which provides an approximation between internal (mental/conceptual) and external reality" (Bannerji, 1991:93).[40] As an analytical tool, the concept of mediation enables us to demonstrate "what is not evident in the appearance of things" and to examine the "underlying reality" of social forms (Jameson, 1981:39). Mediation is therefore a device of the analyst through which

> the fragmentation and autonomization, the compartmentalization and specialization of the various regions of social life . . . is at least locally overcome, on the occasion of a particular analysis. (Jameson, 1981:40)

Moreover, in dialectical narratives, social phenomena are not conceived of as objects removed from human history and action, but rather as products of human praxis. Dialectical social theory also incorporates an historical sensibility in order to grasp the traditions and conditions that mold our present-day experiences. However, unlike the fetishization of experience that has plagued various manifestations of identity politics and post-al discourses that simply and unproblematically privilege the "local," dialectical analyses historicize experience by revealing the social relations which give rise to particular experiences. It thereby seeks to make connections between seemingly isolated situations/experiences by revealing how they are constituted in and circumscribed by broader historical and cultural frameworks of the larger social organization. The importance of a dialectical social theory that is attentive to material conditions and concrete social forms lies in its ability to develop historical knowledge—that is, an understanding of how existing social institutions and social formations have come about and how they can be changed. In this regard, dialectical social theory is inherently political: it attempts to link theory and practice while searching for "potentialities for change in a given society" (Best and Kellner, 1991:264).

Perhaps the most crucial aspect of Marxist-oriented critique is its sustained interrogation of capitalist social relations. Since capitalism continues to be the major constitutive force in our society, the Marxian theory and critique of capitalism continues to be a necessary component of critical social theory. Of course, capitalism has undergone significant transformations since Marx's time, and many of the concepts used to analyze nineteenth-century capitalism cannot simply be applied to the present. But rather than abandoning the analysis of capitalism, as so many postmodernists have done, Marxian categories demand updating in order to account for changes in capitalist social organization. Indeed, given the salience of capitalism in shaping our social, cultural, and political milieu, a thorough and comprehensive understanding of its inner workings is needed.

Yet there is real resistance to Marxist formulations among many leftists, since it is so often assumed that foregrounding capitalist social organization necessarily undermines the importance of "difference" or trivializes struggles against racism and sexism in favor of an abstractly defined class-based politics. In far too many nascent debates, especially between Marxists and identity politicians, there has been a tendency to cast identity and class as two mutually exclusive forms of politics. Many orthodox Marxists persist in valorizing economistic and reductionist strands of Marxism, which do not accord adequate attention to forms of oppression other than those constituted by class. For these stalwarts, other concerns are seen as epiphenomenon, marginal to the "real" and "true" class struggle.

On the other hand, multiculturalists and identity politicians have not adequately addressed class and infrastructural issues. How, then, might a way out of this impasse be found? The starting point is to recognize that the "identity or class" stance creates a debilitating and unnecessary dichotomy. By drawing upon the concept of mediation to unsettle our categorical approaches to both class and identity, Himani Bannerji argues that:

> It is curious how many times in history we have come to face an utterly false dichotomy, a superficial view of the situation in our politics. As Marx pointed out—it is absurd to choose between consciousness and the world, subjectivity and social organization, personal or collective will and historical or structural determination. It is equally absurd then, to see identity and difference as historical forms of consciousness unconnected to class formation, development of capital and class politics. The mutually formative nature of identity, difference and class becomes apparent if we begin by taking a practical approach to the issue, or their relation of "intersection." If "difference" implies more than classificatory diversity, and encodes social and moral-cultural relations and forms of ruling, and establishes identities by measuring the distance between ruler and ruled, all the while constructing knowledge through power—then let us try to imagine "class" or class politics without these forms and content. (Bannerji, 1995:30)

The point of Bannerji's formulation is to historize identity and difference in relation to the history and social organization of capital and class—which includes imperialist and colonialist legacies. By drawing upon a materialist and historical formulation, Bannerji is able to (re)conceptualize "difference" and "identity" in relation to social and economic organization rather than seeing difference as free-floating and/or identities as fixed and static.

In a somewhat different but not unrelated vein, Ebert (1996:134) points to the necessity of historically grounding our understanding of difference. She contends that difference (rather than being conceptualized as dislocated and free-floating in the ludic postmodern sense), needs to be understood as the product of social contradictions. We need to acknowledge that otherness is not something that passively happens, but rather is actively produced. In other words, since systems of differences almost always involve relations of domination, oppression, marginalization, and exploitation, we must concern ourselves with the economies of relations of difference that exist in an historically specific social formation. Apprehending the meaning and function of difference in this manner necessarily highlights the importance of understanding the structural and institutional parameters that produce difference as well as the complexities and contradictions of capitalism.[41]

At a time when *Fortune* magazine boasts of 1995 as "a year for the books" in terms of soaring corporate profits; when the wealthiest 1 percent of families in the United States have nearly as much wealth as the entire bottom 95 percent; when real wages are plummeting and unemployment increasing, especially in communities of color; when two-thirds of the world's labor is done by women who are exploited and underpaid in various "free production zones" of the Third World and North American sweatshops; when control over the global economy by multinationals increasingly resembles the frightening scenarios of William Gibson's *Neuromancer*, we must necessarily retain the centrality of class formations in our social analyses and engage in an unrelenting critique of capitalism. But this requires that we work to deepen and extend Marxist formulations rather than abandoning them. We would also do well to remind ourselves of Marx's famous dictum about the need to change the world, rather than merely interpret it. But if the task of changing the world in progressive and emancipatory ways is to be met with any measure of success, the Left, or whatever remains of it, must work to build bridges and create a common vision.

Cultivating Common Dreams

If all we have are identity politics . . . then capital, now with hardly any barriers, will rule supreme, leaving more dead bodies, and more wasted energies. (West, 1993:240)

In terms of effecting change, what counts now as always is collective action . . . The future will of course have to be struggled for. It cannot be willed into place. But nonetheless we still have to dream and to know in what direction to desire. (Hebdige, 1988:34-35)

The impossible must be imagined if it is to be realized, and it is true sanity to do so. (Kovel, 1991:13)

In *The Philosophy of The Future*, Ernst Bloch (1970:86) writes of dreams: daydreams and night dreams which, as he points out, differ in at least one fundamental regard. Whereas night dreams generally entail a journey back into the dark recesses of repressed experiences, the daydream represents an "unrestricted journey forward," an envisaging of "circumstances and images of a desired, better life." At this critical historical juncture, it is incumbent upon progressives to take up the task of articulating a common dream, a common set of visions, with the clarity and lucidity that only *collective* daydreaming can engender. Indeed, in order for a viable Left to re-emerge and, in order for such a movement to have any impact in the struggle for progressive social change, it will have to cultivate a common project. As Ahmad (1992), Gitlin (1995), Hobsbawn (1996), and others have aptly pointed out, without some common ground, there can be no Left at all. And yet, there is a profound resistance to the very notion of the "common," a fear that any emphasis on commonality or community will necessarily entail a suppression of diversity and difference. I would argue, however, that such suspicions are, more often than not, misguided and politically debilitating. As Kruks (1996:132) points out:

Both reified notions of difference and postmodern claims that the
search for common ground is implicitly "totalitarian" too frequently
lead to a politics that eschews engagement (either analytical or practical) with the wider world of structures, institutions, and macro-his-
torical processes.

Of course, we *would* do well to remind ourselves that difference and diversity are values that were not always well-received
on the Left. The proliferation of identity politics in the late
1960s and early 1970s stemmed in large part from the inad-
equacies of the New Left and its failure to deal with the real
implications of political diversity.[42] One would hope that the
benefit of hindsight and historical memory have taught us some
valuable lessons. On the other hand, we need to recognize as
June Jordan (cited in Parmar, 1990:109) does, that organizing
on the basis of discrete and unconnected identities doesn't
seem to have worked in furthering the cause of broad-based
progressive change and the eradication of oppressive social
relations. If anything, identity politics may have sent us in quite
the opposite direction.[43] On the one hand, we have the pluralist "anything-goes" farrago which undergirds some forms of
"difference" politics, and on the other, a "more-radical-than
thou" logic in various manifestations of essentialist identity
politics. Neither, however, is adequate to the task of anchoring
a broad-based progressive agenda. It is therefore imperative
to acknowledge that calls for unity and common cause among
leftists need not mean a call for homogeneity. As Audre Lorde
reminds us:

Without community there is no liberation . . . But community must
not mean a shedding of differences . . . It is learning . . . how to make
common cause with . . . others . . . in order to define and seek a world
in which we all can flourish. (Lorde, 1984:112)

Cultivating common dreams does, however, necessitate
moving beyond the particularism of identity politics. It demands building forms of solidarity that do not suppress the
real heterogeneity of interests but are committed to constructing a common ground where visions of social transformation
(rather than liberal pluralism) may be collectively dreamed of
and fought for. It requires embarking on a quest to forge a
"new" identity, premised on the notion of "becoming" rather
than "being." Identities of becoming are politically motivated

and historically situated. They are not grounded in essential-ist, individualist prerogatives. Rather, they are spawned by a thorough and critical understanding of the social totality and the forces that mediate reality and social relations. Nurtured in collective struggle, they ask not "who are you?" according to a reified identity scale, but rather "where are you?" in terms of political commitment. The significant distinction between these questions lies in the fact that the latter demands an ethi-cal response (McLaren cited in Borg et al., 1994).

Indeed, it is very difficult to imagine a Left politics without an ethical stance and without a vision of the future, no matter how provisional.[44] The ability to imagine a better future and a freer, less alienating society demands, as Hebdige (quoted above) intimates, that we have a map in order to know in what direction we must desire. I would contend that such a map must be grounded upon a socialist vision. Of course, the very idea of socialism has been junked by many factions on the Left or proclaimed dead by others. Such reactions are due, in some measure, to the baggage of historical failure and the memo-ries of authoritarian and repressive regimes created in the name of socialism. Yet I agree with Kanpol and McLaren (1995), that although the transformation of capitalism and the fragmenta-tion engendered by identity politics pose significant challenges to conventional ways of imagining socialist democracy, it need not sound the death knell for the idea of socialist struggle. We need to follow Epstein's (1994:108) suggestion that socialism can function for progressive movements, not so much as an immediate goal but as a basic set of values, a long-range per-spective from which to develop a viable Left movement. The concept of socialism could be used as a practical guide to ad-vance the democratization of social institutions, further the cause of equality, and challenge the organization of capital and the social relations that breed alienation and inequality in *all* their manifestations.

Creating what West (1993:241) refers to as a "substantive socialist identity," however, requires the articulation of com-mon interests founded upon universalist principles, for Hobsbawn reminds us that:

> the mass social and political movements of the Left, that is, those inspired by the American and French Revolutions and socialism were indeed coalitions of group alliances, but held together not by aims

that were specific to the group, but by great, universal causes through
which each group believed its particular aims could be realized . . . The
political project of the Left is universalist: it is for *all* human beings
[while] . . . identity politics is essentially not for everybody but for
the members of a specific group only . . . That is why the Left cannot
base itself on identity politics. It has a wider agenda. (Hobsbawn,
1996:42-43)

Hobsbawn's description of, and prescription for, the Left undoubtedly raises some serious issues. These become all the
more apparent when one considers his appeals to Left universalism in the context of current hostility towards both universalism and humanistic principles. Indeed, anti-humanism has
been one of the defining features of postmodern and
poststructuralist discourse for the last two decades. The many
and varied critiques of humanism need not be rehearsed here;
nor can the philosophical objections to universality and humanism be fully explored in this context. Yet it is worth briefly
noting that much of the "post-al" hostility directed towards
humanism has been both intellectually disingenuous and politically suspect. Most of these narratives treat humanism as
though it existed as a monolithic discourse. Their error consists in identifying humanism as such with bourgeois or petty-
bourgeois movements, when there are, in fact, a number of
historical variants of humanism, bourgeois liberal humanism
being but one manifestation. The homogenization of all humanisms into one neglects the attempts by Marxists and others such as Sartre and Fanon to found a "new humanism" which
would substitute for the "Enlightenment's conception of man's
unchanging nature," a new historical and revolutionary humanism that would see humans as products of themselves and their
own activity in history (Young, 1992:245).

An important distinction can and should be made between
liberal humanism, which has played a colonizing role in history, and the revolutionary humanism espoused by Marx and
others like Paulo Freire and Frantz Fanon, who drew upon
Marxist formulations.[45] This humanism is as yet unrealized in
its most profound sense.[46] This variant of humanism gives expression to the pain, sorrow, and degradation of the oppressed,
the wretched of the earth, and victims of the culture of silence. It is predicated on a firm commitment to human eman-

cipation and the extension of human dignity, freedom, and social justice to all people—a commitment to *really* universalize these values and promises in practical terms, rather than merely giving lip service to them in an abstractly delineated discourse of rights. It calls for the transformation of those oppressive institutions and alienating relations that have prevented the bulk of humankind from fulfilling its potential. It vests its hopes for progressive change in the development of critical consciousness and social agents who make history, although not always in conditions of their choosing. As such, it believes in the power and the cultivation of consciousness, but it does not err in making an idol of "reason" detached from the social context, as do the idealistic humanists who valorize the omnipotence of reason regardless of time, place, and social circumstances (Novack, 1973). It is this revolutionary tradition of humanism—one that, as Appiah (1992:155) points out, can be provisional and historically contigent—that must be resuscitated from the postmodern dustbin of history.

Equally important is the need to rethink the categorical rejection of universalism. Undoubtedly, part of the resistance to universalist principles stems from the fear that the specificity of human experience and struggle will be undermined by appeals to universalism. Appeals to pure particularism, however, do not necessarily offer solutions to the problems we currently face. In fact, the "assertion of pure particularism, independent of any content and of any appeal to a universality is a self-defeating enterprise" since various demands for equality and recognition cannot be made in terms of difference; rather, they must be made on the "basis of some universal principles." In fact, Laclau claims that if a "particularity asserts itself as a mere particularity, in a purely differential relation with other particularities" it is, in effect, "sanctioning the status quo in power relations between the groups" (Laclau, 1992:88). Hence, rejecting universalism in toto can only lead to a political blind alley. It is also worth remembering that while anti-humanism "may look well on one's office door" and the trashing of universalism hard to resist, too much of the world "still starves, dies young and is wasted by systematic greed and evil for anyone to write" the obituaries of humanism, universalism, and the socialist project (O'Neill, 1995:17, 196). Indeed, Eagleton

(1996: 118) notes that one is a socialist precisely because universality "*doesn't* exist at present in any positive, as opposed to merely descriptive or ideological, sense." He goes on to state:

> Not everyone, as yet, enjoys freedom, happiness and justice. Part of what prevents this from coming about is precisely the false universalism which holds that it can be achieved by extending the values and liberties of a particular sector of humankind, roughly speaking Western Man, to the entire globe . . . Socialism is a critique of this false universalism, not in the name of cultural particularism . . . but in the name of the right of everyone to negotitate their own difference in terms of everyone else's. (Eagleton, 1996:118)

Hence, we might ask ourselves whose interests are actually served by the penning of such obituaries.

Finally, the task of articulating a common dream for the future can surely learn from the past. Of course, there is often a proclivity to romanticize the past, to crown it with a nostalgic halo, especially at a time of scepticism, dolor and disillusionment. Yet historical memory possesses the profound potential to help us navigate the course for the future. To this end, the legacy of the Sixties provides a critical frame of reference for contemporary Leftists: romanticizing the Sixties, however, is perilous for they were marked with mistakes and illusions (some inconsequential, others abysmal). Yet one cannot repudiate the fervent political intensity which characterized the uprisings and protests of that decade. For a brief moment, an intoxicating and unabashedly radical spirit was unleashed and flung in the sombre faces of capitalist demagogues. There were endless questions inspired by the premise that change was possible, that history could be made collectively, and that it was therefore important to think without limits.

Undoubtedly, the "new times" in which we now find ourselves present new challenges. The proliferation of social antagonisms make the prospect of securing a unified, collective political will all the more difficult to imagine. Nonetheless, I concur with Lorde (1984) and hooks (1991) that if we want signs of hope in this age of despair and cynicism, we cannot ignore the legacy of the 1960s, even as we see its weaknesses. The task is to take the valuable lessons from the mass movements of that era and to learn from them, for much of how we imagine the future is contingent not only upon how we interpret the present, but also on how we remember the past. We must resuscitate the "dangerous" memories and the radical spirit of that era, especially at a time when the New Right has done everything to obfuscate and demonize the 1960s. We need to counter the Right's rewriting of history and its retreat into social amnesia by remembering that the challenges mounted against entrenched ideas and the establishment brought about a sense of possibility. It is these "dangerous" memories, the emancipatory potential of dreaming collectively, and the willingness to think and dream the impossible that must be rescued—and as Kovel (1991:13) reminds us, it is true sanity to do so.

Notes

1. The debates about identity politics and the poststructuralist accounts of the subject are often constructed in binary terms—that is, between the "anti-essentialist" poststructuralist and the "essentialist" advocates of identity politics. This posturing, however, is somewhat misleading, given that both these phenomena share, to a large extent, a similar genealogy. For some this may sound like heresy; but when these developments are apprehended within an historical framework it is fairly clear that both are reactions, albeit in different forms, to Marxism as both a theoretical and political project. For poststructuralists, it is the universalistic pretensions and totalizing tendencies that allegedly inform Marxism which are denounced, as are its humanistic appeals to rationality. For those who subscribe to identity politics, it is Marxism's valorization of the "class" subject of history and its concomitant failure to address the possibility of social mobilizations based on categories other than class which are deemed problematic. Needless to say, both these formulations are intrinsically related, for the renunciation of several Marxist categories are common to both the discourse of identity politics and poststructuralism.

2. Indeed, many on the Left were disturbed by the contempt which the Communist Party displayed toward the student protesters. The PCF (the French Communist Party) had adopted a generally unsympathetic and rather conservative disdain towards the popular demonstrations involving students and workers between May 3 and June 1, 1968.

3. Given the salience of the theory-praxis nexus within Marxism it is no surprise that the events of 1968 are often identified as the locus of the "crisis of Marxism" and the dawning of a new era of re-examining the promises and prospects encapsulated in Marxist theory. Barry Smart (1983:6-7) points out that the events of 1968 signalled a crisis of conventional Marxist thought and politics for a number of reasons. First, the forms of popular protest and political action involved mass movements of people that were formed "independently and outside of the conventional political institutions of opposition, namely the trade unions and the political parties of the Left." Furthermore, the emergence of "new social subjects" or new political groupings around specific issues such as womens' rights, gay liberation and the environment constituted a problem for conventional Marxist political analysis, which tended to conceptualize politics almost exclusively in terms of class politics.

4. Structuralism itself is not a monolithic entity, and attempting to define it as such would, as Culler (1976) suggests, lead to little more

than despair. Nonetheless, there are some common characteristics that various proponents of structuralism did share. Although the intellectual roots of the structuralist turn can be traced to Marx, Freud, and even Comte and Durkheim, the most distinguishing feature of structuralism was its engagement with linguistics, especially the works of Saussure. In particular, four central themes developed by Saussure had a profound impact on structuralism. First, was Saussure's insistence that language be studied synchronically, rather than diachronically—that is, rather than looking at language in terms of its history, it should be looked at in terms of its extant structures. Second was his conceptualization of language as a system of signs constituted by signifiers and signifieds whose relationship was arbitrary and culturally determined. Third was the distinction he made between "langue" and "parole"—language and speech—where "langue" referred to the total collectivity of signs that made up a particular language and "parole" to the empirical reality of "langue," its concrete embodiment (Caws, 1988). Finally was Saussure's argument that meaning was generated not by some inherent correspondence between words and things but by the sign's and signifier's difference from other signs and signifiers. Of course, the revolution in linguistics ushered in by the work of Noam Chomsky discredited Saussure's theory in several respects. Ironically, this is most often overlooked by many who continue to rely on Saussurean formulations (Holland, 1992; Turner, 1987).

5. Berube's stance may be contrasted with Giroux's view on the role of public intellectuals. He writes that "critical public intellectuals must define themselves not merely as marginal figures, professionals, or academics . . . but as citizens whose collective knowledge and actions presuppose specific visions of public life, community and moral accountability . . . The very definition of what it means to be a public intellectual must be linked to the imperatives of working educationally and politically to extend and deepen the possibilities of democratic public life" (Giroux, 1995:5).

6. In singling out Berube's treatise on the politics of political correctness, I am in no way suggesting that he is the lone intellectual to hold such views, for in the smattering of articles and essays on P.C., several scholars have espoused the same views, albeit in different forms.

7. There are a number of disturbing issues emanating from the Sokal affair. First and foremost is the fact that Sokal's account tends to paint the entire enterprise of cultural studies as foolish, trivial, and meaningless. While this is applicable to some manifestations of cultural studies, there are many cultural studies practitioners who greet the moral and epistemological relativism of postmodernism with as much scorn as Sokal. To paint all the scholarship which falls under the ever-widening umbrella of cultural studies with the same theoretical and

political brush is both misleading and disingenuous. Furthermore, those engaged in science studies have produced a rich and interesting literature on the ideological underpinnings of science and scientific inquiry—that is to say, many of the critiques of science raise serious political questions and do not necessarily lead to the ridiculousness suggested by Sokal.

8. Of course, one cannot ignore that there are significant differences between postmodernism and poststructuralism, including the fact that postmodernism is often seen as both a theoretical trend and a cultural phenomenon. For example, in its narrowest sense, the term postmodernism is often used to refer to trends in architecture or art, while in a broader sense it is used to refer to various social trends including the fragmentation of social structures and identities, the proliferation of new information technologies, etc.

9. The aforementioned theorists have been linked in various trajectories with postmodernism (Baudrillard, Lyotard), deconstruction (Derrida), and poststructuralism (Foucault, Lacan and Derrida again). These terms, however, have often been used interchangeably, as Sarup (1989) and others have pointed out. My use of "poststructuralism" as a rubric under which to situate these theories and theorists is based on two observations. First, postmodernism is often used in different ways, sometimes to describe a new cultural landscape or historical moment and in others to describe a new theoretical paradigm. Its inclusiveness, however, has in a sense made it "empty" as a category (Pinar et al.,1995) and rather "slippery." Second, because deconstruction is often construed as one among many methods of analyses within poststructuralism, it is often subsumed under the rubric of poststructuralism. Therefore, for purposes of clarity, I have chosen to employ poststructuralism as a category which encompasses postmodernist as well as deconstructionist theories and approaches.

10. Although Derrida's work is often interpreted (especially by American literary theorists) as a radical departure from the Enlightenment tradition, Christopher Norris (1990) argues that a close engagement with Derrida's work reveals Derrida to be a defender of Enlightenment reason against various manifestations of French Nietzscheanism. But he concedes that Derrida's work has been appropriated and interpreted, especially among literary critics and theorists, in ways which obfuscate Derrida's commitment to Enlightenment values.

11. Perhaps one of the most troubling aspects of Foucault's analysis of power is that it seems to emerge as an effect without a cause. In much poststructuralist thought, power moves without human agents or purpose. As O'Neill (1995:21) states: "Poststructuralists seem to believe that the cart of history and politics can lurch along without any horse in front of it—they do not notice the masses pushing from behind."

12.   It is worth noting that the critique of the Cartesian subject began long before the emergence of "post" theories and can be found in the narratives of Marx, Gramsci, Freud and others. For example, Marx opposed the bourgeois liberal humanist view of the subject and the point of his critique of a pre-given, static consciousness was to advance the possibility of an oppositional political identity. The seeming freedom and autonomy of the subject to act in any way he or she chooses are circumscribed by the material and historical conditions or "circumstances" (as Marx said in *The Eighteenth Brumaire of Louis Bonaparte*). However, the potential for the abolition or transformation of oppressive circumstances by embodied actors located in history and seeking to overcome denigration is a recurring theme. Although it is often overlooked or downplayed, Marx's own formulations rely not on an abstract "theoretical subject" but rather are rooted in concrete praxis and notions of experiential selfhood. For a more in-depth critique of the postmodern/poststructuralist treatment of the subject see Langman and Scatamburlo, 1996.

13.   Of course, this notion of the subject is indebted in large part to the work of Lacan (1977) whose post-Saussurean models of language and re-reading of Freud emphatically repudiated the attribution of consciousness to the subject. In this formulation, it is believed that the subject cannot completely know itself or its own identity, since its self-constitution is never completely disclosed in consciousness. In contrast to humanism's valorization of consciousness and its belief in the subject as the origin and destination of discourse, Lacan's work suggests that the subject is produced by its entry into language. This entry into the symbolic order produces a subject that is not the origin of discourse, but rather is spoken through discourse. The critique of the subject is also a focal point in the work of Foucault (1980; 1982) whose Nietzscheanism and anti-humanist posturing led him to conceive of and analyze the subject not as an agent of history but rather as part of the complex function of discourse, as a rather docile object of disciplinary knowledge.

14.   As I have argued elsewhere (Langman and Scatamburlo, 1996), however, the *tout court* disavowal of humanism characteristic of poststructuralism is both politically debilitating and intellectually misleading. Humanism, in and of itself, is not a monolithic discourse, despite the fact that it is treated as such by various post-al theorists. Indeed, there are a number of identifiable humanisms, of which bourgeois liberal humanism is but one manifestation, while other forms of revolutionary humanism undergird the work of theorists ranging from Marx and Gramsci to Fanon and Freire.

15.   Recently, Derrida (1994:13) has claimed that:

It will always be a fault not to read and reread and discuss Marx . . . It will be more and more a fault, a failing of theoretical, philosophical, political responsibility . . . There will be . . . no future without Marx, without the memory and the inheritance of Marx.

However, despite the fact that Derrida has reiterated the importance of Marx, his rendering of Marx is still bound up with textual and poststructuralist overtures, for it continues to deconstruct Marx, thereby "turning his fundamental concepts into tropes, at the very same time it affirms the necessity of Marx's theories" (Ebert, 1996:x-xi).

16. It is important to note, however, that despite its ardent disavowal and repudiations of Enlightenment epistemology and its inherent dualisms, poststructuralism and postmodernism generally fall short on their promise of abandoning them and have in essence reinscribed them (albeit inversely). In other words, the "other" in binary constructs such as mind/body, universal/particular, and sameness/difference, has simply been exalted.

17. Elaborating on Hal Foster's (1983:ix-xvi) distinction between reactionary and resistant postmodernisms, Ebert (1992/93;1996) and others have sought to differentiate between "ludic" and "resistant" manifestations of postmodernism. While ludic postmodernism often takes on an apolitical, ahistorical character and concerns itself exclusively with signs, significations, and the discursive, more resistant forms of postmodern theory seek to challenge received assumptions and the status quo from critical and politically committed perspectives.

18. For critiques of Laclau and Mouffe's reading of Gramsci, see for example Geras (1987); Hennessy (1993) and Wood (1986).

19. Ebert (1992/93:42) notes that even when language and discourse are viewed as "material" in ludic postmodernism, it is an idealist understanding of discourse. That is, it is "transhistorical" and refers mostly to "the material in the sense of 'medium'; it is in other words, a form of 'matterism' rather than materialism."

20. This romance with language and the "sign" and its political implications is articulated eloquently by Terry Eagleton (1996:18) who claims that:

> If it is no longer possible to realize one's political desires in action, then one might direct them instead to the sign, cleansing it, for example of its political impurities, and channelling into some linguistic campaign all the pent-up energies which can no longer help to end an imperialist war or bring down the White House. Language, of course, is as real as anything else, as those who are the objects of racial or sexist slurs have reason to know . . . [but] . . . to deny that there is any significant distinction between discourse and reality, between practising genocide and talking about it, is among other things a rationalization of this condition.

21. While there are undoubtedly significant differences between Foucault and Rorty's treatment of "truth", they nonetheless converge to some degree as Dasenbrock (1995:175) aptly points out.

22. Foucault (1980:118) rejected the notion of ideology because it was, more often than not, posited as something which stood "in virtual opposition to something else" which supposedly counted as truth. Foucault's critique of ideology was, however, fairly one-dimensional since he focused almost exclusively on the orthodox Marxist notion of ideology as something opposed to science. He did not consider alternative renderings of Marx's concept of ideology.

23. Eagleton reminds us that the displacement of ideology by discourse is all the more absurd given that the last decade or so has witnessed the resurgence of ideological movements throughout the world. He further remarks on the limitations of the concept of discourse common in poststructuralist narratives. He states that the "category of discourse is inflated to the point where it imperialises the whole world eliding the distinction between thought and material reality. The effect of this is to undercut the critique of ideology—for if ideas and material reality are given indissolubly together, there can be no question of asking where social ideas actually hail from" (Eagleton, 1991:219).

24. See Marx and Engels articulation of ideology as delineated in Part One of *The German Ideology*.

25. Burbules (1995:53-69) identifies a loose topology of five different modes of ideology critique. The first and most common form is "scientific" or "rational" critique. According to this approach, ideologies lack certain formal attributes of rational discourse. That is, they may ignore facts, argue fallaciously, etc. Burbules claims that this position is based on the orthodox Marxian conception of ideology, which treats it as a belief system that makes "pretentious" and/or "unjustified" claims to scientificity—ideology, in other words is a failed rather than "authentic" science. This approach regards ideology as a "subject of epistemic scrutiny and judges it against traditional measures of truth, clarity and validity" (Burbules, 1995:57). The epistemological assumptions of such a position assume that there is "objective" evidence against which purportedly "ideological" claims can be compared.

   The second form of ideology critique, immanent critique, was emphasized by early proponents of critical theory, namely the Frankfurt School. In attempting to move beyond the traditional Marxist conceptions of ideology, the Frankfurt School opted for a stance that sought to disclose hypocrisies and contradictions inherent within cultural formations and texts. Burbules points out that by employing this framework, one attempts to discredit or challenge a belief system not by comparing it against a set of external, objective standards but by demonstrating its internal incongruities.

He identifies the third form of ideology critique as deconstructionist. A deconstructionist critic does not argue for a position of epistemic superiority. Indeed, most proponents of this method embrace the postmodern rejection of notions of evidence, truth, or logical validity. Burbules notes that advocates of this approach define apparently neutral criteria such as clarity and consistency as "remnants of an anachronistic search for intellectual order." Moreover, deconstructive criticism seeks to disclose mechanisms for revealing truth, meaning, and value as ultimately arbitrary and culturally particularistic. Far from being radical, however, ludic deconstructionist critique does not substantively contest ideology but rather deconstructs "discursively" the "truth" of ideology. Zavarzadeh and Morton (1991:194) illustrate the ways in which deconstruction has become a device for "systems-maintenance and the conservation of the status quo." They maintain, for example, that since the ideological function of deconstructive "dehierarchization" reinforces pluralism, it also reinscribes political pluralism which conceals relations of domination by representing "the elements of power as sovereign, individual and equal"(Zavarzadeh & Morton, 1991:213).

The fourth type of ideology critique outlined by Burbules is an "argument from effects." From this perspective, all systems of belief and value exist in a socio-political context and have consequences within the dynamics of that context. Burbules claims that an alternative reading of Marx engenders this form of ideology critique. This mode differs from the first three in that its basis for judgement does not "pertain to epistemic adequacy, reasonableness, consistency, and so on, but to the ways in which ideologies legitimate and support a social system that itself is judged" (Burbules, 1995:60).

The last type of ideology critique outlined by Burbules is that which advocates the development of a counter-ideology. He suggests that to a certain extent, this formulation is often advanced by those who espouse relativistic epistemologies; that is, by those who do not "believe that it is possible to apply criteria of comparison or assessment across systems of belief and value"(1995:60). Burbules points out that such approaches do nonetheless rely implicitly on nonrelativistic claims, since in proffering alternative ideologies one is making claims about what is better or worse, not only in line with one's own preferences but for others as well. This might then be deemed a vanguard form of ideology critique.

26. See Foucault (1980:118).

27. Moreover, a theory of ideology and the practice of political ideology critique necessitates that intellectuals reflect upon their own social locatedness and academic practices. Indeed, the importance of ideology in relation to intellectual production is something that Spivak (1988) foregrounded in her seminal essay, "Can The Subaltern Speak?" The thrust of Spivak's critique of Foucault and Deleuze for their lack

of attention to ideology is expressly evident in her respective discussions of Deleuze's notion of desire and Foucault's genealogical speculation. One of the most important points made by Spivak is that both Foucault and Deleuze, lacking an adequate theory of ideology, render themselves transparent and fail to locate themselves within the international division of intellectual labor as First World, Western, metropolitan intellectuals. Interestingly enough, while Foucault saw nothing more ignominious than speaking for "others" and viewed representation as panoptic, coercive, and disciplinary, it was Foucault perhaps more than any other contemporary theorist who tried to "voice" the other in his various works. It is this paradox that Spivak perceptively illuminates. In addition, she also argues that a well-developed theory of ideology foregrounds the notion of critical self-reflection and recognizes that various forms of intellectual production also work ideologically, both consciously and unconsciously.

28. Steven Best (1995:230) aptly points out that postmodern theory commits us to an either/or fallacy that undermines a third alternative to absolutism and relativism. This alternative, according to Best, "provides a nonarbitrary, extralocal means of grounding normative claims, without appealing to any ahistorical criteria.

29. Eagleton (1996:123) argues that far too many postmodern discourses confuse objectivity and objectivism, which in turn, leads them to embrace forms of relativism which are politically debilitating and ethically vacuous. For an elaboration on the differences between objectivism and objective relations, see Gramsci's (1971:381-472) discussion on the "problems of Marxism" in the *Prison Notebooks*, and for an insightful commentary on Gramsci's critique of objectivism, see Nemeth (1980).

30. These issues are elaborated upon briefly at the conclusion of this chapter.

31. Quite simply, pre-given, essentialist identities or subject positions cannot define and predict one's political direction. Nor for that matter can we naively assume that identity-based movements have emerged solely within subaltern populations and left-leaning constituencies. One need only look to the proliferation of xenophobic movements in Europe and the United States—mobilizations which are based on White resentment to see the folly of such an assertion.

32. Marable (1992) cited in Yudice (1995:274).

33. Even more disturbing is the fact that 45 percent of union members voted for Republican "Contract with America" candidates who "promised to make the U.S. a union busting country" (Ziedenberg, 1996:19). This trend was, of course, evident in the 1980s when many frustrated White working-class and downwardly mobile middle-class Americans jumped on Reagan's anti-welfare, anti-affirmative action bandwagon

even though Reagan did more damage to workers' rights than any president in recent history.

34. It is equally important to note, however, that while the income of White males has declined over the last two decades, they still earn more than White women and far more than Blacks of either gender.

35. For an insightful look at talk radio's role in contemporary society, see Giroux (1996:141-161).

36. The debates about Fordism and post-Fordism continue to rage and the issues they have raised go far beyond the scope of this text. Nonetheless, it bears mentioning that post-Fordist tendencies (including the decline in the proportion of skilled, manual labor; the "feminization" of the work force and an economy dominated by relatively autonomous multinationals and their "new" international division of labor), have had a significant impact on the plight of the working classes. For more detailed analyses of post-Fordism, see for example Allen (1996); Harvey (1989, 1991) and Hall (1991).

37. According to Zeskind (1996:22), MARs were discovered by Michigan sociologist Donald Warren in his 1976 study of George Wallace's presidential campaigns, entitled *The Radical Center*. Warren identified them as middle-class political radicals who believed that the rich give in to the demands of the poor, while the middle-income people foot the bill. Zeskind contends that in 1968 and 1972, MARs supported Wallace, and in the 1990s voted for Perot and Buchanan.

38. A similar argument is put forth by Tomasky (1996), however, in my view, Tomasky goes too far in advocating an almost exclusive focus on class-based economic politics and an accompanying class politics of culture, while ignoring the intersections of race, class, gender, and other factors in the United States.

39. Echoing these sentiments Eagleton (1996: 128) invites us to interrogate why it is that so many radical intellectuals denounce the notion of totality at a time when the system and capitalism are becoming even more "total."

40. The concept of mediation also enables us to problematize the autonomous, volitional subject of liberal humanism, for it points to the way in which the social, historical, and structural are always imbricated in the constitution of subjectivity and experience. At the same time, however, it refuses those formulations that present an objectified and oversocialized conceptualization of human existence, while denying the importance of consciousness, subjectivity, and agency. In this regard, the relevance of the concept of mediation is that it allows us to avoid both debilitating forms of subjectivism, which ignore the historical limits and conditions of social structure, as well as forms of objectivism which delegitimate human activity and praxis.

41. Best and Kellner (1991) argue that the exploitation and repression of diverse groups and individuals by the forces of capitalism and the state provide a fundamental point of commonality. Of course, while racism and sexism are virtually inseparable from economic exploitation and state repression, they are not identical to them. In other words, these forms of oppression are not reducible solely to economic conditions, but they are conditioned by them insofar as racism and sexism are "necessary social relations" for the organization of "modern imperialist capitalism in the West" (Bannerji, 1991:87). Equally important is acknowledging the role of the state in terms of its function as a moral regulator. This is particularly evident if one considers the regulation of homosexuality and the denial of civil liberties to gays and lesbians through various state and judicial apparatuses.

42. For an in-depth and insightful look at this issue, see Aronowitz (1996).

43. Tomasky aptly points out that in the years that identity has triumphed on the Left, little has actually been done to improve the material conditions of people's lives. In fact,

    the lives of poor black people . . . have simply gotten worse . . . and now, for the first time in our modern history, laws are being written that penalize poor women for having babies. It's no accident, in other words, that the right has taken over the country just as the left has permitted itself to disintegrate into ever more discrete race and gender-based camps. (Tomasky, 1996:81)

44. For a fuller elaboration of some of the arguments here, see Grossberg (1996[b]).

45. Recently, a number of critical scholars have begun to reassess the significance of the revolutionary and radical humanism undergirding the work of Paulo Freire (Aronowitz, 1994:218-237) and Frantz Fanon (Bernasconi, 1996; Gordon, 1995), in light of the postmodern assault on humanism. These themes are also addressed in Langman and Scatamburlo (1996).

46. Marxism is profoundly humanistic, although the kind of humanism it stands for differs radically from previous humanisms for revolutionary socialist humanism is consistently materialist and historical (Novack, 1973).

Conclusion: Towards a
Politically Committed Pedagogy

Is "Teaching the Conflicts" Enough?

To say that the past few years have been a tumultuous period in higher education is to state the obvious. For progressive educators engaged in a project of re-imagining the academy and its contours, it has been a time of struggle and contestation, in which they have become the targets of an insidious attempt to undermine the very notion of democratic education. The debates, issues, and questions spawned by P.C. are many and varied, pointing to the contradictions and complexities of multiculturalism, identity politics, and the very future of progressive politics. They also raise serious pedagogical questions—they bring to the fore the issue, not only of what is taught, but how it is taught and with what purpose in mind.

One of the most widely touted pedagogical solutions offered as a way out of the impasse generated by the culture wars has been Gerald Graff's suggestion to teach the "conflicts" spawned by the P.C. debates. In *Beyond the Culture Wars*, Graff (1992:3-15) advocates this pedagogical approach, which purports to be *neither* a liberal pluralist perspective "content to let cultural and intellectual diversity proliferate without addressing the conflicts and contradictions that would result," *nor* a conservative approach that would "exclude or shut down those conflicts." Graff's liberal pedagogical approach, however, reveals a number of shortcomings.

First is the underlying assumption that there exists two "sides" when in fact there are many.[1] Those seeking pedagogical change cannot neatly be categorized under the umbrella of liberal pluralism; several of them in fact, would eschew such a label. A number of radical education theorists and critical pedagogues have been among the most vocal critics of liberal pluralist approaches to multicultural pedagogical reform (McLaren, 1995; Mohanty, 1994; Zavarzadeh and Morton, 1994). Even if one were to accept Graff's binary formulation, it is misleading to suggest that the two sides are equally weighted, for they are not. Contrary to the overblown charges that multiculturalists and leftists wield the wand of academic power, universities are by and large still under the control of traditionalists and conservatives who have the deep pockets of corporate-sponsored think-tanks to promote their monocultural agendas.

Second, the suggestion to teach the conflicts as if they were fixed, stable, and immobile does not provide any grounds for exploring how "the conflictual" gets articulated in specific contexts. It also ignores that the subject of conflict is rarely constant, but rather, continuously changes and takes on new forms. If the conflicts are treated as hard and fast categories, placed at the center of a curriculum, and made into its structuring principle, the parameters of academic discourse become rigid, and other conflicts which may not fit neatly into already designated categories are suppressed.

Third, Graff's formulation seeks to impose a discourse of value-neutrality on an enterprise (education) that is inherently political and always mediated by power relations. In a recent essay (a rather distorted critique of critical pedagogy), Gregory Jay and Gerald Graff (1995) present a case for not "politicizing" the classroom. In their idyllic scenario, the conflicts are presented impartially by the teacher to students who are then to formulate their own opinions. What Jay and Graff fail to acknowledge, however, is that the educator who simply teaches the conflicts from a seemingly "objective" viewpoint is denuded of his or her's own embodied subjectivity and falsely projected as neutral. This educator is conceived of as a disembodied purveyor or transmitter of "knowledge" rather than a social actor embedded in a network of differential power relations. Not only does this logic reinscribe a vulgar form of positivist rationality, it also implies that intellectuals can suspend their own political viewpoints and affective investments in the context of the classroom.

It is also a form of intellectual dishonesty—assuming an allegedly apolitical posture is in itself a form of "political" posturing. Even when the political may not be overt, an educator's own social locatedness mediates pedagogical practices—something which an assumed "view from nowhere" obscures. The notion of an objective educator who simply teaches the conflicts also begs some obvious questions. If objectivity, detachment, and impartiality are necessary to the process of educating, how does education connect with ordinary life, with society, or with the world outside of the academy? How does the objective purveyor of "knowledge" even have a social conscience? Moreover, Jay and Graff's position is based on a confusion between political education and the practice of politicizing education. Political education refers to teaching

> students how to think in ways that cultivate the capacity for judgement essential for the exercise of power and responsibility by a democratic citizenry . . . A political, as distinct from a politicizing education would encourage students to become better citizens to challenge those with political and cultural power as well as to honor the critical traditions within the dominant culture that make such a critique possible and intelligible. (Euben, cited in Giroux, 1996:126)

Giroux goes to argue that a political education

> means decentering power in the classroom and other pedagogical sites so the dynamics of those institutional and cultural inequalities that marginalize some groups, repress particular types of knowledge, and suppress cultural dialogue can be addressed. On the other hand, politicizing education . . . is determined by a doctrinaire political agenda that refuses to examine its own values, beliefs, and ideological construction. (Giroux, 1996:126-127)

Although Jay and Graff seek to disavow critically engaged pedagogies, I would contend that such critical discourses have assumed even greater importance in light of the New Right's ascendency and their mean-spirited assaults on Left activism, critical multiculturalism, and other progressive initiatives. Therefore, rather than arguing for a "teaching the conflicts" strategy, the task should be the cultivation of a *politically committed* pedagogy which, among other things, would historicize and contextualize the advent of P.C. itself. Because the phrase floats so freely in our culture and in our classrooms, often with little regard for the social relations that gave rise to its demonization, it is imperative to situate the culture wars within the broader and more complex field of social and material conditions. A politically committed pedagogy does not satisfy itself with teaching the conflicts in antiseptic isolation from the concerns of the world outside the academy, but rather seeks to produce and develop historical knowledge about P.C. and the culture wars and to confront their implications.

Furthermore, a politically committed pedagogy is not one that is mired in the dogmatism of political correctness. Unfortunately, much of Jay and Graff's critique is predicated on the idea that teaching from an ethically committed standpoint is commensurate with ideological indoctrination. Clear distinctions must be made between a "politically correct" pedagogy and a "politically committed" pedagogy. Of course, it is necessary to acknowledge that for educators seeking to grapple with pressing social issues like racism, sexism, and various other forms of oppression in the classroom, there *is* often a fine line between imposing a dogmatic view and cultivating in students a willingness to engage such concerns seriously, openly, and earnestly. Even some of the most dedicated and well-intentioned pedagogues are not immune to falling into the trap of pedagogical terrorism and imposing the edicts of P.C. on their students. Often times this occurs in situations where educators declare that certain utterances (such as racist, sexist, or homophobic remarks) will not be tolerated in a given classroom setting. Such posturing, while undoubtedly motivated by noble intentions, nonetheless has a chilling effect. It imposes closure before dialogue can even begin. In such situations, there is often a profound reluctance on the part of students to speak for fear that they may be accused of one of the growing list of "isms." In this regard, Benjamin Barber's (1992) observation that what we must fear is not the closing of the American mind, but rather the closing of the American mouth, is dangerously accurate.

Unlike the silencing effects that often accompany a rigid P.C. posturing, a politically committed pedagogy takes seriously the "politics of voice" and is willing to extend it to all, including those whose voices may be disturbing and unsettling. Censoring and silencing what may be unpopular opinions (those that convey racist, sexist, and homophobic views) in the classroom is incompatible with the task of educating for critical consciousness. In fact, it may fuel resentment and actually reinforce and promote such views outside of the classroom

(Cohen, 1991). This does not imply that racism, sexism, and the like should be condoned, only that educators provide the space for the articulation of disturbing voices so that they may then be engaged critically (by students and educators alike) in the context of the classroom, rather than going uncontested or unexplored in other forums. Writing in reference to teaching about race, Stuart Hall (1981:58-59) discusses the necessity of creating

> an atmosphere which allows people to say unpopular things . . . What I am talking about here are the problems of handling the racist time-bomb and doing so adequately so that we connect with our students' experience and can therefore be sure of defusing it. That experience has to surface in the classroom even if it's pretty horrendous to hear: better to hear it than not because what you don't hear you can't engage with.

Hall's astute observations highlight the importance of developing forms of pedagogical practice that do not deny disturbing voices. While these pedagogical practices must necessarily be grounded in an ethical stance that contests dehumanizing and oppressive social relations, they cannot do so by silencing students. Rather, courageous attempts must be made to challenge unpopular views, not by tossing epithets about, but by examining the bases for such views and their affective appeal, and exploring the social relations which give rise to their articulation. Only a thorough engagement with unpopular voices has any hope of promoting the kind of critical self-reflective capacity in students that may enable them to better understand the mediating influences and social structures that shape their experience and their views. In this regard, it is not simply "individual" attitudes which are challenged and explored but the very social relations that engender and nurture such attitudes. Although such an exercise cannot guarantee that students will embrace more progressive views, the failure to engage unpopular voices in the classroom leaves them more receptive and vulnerable to the vitriolic propaganda of right-wing public intellectuals like Rush Limbaugh.

Moreover, a politically committed pedagogy moves beyond the pluralism that undergirds liberal forms of multiculturalism. While liberal multiculturalism relies on pluralism and the rhetoric of tolerance and diversity to obscure the economic

and political inequities that are related to racial, ethnic, and
gender differences, politically committed pedagogues attempt
to illuminate them in relation to the social organization of
capital. Rather than seeking a mere "symbolic" multiculturalism, politically committed pedagogy seeks to demystify
the ideological functions of liberal forms of multiculturalism
which, more often than not, operate in ways that thwart a serious engagement with institutionalized and structural forms of
oppression and exclusion.

 A politically committed approach also takes issue with liberal pedagogical prescriptions for "teaching the conflicts"
because of their decontextualized and depoliticized underpinnings. The "culture wars" are not limited to questions about
what texts to teach or how they should be taught. They signal
much broader struggles over the very meanings of democracy,
critical citizenship, and the future complexion of our political
and social topography. The culture war waged by the New Right
is not, therefore, merely a struggle over the teaching of *I,
Rigoberta Menchu* or the importance of taking "gender, race or
class" as categories of "literary and philosophical analysis" (Jay
and Graff, 1995:213). It is a broad-based assault funded by a
vast network of corporate-sponsored think-tanks intent on furthering a regressive social and political agenda. In failing to
adequately contextualize the breadth and scope of the right-
wing assault, Jay and Graff sidestep important questions about
the political implications of their pedagogical prescriptions.
Does simply teaching the conflicts of the culture wars help to
explain how these culture wars started in the first place? Does
it take into account the funding and organizations that have
been behind the culture wars? Does it address how the New
Right's agenda cuts much deeper than fights over curricula?
Does it help to illuminate the social relations and material
conditions that have given rise to the Right's assault? Does it
address the New Right's agenda in all its ugliness and inhu-
manity? For if we truly want to teach the "conflicts," we need
to understand these conflicts in much broader historical terms.
These conflicts are deeply embedded in power relations; they
are, in short, conflicts about different ways of envisioning the
future. As such, they are inherently political. Hence, whereas
liberal pedagogues limit their concern solely to the privileged

space of the university, politically committed pedagogues seek to link struggles in the university with larger social struggles. They do not limit their interventions into the "culture wars" to those made in college curricula. Rather, they attempt to elucidate how the culture wars are imbricated in power/knowledge arrangements which extend far beyond the hallowed halls of academe; they understand clearly that there is much more at stake in the culture wars than liberals are willing to admit.

Beyond the Ivory Tower

> . . . many . . . do not eat at all. But that cannot be the question. There is no justice for them. But that cannot be the question. Nor is there any truth for them. But that cannot be the question. Who, then, owns these questions? Why are they not raised without irritation and scorn, if not impatience and ridicule? These questions go unasked because those of us who own knowledge . . . have chosen to rage against our own gifts rather than to fight for their enlargement in the general public. (O'Neill, 1995:2)

If nothing else, the skirmishes over P.C. have thrust critical questions about the relationship between intellectual life, knowledge, power, and the struggle for social change to the fore. These questions become all the more urgent when one considers O'Neill's remarks, for they serve to remind us about the importance of bridging the intellectual work carried out in the academy with concerns raging outside of its walls. They also provide a chilling reminder of the detachment and cynicism that has infected the political soul of many leftists.

Well over thirty years ago, C. Wright Mills (1959) complained about the retreat of the intellectual and the failure of scholars to ask the "big" questions. Of course, Mills was then lamenting the methodological inhibition and fact fetishism of positivist social science, which provided intellectuals with "busy work" by counting more and more about less and less. Yet the point of his polemic rings true today, albeit in a somewhat different form. To be sure, a great deal of busy work still goes on in the name of a narrow empiricism. But equal amounts of busy work are carried out by "Left" intellectuals, in the form of a flighty theoreticism which often bears little connection to the realities of our contemporary social world. The result is a scenario in which Left intellectuals engage in critique within universities and the privileged purview of scholarly journals yet surrender the possibility for more public interventions.

Rather than retreating from the exigencies of the real world into the intellectual tower of Babel and babble, committed leftists working in the academy must seize the opportunities to produce "activist" knowledges intended to further the cause of progressive change not just in the university but in the general public as well. This task becomes all the more pressing if we consider the vigor with which the New Right has cultivated its cache of "intellectuals" for the purpose of advancing regressive social measures. Of course, one cannot ignore the fact that the New Right's intellectual base has been courted by a corporate establishment that has generously funded many of the diatribes about higher education and other issues. Yet, if progressives hope to have a hand in shaping the future, they must engage less in arcane debates among themselves and more in producing activist knowledge, which the New Right has shown to be an effective mode of intervention in the political domain (Messer-Davidow, 1993).[2]

To this end, a number of strategies are needed. First, it is imperative for progressives to assume the role of "public intellectuals" and to engage in what hooks and West (1991) refer to as insurgent intellectualism. The aim of insurgent intellectualism is to link theory with practice and the academy to the wider community, thereby highlighting the importance of defining academic work within its broader social, political, and cultural context. This would compel academics to develop their research agendas and theoretical frameworks in connection with cultural workers doing oppositional work in other arenas. These may include, for example, alternative media projects, labor organizations, artistic communities, homeless activists, antiracist groups, or any one of a number of sites or community organizations outside the academy (Giroux, 1996:123).[3] The forging of such alliances and the crossing of such borders could possibly assist in overcoming the current chasm between Left academics and activists.[4]

Furthermore, progressives also need to acknowledge that the concept of public intellectual is no longer the sole preserve of the Left. Given the impact of right-wing "organic" intellectuals like Rush Limbaugh and Newt Gingrich in defining the parameters of political, cultural, and moral discourse, we need to seriously engage such popular, public figures. Rather than merely dismissing them as bigoted malcontents, there is a need to explore, in concrete terms, both the basis of their affective appeal and the power relations that enable them to speak authoritatively to contemporary social concerns. Hence, the terrain of popular culture as a site where forms of consciousness are constantly created and negotiated needs to be critically engaged. This becomes all the more pressing at a time when talk radio and reactionary figures are assuming an educative role in public life.

Second, if we take seriously the premise that the university can be used as a site for constructing oppositional knowledge, there is a need to translate critical intellectual work in a way that makes it accessible to publics other than one's own academic cohort. Pratt points out that there has been a remarkable inability among intellectuals to translate their views into a "politically effective public discourse." In fact, she reports that once some professors began to speak out amid the P.C. ballyhoo, it was such "a departure from the ordinary that the *Chronicle of Higher Education* considered it a news event" (Pratt, 1995:35). Unfortunately, the motivation to "go public" was rather short-lived and was largely a reaction to the New Right's very public attack on higher education. On other issues, Left intellectuals rarely make proactive interventions into public life, leaving that to the likes of right-wing scions like Limbaugh and others cut from similar political cloth. This, however, is not intended to advocate a brand of intellectual populism nor to relegate intellectuals to the realm of "plainspeak" or "soundbite" simplicity, for any form of anti-intellectualism on the Left would be a service to the Establishment.[5] However, there is a tendency for many Left intellectuals to write in ways that are inaccessible and overly cryptic. If we hope to intervene in the culture wars raging both inside and outside the walls of academe, a concerted effort must be made to transcend the rarified discourses of academia and to communicate in ways that are intelligible to audiences outside the academic world.[6]

Progressives need to cultivate the ability to write in many different modes depending on the audience or public they are attempting to reach. Of course, the sad truth of "profession-

alization" is that it often demands that intellectuals write in
languages specific to a particular field of inquiry or to a particular audience of academic cohorts, yet this is but one public among many. The task is to be able to move in and out of
different publics, to cross boundaries created by intellectual
borders, and to adjust our languages in diverse settings. It is
necessary to create modes of understanding that help to explain the complexities of our social world in a manner that
communicates them effectively and convincingly. In this regard, simple and often self-serving defences of obscurantist
language do not further the cause of democratizing knowledge in the interest of social change.

   Finally, although the academy is circumscribed by its socio-
economic context and most often contributes to the manufacturing of an intelligentsia which produces knowledge conducive to the maintenance of repressive conditions, we would do
well to remind ourselves that it nonetheless remains one of
the principal locations in advanced capitalist society for the
articulation of radically oppositional knowledge. The university as a space for radical intervention must therefore be engaged extensively and unrelentingly. Progressive intellectuals
must participate in what Marcuse (1972:131) called the "absolute refusal of the intellect" to lend "support to the Establishment, and the mobilization of the power of theoretical and
practical reason for the work of change." This is no part-time
or easy task; it requires the dedication of progressive Left intellectuals who are willing to commit themselves to the struggle
for a more just and humane world. And, it requires, as O'Neill
suggests, that we start asking the right questions.

Notes

1. The "conflicts" among leftists alone are evidence of this.

2. In making this assertion, I am not advocating a form of anti-intellectualism; nor am I dismissing the importance of academic politics as a form of critical political intervention.

3. It is important to note, however, that such connections and alliances should not suggest that the university define its public function solely in terms of its associations with other public spheres. As Giroux (1996:123) and Ross (1993:261) argue, the university must be defended as a vital public sphere in its own right, as a space with profound moral and educative dimensions that impact on civic life.

4. In cultivating such alliances, however, there is always the danger that intellectuals will assume the role of the "expert." The problems inherent in such posturing are many, and care must be taken to avoid succumbing to this tendency. Nonetheless, intellectuals do have the responsibility to speak critically to various issues and to share whatever knowledge they possess with non-academic cultural workers. However, this sharing of knowledge should be reciprocal: intellectuals should be open to being educated to new conceptions or ways of seeing in the dialogic encounter with community activists and members of marginalized groups.

5. See Marcuse (1972).

6. This issue of "clarity" has recently spawned fierce debates. Critics (Agger, 1990; Apple, 1995) of the recondite writing which has characterized much critical intellectual work argue that if the overt aim of the Left is to intervene meaningfully in the realm of public discourse, it must avoid the tendency to write in a language that is largely inaccessible. Defenders of the "new languages" view the calls for lucid prose with a certain degree of derision, arguing instead that the complexity of social life demands complex concepts and specialized discourses. It is also held that demands for clarity and intelligibility amount, in the end, to a suppression of diversity and different ways of speaking, writing and communicating (Giroux, 1993). While there is a great deal of merit to these observations, it is nonetheless important to note that the diversity of voices, meanings and languages means precious little if no one can hear them for lack of understanding.

References

"A Most Uncommon Scold." Interview with Allan Bloom. *Time* (Oct. 17, 1988):74-76.

Adler, Jerry, et al. "Taking Offense." *Newsweek* (Dec. 24, 1990):48-54.

Agresto, John. "The Politicization of Liberal Education." *Academic Questions* (Fall, 1990):69-73.

Agger, Ben. *The Decline of Discourse: Reading, Writing and Resistance in Postmodern Capitalism.* Bristol, Pennsylvania: The Falmer Press, 1990.

Ahmad, Aijaz. *In Theory.* London and New York: Verso Press, 1992.

Alcoff, Linda. "The Problem of Speaking For Others." *Cultural Critique* (1991/92, no. 20):5-32.

————. "How Is Epistemology Political?" in *Radical Philosophy: Tradition, Counter-Tradition, Politics.* Ed. Roger Gottlieb. Philadelphia: Temple University Press, 1993, pp. 65-85.

Allen, John. "Post-Industrialism/Post-Fordism," in *Modernity: An Introduction to Modern Societies.* Eds. Stuart Hall et al. Cambridge, Massachusetts: Blackwell, 1996, pp. 533-563.

Anderson, Benedict. *Imagined Communities: Reflections on the Origin and Spread of Nationalism.* London: Verso Books, 1983.

Anderson, Margaret. "From The Editor." *Gender & Society* (Dec., 1991):454.

Appiah, Kwame Anthony. *In My Father's House: Africa in the Philosophy of Culture.* New York and Oxford: Oxford University Press, 1992.

Apple, Michael. "The Politics Of Common Sense: Schooling, Populism, And The New Right," in *Critical Pedagogy, The State And Cultural Struggle.* Eds. Henry Giroux and Peter McLaren. New York: State University of New York Press, 1989, pp. 32-49.

————. "Cultural Capital and Official Knowledge," in *Higher Education Under Fire: Politics, Economics, and the Crisis of the Humanities.* Eds. Michael Berube and Cary Nelson. New York and London: Routledge, 1995, pp. 91-107.

Arnold, Matthew. "Culture and Anarchy: An Essay in Political and Social Criticism," in *Arnold: Culture and Anarchy and Other Writings*. Ed. Stefan Collini. Cambridge, Massachusetts: Cambridge University Press, 1993, pp. 53-211.

Aronowitz, Stanley, and Giroux, Henry. *Education Under Siege*. New York: Bergin and Garvey, 1985.

Aronowitz, Stanley. *Science As Power: Discourse and Ideology in Modern Society*. Minneapolis: University of Minnesota Press, 1988.

Aronowitz, Stanley, and Giroux, Henry. *Postmodern Education: Politics, Culture and Social Criticism*. Minneapolis: University of Minnesota Press, 1991.

———. *Education Still Under Siege*. Toronto: OISE Press, 1993.

Aronowitz, Stanley. *Roll Over Beethoven: The Return of Cultural Strife*. Hanover and London: University of New England Press, 1993.

———. "The Situation of the Left in the United States." *Socialist Review* (1994; vol. 23, no. 3):5-79.

———. *Dead Artists, Live Theories*. New York: Routledge, 1994.

———. *The Death and Rebirth of American Radicalism*. New York: Routledge, 1996.

Asante, Molefi Kete. "Multiculturalism: An Exchange," in *Debating P.C.* Ed. Paul Berman. New York: Dell Publishing, 1992, pp. 299-311.

Balch, Stephen, and London, Herbert. "The Tenured Left." *Commentary* (Oct. 1986):41-51.

Bannerji, Himani. "But Who Speaks For Us? Experience And Agency In Conventional Feminist Paradigms" in *Unsettling Relations*. Toronto: Women's Press, 1991, pp. 67-108.

———. *Thinking Through: Essays on Feminism, Marxism and Anti-Racism*. Toronto: Women's Press, 1995.

Barber, Benjamin R. "Cultural Conservatism and DemocraticEducation: Lessons From The Sixties." *Salmagundi* (Winter, 1989, no. 81):159-173.

———. *An Aristocracy of Everyone*. New York: Oxford University Press, 1992.

Barkan, Elazar. "Fin de Siècle Cultural Studies." *Tikkun* (1993, vol. 8, no. 4):49-51, 92-93.

Barthes, Roland. *Mythologies*. London: Paladin Press, 1972 [orig.1957].

Baudrillard, Jean. *Simulations*. New York: Semiotext(e), 1983.

Bellant, Russ. *Old Nazis, The New Right, and the Republican Party: Domestic Fascist Networks andTtheir Effect on U.S. Cold War Politics.* Boston: South End Press, 1988.

———. *The Coors Connection: How Coors Family Philanthropy Undermines Democratic Pluralism.* Boston: South End Press, 1991.

Benjamin, Walter. *Illuminations.* New York: Schoken, 1968.

Berger, John. *Ways of Seeing.* London: BBC and Penguin Books Ltd., 1972.

Berlant, Lauren, and Warner, Michael. "Introduction to Critical Multiculturalism," in *Multiculturalism: A Critical Reader.* Ed. David Theo Goldberg. Cambridge, Massachusetts: Blackwell, 1994, pp. 107-113.

Berlet, Chip. Preface to *The Coors Connection.* Boston: South End Press, 1991.

Berman, Marshall. *All That Is Solid Melts Into Air.* New York: Simon and Schuster, 1982.

Berman, Marshall. "Why Modernism Still Matters." *Tikkun* (1989, vol. 4, no. 1):11-14, 81-86.

Berman, Paul, Ed. *Debating P.C.: The Controversy Over Political Correctness On College Campuses.* New York: Dell Publishing, 1992.

Bernasconi, Robert. "Casting the Slough: Fanon's New Humanism for a New Humanity," in *Fanon: A Critical Reader.* Ed. Lewis Gordon et al. Cambridge, Massachusetts: Blackwell, 1996, pp. 113-121.

Bernstein, Charles. "Centering The Postmodern: In The Middle of Modernism, In The Middle of Capitalism." *Socialist Review* (Nov.-Dec., 1987, vol. 17, no. 6):45-58.

Bernstein, Richard. "The Rising Hegemony of the Politically Correct." *New York Times* (Oct. 28, 1990, sec. 4):1.

——— *Dictatorship of Virtue.* New York: Simon and Schuster, 1994.

Bertsch, Charlie. "Gramsci Rush: Limbaugh on the 'Culture War.'" *Bad Subjects* (March, 1994, no. 12).

Berube, Michael. "Public Image Limited: Political Correctness and the Media's Big Lie," in *Debating P.C.: The Controversy over Political Correctness on College Campuses.* Ed. Paul Berman New York: Dell Publishing, 1992, pp.124-149.

———. *Public Access: Literary Theory and American Cultural Politics.* London and New York: Verso Press, 1994.

———. "Truth, Justice and the American Way: A Response to Joan Wallach Scott," in *PC Wars: Politics and Theory in the Academy.* Ed. Jeffrey Williams. New York and London: Routledge, 1995, pp. 44-59.

Best, Steven. "Jameson, Totality, and the Poststructuralist Critique," in *Postmodernism, Jameson, Critique.* Ed. Douglas Kellner. Washington, D.C.: Maisonneuve Press, 1989, pp. 333-368.

Best, Steven, and Kellner, Douglas. *Postmodern Theory: Critical Interrogations.* New York: Guilford Press, 1991.

Best, Steven. *The Politics of Historical Vision: Marx, Foucault, Habermas.* New York and London: Guilford Press, 1995.

Blaut, J.M. *The Colonizer's Model of the World: Geographical Diffusionism and Eurocentric History.* New York: Guilford Press, 1993.

Bloch, Ernst. *The Principle of Hope, Vol. 1.* Trans. Neville Plaice, Stephen Plaice and Paul Knight. Cambridge, Massachusetts: MIT Press, 1995.

Bloom, Allan. *The Closing of the American Mind.* New York: Simon and Schuster, 1987.

Blumenthal, Sidney. *The Rise of the Counter-Establishment: From Conservative Ideology to Political Power.* New York: Harper and Row, 1988.

Boettcher, Robert, and Freeman, Gordon L. *Gifts of Deceit: Sun Myung Moon, Tongsun Park, and the Korean Scandal.* New York: Holt, Rinehart and Winston, 1980.

Boland, Harland G. and Sue M. *American Learned Societies In Transition: The Impact of Dissent and Recession.* New York: McGraw-Hill, 1974.

Bologh, Roslyn Wallach, and Mell, Leonard. "Modernism, Postmodernism, and the New World (Dis)order: A Dialectical Analysis and Alternative." *Critical Sociology* (1994, vol. 20, no. 2):81-120.

Bondi, Liz. "Locating Identity Politics," in *Place and the Politics of Identity.* Eds. Michael Keith and Steven Pile. New York: Routledge, 1993, pp. 84-101.

Bordo, Susan. "Feminism, Postmodernism, and Gender-Scepticism," in *Feminism/Postmodernism.* Ed. Linda Nicholson. New York and London: Routledge, 1990, pp. 133-156.

Borg, Carmel, Mayo, Peter and Sultana, Ronald. "Revolution and Reality: An Interview with Peter McLaren." *Education (Malta)* (1994, vol.5, no.2):2-12.

Bork, Robert H., Krane, Howard and Krane, George. *Political Activities of Colleges and Universities: Some Policy and Legal Implications.* Washington, D.C.: American Enterprise Institute, 1970.

Bourdieu, Pierre. *The Political Ontology of Martin Heidegger* Stanford, California: Stanford University Press, 1991.

Bourne, Jenny. "Homelands of the Mind: Jewish Feminism and Identity Politics." *Race & Class* (Summer 1987, vol. 29, no. 1):1-24.

Brennan, Tim. "PC and the Decline of the American Empire." *Social Policy* (Summer 1991):16-29.

Brodkey, Linda, and Fowler, Shelli. "Political Suspects." *Village Voice Education Supplement* (August 20, 1991):6.

Brunt, Rosalind. "The Politics of Identity," in *New Times: The Changing Face of Politics in the 1990s*. Eds. Stuart Hall and Martin Jacques. London: Verso Books, 1990, pp. 150-159.

Buckley, William F., and Bozell, Brent. *McCarthy and His Enemies: The Record and Its Meaning*. Chicago: Henry Regnery Co., 1954.

Buckley, William F. *God and Man at Yale: The Superstitions of "Academic Freedom."* Illinois: Regnery Gateway, 1986 [orig. 1951].

Buhle, Mari Jo. "Irving Howe," in *Encyclopedia of the American Left*. Eds. Buhle et al. Urbana, Illinois: University of Illinois Press, 1992, pp. 336-337.

Buhle, Paul. *Marxism in the United States*. London and New York: Verso Press, 1987.

Burbules, Nicholas. "Forms of Ideology-Critique: A Pedagogical Perspective," in *Critical Theory and Educational Research*. Eds. Peter McLaren and James Giarelli. Albany: SUNY Press, 1995, pp. 53-69.

Butler, Judith. *Gender Trouble: Feminism and the Subversion of Identity*. New York: Routledge, 1990.

———. "Contingent Foundations: Feminism and the Question of 'Postmodernism,'" in *Feminists Theorize The Political*. Eds. Judith Butler and Joan W. Scott. New York and London: Routledge, 1992, pp. 3-21.

———. *Bodies That Matter: On The Discursive Limits of "Sex"*. New York: Routledge, 1993.

Cameron, Deborah. *Verbal Hygiene*. London and New York: Routledge, 1995.

Carby, Hazel. "White Women Listen! Black Feminism and the Boundaries of Sisterhood," in *The Empire Strikes Back: Race and Racism in 70s Britain*. Centre For Contemporary Cultural Studies. London: Hutchinson, 1981, pp. 212-235.

———. "The Canon: Civil War and Reconstruction." *Michigan Quarterly Review* (Winter, 1989, vol. 28, no. 1):35-43.

Carton, Evan. "The Self Besieged: American Identity on Campus and in the Gulf." *Tikkun* (1991, vol. 6, no. 4):40-47.

238   *References*

Caute, David. *The Great Fear: The Anti-Communist Purge Under Truman and Eisenhower*. New York: Simon and Schuster, 1978.

Caws, Peter. *Structuralism: The Art of the Intelligible*. New Jersey: Humanities Press International, 1988.

Ceplair, Larry, and Englund, Steven. *The Inquisition in Hollywood: Politics in the Film Community, 1930-1960*. New York: Anchor Press, 1980.

Chaney, Lynne V. *Humanities In America: A Report to the President, the Congress, and the American People*. Washington, D.C., 1988.

Cherryholmes, C. *Power and Criticism: Poststructural Investigations in Education*. New York: Teachers College Press, 1988.

Chomsky, Noam. "The Responsibility of Intellectuals," in *The Chomsky Reader*. Ed. James B. Peck. New York: Pantheon Books, 1987, pp. 59-82.

———. "The Universities and the Corporations," in *Language And Politics*. Ed. C.P. Otero. Montreal: Black Rose Books, 1988.

———. *Necessary Illusions: Thought Control In Democratic Societies*. Toronto: CBC Enterprises, 1990.

———. *Deterring Democracy*. London and New York: Verso Press, 1991.

———. "Rollback II." *Z Magazine* (February 1995):20-31.

Christian, Barbara. "The Race for Theory." *Cultural Critique* (Spring 1987, no. 6):51-63.

Cockburn, Alexander. "Bush and P.C.—A Conspiracy So Immense." *The Nation* (May 27, 1991):685, 690-691, 704.

Cohen, G., et al. *The New Right: Image and Reality*. London: Runnymeade Trust, 1986.

Cohen, Philip. "Monstrous Images, Perverse Reasons: Cultural Studies in Anti-Racist Education." *Working Paper No. 11*. London: Centre for Multicultural Education, University of London Institute of Education, 1991.

Cohen, Stan. *Folk Devils And Moral Panics: The Creation of the Mods and the Rockers*. London: MacGibbon and Kee, 1972.

Cohen, Jeff, and Solomon, Norman. "Guns, Ammo & Talk Radio," in *Eyes Right: Challenging The Right-Wing Backlash*. Ed. Chip Berlet. Boston: South End Press, 1995, pp. 241-243.

Collier, Peter, and Horowitz, David. *Destructive Generation: Second Thoughts about the Sixties*. New York: Summit Books, 1989.

———. Eds. *Surviving the PC University*. Studio City, California: Center for the Study of Popular Culture, 1993.

Collins Hill, Patricia. *Black Feminist Thought: Knowledge, Consciousness and the Politics of Empowerment.* New York: Routledge, 1991.

Conran, Tom. "Men on the Verge of a Nervous Breakdown: The Dissolution of Privilege, the Deconstruction of Identity, and the Attraction of Violence." Paper presented at the Sixth Annual Midwest Radical Scholars & Activists Conference, Loyola University, Chicago, October 29, 1995.

Crews, Frederick. *Skeptical Engagements.* New York: Oxford University Press, 1986.

Culler, Jonathan. *Structuralist Poetics: Structuralism, Linguistics and the Study of Literature.* Ithaca, New York: Cornell University Press, 1976.

Cultural Conservatism: Toward A New Agenda. Washington, D.C.: Institute for Cultural Conservatism/Free Congress Research and Education Foundation, 1987.

Dasenbrock, Reed Way. "We've Done It To Ourselves: The Critique of Truth and the Attack on Theory," in *PC Wars: Politics And Theory In The Academy.* New York and London: Routledge, 1995, pp. 172-183.

Davidson, Carl. *The New Radicals in the Multiversity.* Chicago: Kerr Publishing, 1967.

Davies, Ioan. *Cultural Studies and Beyond: Fragments of Empire.* London and New York: Routledge, 1995.

Davis, Mike. *City of Quartz: Excavating The Future In Los Angeles.* London and New York: Verso, 1990.

————. "A Prison-Industrial Complex: Hell Factories in the Field." *The Nation* (February 20, 1995, vol. 260, no. 7):229-234.

Davis, Ray. "Anti-Racist Organizing, Then And Now." *Socialist Review* (Oct.-Dec., 1990, vol. 20, no. 4):29-36.

de Lauretis, Teresa. "Displacing Hegemonic Discourses: Reflections on Feminist Theory in the 1980s." *Inscriptions: Feminism & The Critique of Colonial Discourse.* (1988, nos. 3&4):127-144.

Delaney, Lawrence J., and Lenkowsky, Leslie. "The New Voice on Campus: 'Alternative Student Journalism.'" *Academic Questions* (Spring, 1988, vol. 1, no. 2):32-38.

Derrida, Jacques. *Of Grammatology.* Trans. Gayatri Spivak. Baltimore: Johns Hopkins University Press, 1976.

————. *Writing and Difference.* Trans. Alan Bass Chicago: University of Chicago Press, 1978.

————. *Positions.* Trans. Alan Bass. Chicago: University of Chicago Press, 1981.

————. *Specters of Marx: The State of the Debt, the Work of Mourning & the New International.* Trans. Peggy Kamuf. New York and London: Routledge, 1994.

Diamond, Sara. "Endowing The Right-Wing Academic Agenda." *Covert Action: Information Bulletin* (Fall, 1991, no. 38):46-49.

————. *Roads To Dominion: Right-Wing Movements and State Power in the United States, 1945 to the Present.* New York: Guilford Press, 1995[a].

————. "Managing the Anti-P.C. Industry," in *After Political Correctness: The Humanities and Society in the 1990s.* Eds. Christopher Newfield and Ronald Strickland. Boulder, Colorado: Westview Press, 1995[b].

————. "God Stuffs the Ballot Box." *The Nation* (October 9, 1995(c), vol. 261, no. 11):386-388.

Diggins, John Patrick. *The Rise and Fall of the American Left.* New York: W.W. Norton & Co., 1992.

Dirlik, Arif. "Culturalism as Hegemonic Ideology and Liberating Practice." *Cultural Critique* (Spring, 1987, no. 6):13-50.

Dodge, Susan. "A National Network Helps Conservative Students Set Up 58 Newspapers On College Campuses." *Chronicle of Higher Education* (May 9, 1990):35-37.

————. "Campus Codes That Ban Hate Speech Are Rarely Used To Penalize Students." *The Chronicle of Higher Education* (February 12, 1992):A35-A36.

Dorrien, Gary. *The Neoconservative Mind: Politics, Culture and the War of Ideology.* Philadelphia: Temple University Press, 1993.

Draper, Hal. *Berkeley: The New Student Revolt.* New York: Grove Press, 1965.

Duster, Troy. "They're Taking Over and Other Myths about Race on Campus." *Mother Jones* (Sept./Oct., 1991):30-33, 63-64.

————. "What's New in the IQ Debate." *The Black Scholar* (Winter, 1995, vol. 25, no. 1):25-31.

Dyer, Richard. "White." *Screen* (1988, vol. 29, no. 4):44-64.

D'Souza, Dinesh. *Falwell, Before the Millennium: A Critical Biography.* Chicago: Regnery Gateway, 1984.

————. *Illiberal Education: The Politics of Race and Sex on Campus.* New York: Random House, 1992.

————. *The End of Racism: Principles for a Multicultural Society.* New York: The Free Press, 1995.

Eagleton, Terry. *Literary Theory: An Introduction*. Minneapolis: University of Minnesota Press, 1983.

———. *Against The Grain*. London and New York: Verso Press, 1986.

———. *Ideology: An Introduction*. London and New York: Verso Press, 1991.

———. *The Illusions of Postmodernism*. Cambridge, Massachusetts: Blackwell, 1996.

Easterbrook, Gregg. "Blacktop Basketball and The Bell Curve," in *The Bell Curve Debate: History, Documents, Opinions*. Eds. Russell Jacoby and Naomi Glauberman. New York: Random House, 1995, pp. 30-43.

Ebert, Teresa. "Political Semiosis In/Of American Cultural Studies." *American Journal of Semiotics* (1991, vol. 8):113-135.

———. "Ludic Feminism, The Body, Performance, and Labor: Bringing *Materialism* Back Into Feminist Cultural Studies." *Cultural Critique* (Winter, 1992/93, no. 23):5-50.

———. "The Knowable Good: Post-al Politics, Ethics and Red Feminism." *Rethinking Marxism* (Summer, 1995, vol. 8, no. 2):39-59.

———. *Ludic Feminism And After*. Ann Arbor: University of Michigan Press, 1996.

Echols, Alice. "We Gotta Get Out Of This Place": Notes Toward a Remapping of the Sixties," in *Cultural Politics and Social Movements*. Eds. Marcy Darnovsky, Barbara Epstein and Richard Flacks. Philadelphia: Temple University Press, 1995, pp. 110-130.

Eco, Umberto. *Travels In Hyperreality*. New York: Harcourt, Brace and Jovanovich, 1990.

———. "Eternal Fascism." *UTNE Reader* (Nov-Dec. 1995, no. 72):57-59.

Ehrenreich, Barbara. "The Challenge For The Left," in *Debating P.C.: The Controversy Over Political Correctness On College Campuses*. Ed. Paul Berman. New York: Dell Publishing, 1992, pp. 333-338.

Epstein, Barbara. "Responses To Aronowitz." *Socialist Review* (1994, vol. 23, no. 3):107-111.

———. "Political Correctness and Collective Powerless," in *Cultural Politics and Social Movements*. Eds. Marcy Darnovsky, Barbara Epstein and Richard Flacks. Philadelphia: Temple University Press, 1995, pp. 3-19.

———. "Why Poststructuralism Is a Dead End For Progressive Thought," forthcoming in *Socialist Review* (1996).

Evans, M. Stanton. *Revolt On The Campus*. Chicago: Henry Regnery Co., 1961.

Faludi, Susan. *Backlash: The Undeclared War Against American Women*. New York: Crown Publishers, Inc., 1991.

Feagin, Joe, and Vera, Hernan. *White Racism*. New York and London: Routledge, 1995.

Ferguson, Sarah. "The Campus and Beyond." *Village Voice Education Supplement* (August 20, 1991):6.

———. "The Comfort of Being Sad." *UTNE Reader* (July/Aug., 1994, no.64):60-62.

Ferguson, Thomas, and Rogers, Joel. *Right Turn: The Decline of the Democrats and the Future of American Politics*. New York: Hill and Wang, 1986.

Finn, Chester. "The Campus: 'An Island of Repression in a Sea of Freedom.'" *Commentary* (Sept. 1989, vol. 88, no. 3):17-23.

Fish, Stanley. *There's No Such Thing As Free Speech . . . and it's a good thing too*. New York and Oxford: Oxford University Press, 1994.

Flacks, Richard et al. "Port Huron: Agenda For A Generation." *Socialist Review* (May-Aug. 1987, vol. 17, nos. 3&4):105-66.

Foley, Barbara. "Marxism in the Poststructuralist Moment: Some Notes on the Problem of Revising Marx." *Cultural Critique*, (Spring, 1990, no. 15):5-37.

Foner, Eric. "Race and the Conservatives." *Dissent* (Winter, 1996):105-109.

Foster, Douglas. "The Disease is Adolescence." *UTNE Reader* (July/Aug., 1994, no. 64):50-56.

Foster, Hal. "Postmodernism: A Preface." *The Anti-Aesthetic: Essays On Postmodern Culture*. Seattle, Washington: Bay Press, 1983, pp. ix-xvi.

Foucault, Michel. *Power/Knowledge: Selected Interviews and Other Writings, 1972-1977*. Ed. C. Gordon. Brighton: Harverster, 1980.

———. "The Subject and Power," in *Michel Foucault: Beyond Structuralism and Hermeneutics*. Eds. H. Dreyfus and Paul Rabinow. Chicago: Chicago University Press, 1982.

Frankenberg, Ruth. *White Women, Race Matters: The Social Construction of Whiteness*. Minneapolis: University of Minnesota Press, 1993.

Fraser, Steven. "Introduction," in *The Bell Curve Wars*. New York: Harper Collins, 1995, pp. 1-10.

Freire, Paulo. *Pedagogy of the Oppressed*. New York: Seabury Press, 1970.

———. *Pedagogy of the City*. Trans. Donaldo Macedo. New York: Continuum Publishing Co., 1993.

Fusco, Coco. "Fantasies of Oppositionality." *Afterimage* (Dec. 1988, vol. 16, no. 5):6-9.

Gallagher, Charles A. "White Reconstruction in the University." *Socialist Review* (1994, vol. 24, nos. 1&2):165-187.

Gates, Henry Louis. "The Master's Pieces: On Canon Formation and the African-American Tradition," in *The Politics of Liberal Education*. Eds. Darryl J. Gless and Barbara Herrnstein Smith. Durham: Duke University Press, 1992, pp. 95-117.

Genovese, Eugene D. "Living With Inequality," in *The Bell Curve Debate: History, Documents, Opinions*. Eds. Russell Jacoby and Naomi Glauberman. New York: Times Books, 1995, pp. 331-334.

Geras, Norman. "Post-Marxism?" *New Left Review* (1987, no. 163):40-82.

Giddens, Anthony. *The Constitution of Society*. Berkeley and Los Angeles: University of California Press, 1984.

Gilroy, Paul. *'There Ain't No Black in the Union Jack': The Cultural Politics of Race and Nation*. Chicago: University of Chicago Press, 1991.

Ginsberg, Elaine and, Lennox, Sara. "Antifeminism in Scholarship and Publishing," in *AntiFeminism in the Academy*. Eds. Veve Clark et al. New York: Routledge, 1996, pp. 169-199.

Giroux, Henry. *Border Crossings: Cultural Workers and the Politics of Education*. New York and London: Routledge, 1992.

———. *Living Dangerously: Multiculturalism and the Politics of Difference*. New York: Peter Lang Publishing, 1993.

———. *Disturbing Pleasures*. New York and London: Routledge, 1994.

———. "Beyond The Ivory Tower: Public Intellectuals and the Crisis of Higher Education," in *Higher Education Under Fire: Politics, Economics and the Crisis of the Humanities*. Eds. Michael Berube and Cary Nelson. New York and London: Routledge, 1995, pp. 238-258.

———. "White Panic." *Z Magazine* (March, 1995):12-14.

———. "Talk Radio, Public Intellectuals and Right Wing Pedagogy." *The Cultural Studies Times* (Fall, 1995):1, 5.

———. *Fugitive Cultures: Race, Violence and Youth*. New York: Routledge, 1996.

Gitlin, Todd. *The Whole World Is Watching: Mass Media in the Making and Unmaking of the New Left*. Berkeley: University of California Press, 1980.

———. *The Sixties: Years of Hope, Days of Rage*. New York: Bantam Books, 1987.

———. "On The Virtues of a Loose Canon," in *Beyond P.C.: Towards a Politics of Understanding*. Minnesota: Graywolf Press, 1992, pp. 185-190.

———. "From Universality to Difference: Notes on the Fragmentation of the Idea of the Left," in *Social Theory and the Politics of Identity*. Ed. Craig Calhoun. Cambridge, Massachusetts: Blackwell, 1994, pp. 150-174.

———. *The Twilight of Common Dreams: Why America Is Wracked By Culture Wars*. New York: Henry Holt & Co., 1995.

Glick, Brian. *War At Home*. Boston: South End Press, 1989.

Goldberg, David Theo, Ed. "The Social Formation of Racist Discourse," in *Anatomy of Racism*. Minneapolis: University of Minnesota Press, 1990, pp. 295-318.

———. *Racist Culture: Philosophy and the Politics of Meaning*. Cambridge, Massachusetts: Blackwell, 1993.

———. "Introduction: Multicultural Conditions," in *Multiculturalism: A Critical Reader*. Cambridge, Massachusetts: Blackwell, 1994, pp. 1-41.

Goldstein, Richard. "Save the Males: The Making of the Butch Backlash." *Village Voice* (March 7, 1995):25-29.

Goldwater, Barry. *The Conscience of a Conservative*. Washington, D.C.: Regnery Gateway, 1990 [orig. 1960].

Gordon, Lewis. *Fanon and the Crisis of European Man: An Essay on Philosophy and the Human Sciences*. New York and London: Routledge, 1995.

Gottfried, Paul, and Fleming, Thomas. *The Conservative Movement*. Boston: Twayne Publishers, 1988.

Gottfried, Paul. "Populism vs. Neoconservatism." *Telos* (Winter, 1991/92, no. 90)

———. *The Conservative Movement, 2nd Edition*. New York: Twayne Publishers, 1993.

Graff, Gerald. *Beyond The Culture Wars: How Teaching The Conflicts Can Revitalize American Education*. New York and London: W.W. Norton & Co., 1992.

Gramsci, Antonio. *Lettere Dal Carcere*. Ed. Felice Platone. Torino, Italy: Einaudi), 1949.

———. *Selections from the Prison Notebooks*. Ed. and trans. Quintin Hoare and Geoffrey Nowell Smith. New York: International Publishers, 1971.

Grimshaw, Jean. *Philosophy and Feminist Thinking*. Minneapolis: University of Minnesota Press, 1986.

Grossberg, Lawrence. *We Gotta Get Out Of This Place: Popular Conservatism and Postmodern Culture*. New York: Routledge, 1992.

―――. "History, Politics and Postmodernism: Stuart Hall and Cultural Studies," in *Stuart Hall: Critical Dialogues In Cultural Studies*. Eds. David Morley and Kuan-Hsing Chen. London and New York: Routledge, 1996[a], pp. 151-173.

―――. "Identity and Cultural Studies: Is That All There Is?" in *Questions of Cultural Identity*. Eds. Stuart Hall and Paul duGay. London: Sage Publications, 1996[b], pp. 87-107.

Hacker, Andrew. "Affirmative Action: The New Look." *New York Review of Books* (Oct.12, 1989):65.

―――. *Two Nations: Black and White, Separate, Hostile, Unequal*. New York: Charles Scribner's Sons, 1992.

―――. "The Crackdown on African-Americans." *The Nation* (July 10, 1995):45-46, 48-49.

Hager, Mark M. "The Real Orthodoxy Network." *Z Magazine* (April 1992, vol. 5, no. 4):58-62.

Hall, Stuart, et al. *Policing The Crisis: Mugging, The State and Law and Order*. London: Macmillan, 1978.

Hall, Stuart. "Teaching Race," in *The School in the Multicultural Society*. Eds. A. James and R. Jeffcoate. London: Harper and Row, 1981, pp. 58-69.

―――. "Minimal Selves." *Identity: ICA Document #6*. London: Institute For Contemporary Arts, 1987, pp. 44-46.

―――. "The Toad in the Garden: Thatcherism among the Theorists," in *Marxism and the Interpretation of Culture*. Eds. Cary Nelson and Lawrence Grossberg. Urbana and Chicago: University of Illinois Press, 1988, pp. 35-57.

―――. *The Hard Road to Renewal: Thatcherism and the Crisis of the Left*. London and New York: Verso Press, 1988.

―――. "New Ethnicities." *Black Film, British Cinema: ICA Document # 7*. London: Institute For Contemporary Arts, 1988, pp. 27-31.

―――. "Brave New World." *Socialist Review* (Jan.-Mar., 1991, vol. 21, no. 1):57-64.

―――. "Some 'Politically Incorrect' Pathways Through PC," in *The War Of The Words: The Political Correctness Debate* Ed. Sarah Dunant. London: Virago Press, 1994, pp. 164-183.

―――. "Gramsci's Relevance for the Study of Race and Ethnicity," in *Stuart Hall: Critical Dialogues In Cultural Studies*. Eds. David Morley and Kuan-Hsing Chen. London and New York: Routledge, 1996, pp. 411-440.

Hammer, Rhonda. "On Colonization." Unpublished Ph.D. Dissertation, 1997.

Haraway, Donna. "The Promises of Monsters: A Regenerative Politics for Inappropriate/d Others," in *Cultural Studies*. Eds. Grossberg et al. New York and London: Routledge, 1992, pp. 295-337.

Harvey, David. *The Condition of Postmodernity*. Cambridge, Massachusetts: Basil Blackwell, 1989.

———. "Flexibility: Threat or Opportunity?" *Socialist Review* (Jan.-Mar., 1991, vol. 21, no. 1):65-77.

Hayden, Tom, and Rice, Connie. "California Cracks Its Mortarboards." *The Nation* (Sept. 18, 1995):264-266.

Hayes, Floyd W. "Fanon, Oppression, and Resentment: The Black Experience in the United States," in *Fanon: A Critical Reader*. Eds. Lewis Gordon, T. Denean Sharpley-Whiting and Renee T. White. Cambridge, Massachusetts: Blackwell, 1996, pp. 11-23.

Hayward, Steven. "Feminism as a Festering Ideology." *New Perspectives* (Winter, 1988):53-54.

Hebdige, Dick. "Some Sons and Their Fathers." *Borderlines* (Spring, 1988, no. 11):29-35.

Hennessy, Rosemary. *Materialist Feminism and the Politics of Discourse*. New York and London: Routledge, 1993.

Henry, William A. "Upside Down in the Groves of Academe." *Time* (April 1, 1991):66-69.

Henson, Scott. "The Education of Dinesh D'Souza." *The Texas Observer* (Sept. 20, 1991):6-7, 9.

Henson, Scott, and Philpott, Tom. "The Right Declares A Culture War." *The Humanist* (March/April, 1992):10-16, 46.

Hentoff, Nat. "Speech Codes and Free Speech," in *Beyond P.C.: Towards a Politics of Understanding*. Ed. Patricia Aufderheide. Minnesota: Graywolf Press, 1992, pp. 50-58.

Herman, Edward S., and Chomsky, Noam. *Manufacturing Consent*. New York: Pantheon Books, 1988.

Herman, Edward S. *Beyond Hypocrisy: Decoding the News in an Age of Propaganda*. Boston: South End Press, 1992.

Herrnstein, Richard, and Murray, Charles. *The Bell Curve*. New York: The Free Press, 1994.

Himmelstein, Jerome L. *To The Right: The Transformation of American Conservatism*. Berkeley: University of California Press, 1990.

Hobsbawn, E., and Ranger, T. Eds. *The Invention of Tradition*. Cambridge: Cambridge University Press, 1983.

Hobsbawn, Eric. "The Cult of Identity Politics." *New Left Review* (May/June, 1996, no. 217):38-47.

Hoffman, Abbie. *The Best of Abbie Hoffman*. New York: Four Walls, Eight Windows, 1989.

Hofstadter, Richard. *Anti-Intellectualism in American Life*. New York: Vintage Books, 1962.

Hoggart, Richard. *The Way We Live Now*. London: Pimlico, 1996.

Holland, Norman. *The Critical "I"*. New York: Columbia University Press, 1992.

Hollander, Paul. "From Iconoclasm to Conventional Wisdom: The Sixties in the Eighties." *Academic Questions* (Fall, 1989, vol.2, no.4):31- 38.

hooks, bell. *Feminist Theory: From Margin To Centre*. Boston: South End Press, 1984.

―――. *Talking Back: Thinking Feminist, Thinking Black* Boston: South End Press, 1989.

hooks, bell, and West, Cornel. *Breaking Bread: Insurgent Black Intellectual Life*. Toronto: Between The Lines, 1991.

hooks, bell. *Black Looks*. Toronto: Between The Lines, 1992.

―――. *Outlaw Culture: Resisting Representations*. New York and London: Routledge, 1994.

―――. *Killing Rage: Ending Racism*. New York: Henry Holt & Co., 1995[a].

―――. "Intellectual Life In And Beyond The Academy." *Z Magazine* (November, 1995 [b]):25-29.

Horkheimer, Max, and Adorno, Theodor. *Dialectic Of Enlightenment*. Trans. John Cumming. New York: Continuum Publishing Co., 1993 [orig. 1944].

Horkheimer, Max. *Critical Theory*. Trans. Matthew J. O'Connell et al. New York: Seabury Press, 1972.

Houston, Patrick. "He Wants to Pull the Plug on the PC." *Newsweek* (December 24, 1990):52-53.

Howe, Irving. "The Agony of the Campus." *Dissent* (Sept./Oct. (1969):387-394.

Hudson, J. Blaine. "Scientific Racism: The Politics of Tests, Race and Genetics." *The Black Scholar* (Winter, 1995, vol. 25, no. 1):3-10.

Hughes, Robert. *Culture of Complaint.* New York: Warner Books, 1993.

Iannone, Carol. "Feminism and Literature." *New Criterion* (Nov., 1985, vol. 4, no. 3):83-87.

———. "The Barbarism of Feminist Scholarship." *Intercollegiate Review* (Fall, 1987, vol. 23, no. 1):35-41.

———. "Feminist Follies." *Academic Questions* (Winter, 1987/88):45-47.

———. "Analyzing a Feminist Whine." *American Spectator* (May, 1988):30-31.

Institute for First Amendment Studies. "Who To Challenge," in *Eyes Right!: Challenging The Right Wing Backlash.* Ed. Chip Berlet. Boston: South End Press, 1995, pp. 368-370.

Isserman, Maurice. "Travels With Dinesh." *Tikkun* (Sept/Oct., 1991, vol. 6, no. 5):81-84.

Ivins, Molly. "Lyin' Bully." *Mother Jones* (May/June, 1995):36-38.

Jacoby, Russell. *Social Amnesia: A Critique of Contemporary Psychology from Adler to Laing.* Boston: Beacon Press, 1975.

———. *The Last Intellectuals: American Culture in the Age of Academe.* New York: Noonday Press, 1987.

———. *Dogmatic Wisdom: How The Culture Wars Divert Education and Distract America.* New York: Doubleday, 1994.

Jacoby, Russell, and Glauberman, Naomi, eds. *The Bell Curve Debate: History, Documents, Opinions.* New York: Random House, 1995.

Jameson, Fredric. *The Political Unconscious: Narrative as a Socially Symbolic Act.* Ithaca, New York: Cornell University Press, 1981.

———. *Late Marxism: Adorno, or, The Persistence of the Dialectic.* London: Verso Books, 1990.

Jay, Gregory, and Graff, Gerald. "A Critique of Critical Pedagogy," in *Higher Education Under Fire: Politics, Economics and the Crisis of the Humanities.* Eds. Michael Berube and Cary Nelson. New York and London: Routledge, 1995, pp. 201-213.

Jay, Martin. *The Dialectical Imagination.* Berkeley: University of California Press, 1996 [orig.1973].

Jewett, Robert, and Lawrence, John. *The American Monomyth.* Lanham, Maryland: University Press of America, 1988.

Jordan, June. *On Call: Political Essays.* Boston: South End Press, 1985.

Junas, Daniel. "Rev. Moon Goes To College." *Covert Action* (Fall, 1991, no. 38):22-27.

————. "The Rise of Citizen Militias: Angry White Guys with Guns," in *Eyes Right: Challenging The Right Wing Backlash*. Ed. Chip Berlet. Boston: South End Press, 1995, pp. 226-235.

Kamin, Leon J. "Lies, Damned Lies, and Statistics," in *The Bell Curve Debate: History, Documents, Opinions*. Eds. Russel Jacoby and Naomi Glauberman. New York: Random House, 1995, pp. 81-105.

Kang, Liu. "Subjectivity, Marxism and Culture Theory in China." *Social Text* (1992, vol. 10, nos. 2&3):114-140.

Kauffman, L.A. "The Anti-Politics of Identity." *Socialist Review* (1990, vol. 20, no. 1):67-80.

Kellner, Douglas. "Ideology, Marxism, And Advanced Capitalism." *Socialist Review* (1978, vol. 8, no. 6):37-65.

————. *Herbert Marcuse and the Crisis of Marxism*. California: University of California Press, 1984.

————. "Critical Theory and the Crisis of Social Theory." *Sociological Perspectives* (1990, vol. 33, no. 1):11-33.

————. *The Persian Gulf TV War*. Boulder, Colorado: Westview Press, 1992.

————. *Media Culture*. London and New York: Routledge, 1995.

Kennedy, Randall. "The Phony War," in *The Bell Curve Wars*. Ed. Steven Fraser. New York: Harper Collins, 1995, pp. 179-186.

Kenway, Jane. "Education and the Right's Discursive Politics," in *Foucault and Education: Disciplines and Knowledge*. Ed. Stephen J. Ball. London and New York: Routledge, 1990, pp. 167-296.

Kimball, Roger. "Review of *The Closing of the American Mind*." *The New York Times Book Review* (April, 5, 1987):7.

————. *Tenured Radicals: How Politics Has Corrupted Our Higher Education*. New York: Harper and Row, 1991.

————. "Dragon Lady of Academe." *Wall Street Journal* (Sept. 17, 1992):A14.

Kincheloe, Joe, and McLaren, Peter. "Rethinking Critical Theory and Qualitative Research," in *Handbook of Qualitative Research*. California: Sage Publications, 1994, pp. 138-157.

Kincheloe, Joe. "Afterword," in *Politics of Liberation: Paths from Freire*. Eds. Peter McLaren and Colin Lankshear. New York and London: Routledge, 1994, pp. 216-218.

————, Steinberg, Shirley, R. and Gresson, Aaron, D. Eds. *Measured Lies: The Bell Curve Examined*. Toronto: OISE Press, 1996

Kirk, Russell. *A Program for Conservatives*. Chicago: Henry Regnery Co., 1962.

Kohl, Herbert. "The Politically Correct Bypass: Multiculturalism and the Public Schools." *Social Policy* (Summer, 1991):33-40.

Kovel, Joel. *History And Spirit: An Inquiry Into The Philosophy of Liberation.* Boston: Beacon Press, 1991.

———. *Red Hunting in the Promised Land: Anticommunism and the Making of America.* New York: Harper Collins, 1994.

Kristol, Irving. "Teaching In, Speaking Out: The Controversy over VietNam." *Encounter* (August 2, 1965, vol. 25, no. 2):66-69.

———. "A Different Way to Restructure the University." *New York Times Magazine* (December 8, 1968).

———. *Two Cheers for Capitalism.* New York: Basic Books, 1978.

Kruks, Sonia. "Fanon, Sartre and Identity Politics," in *Fanon: A Critical Reader.* Eds. Gordon et al. Cambridge, Massachusetts: Blackwell, 1996, pp. 122-133.

Lacan, Jacques *Ecrits.* Trans. Alan Sheridan. New York: W.W. Norton & Co., 1977.

Laclau, Ernesto, and Mouffe, Chantal. *Hegemony and Socialist Strategy.* London: Verso Books, 1985.

Laclau, Ernesto. "Universalism, Particularism, and the Question of Identity." *October* (Summer, 1992, no. 61):83-90.

Lambrose, R.J. "Culture and Anarchy." *The Nation* (June 4, 1990):791-795.

Langman, Lauren, and Scatamburlo, Valerie. "The Self Strikes Back: Identity Politics in the Postmodern Age," in *Alienation, Ethnicity And Postmodernism.* Ed. Felix Geyer. Connecticut: Greenwood Publishing, 1996, pp. 127-138.

Larew, John. "Why Are Droves of Unqualified, Unprepared Kids Getting Into Our Top Colleges? Because Their Dads Are Alumni." *Washington Monthly* (June, 1991):10-14.

Lazere, Donald. "Cultural Studies: Countering a Depoliticized Culture," in *After Political Correctness: The Humanities and Society in the 1990s.* Eds. Christopher Newfield and Ronald Strickland. Boulder, Colorado: Westview Press, 1995, pp. 340-360.

Lee, Martin A., and Shlain, Bruce. *Acid Dreams: The Complete Social History of LSD: The CIA, The Sixties, and Beyond.* New York: Grove Weidenfeld, 1985.

Lee, Martin, and Solomon, Norman. *Unreliable Sources.* U.S.A.: Lyle Stuart, 1990.

Levin, Michael. "Affirmative Action Philosophy." *Academic Questions* (Spring, 1988, vol. 1, no. 2):16-22.

Levitas, Ruth, ed. *The Ideology of the New Right.* Cambridge: Polity Press, 1986.

Limbaugh, Rush. *See, I Told You So.* New York: Pocket Books, 1994.

Lind, Michael. "Brave New Right," in *The Bell Curve Wars.* Ed. Steven Fraser. New York: Harper Collins, 1995, pp.172-178.

Lind, William. "What Is Cultural Conservatism?" *Essays in Our Times* (March, 1986, vol. 2, no. 1):1-8.

Lind, William S., and Marshner, William H. eds. *Cultural Conservatism: Theory And Practice.* Washington, D.C.: Free Congress Foundation, 1991.

Lipsitz, George. *Time Passages.* Minneapolis: University of Minnesota Press, 1990.

Lloyd, Genevieve. *The Man of Reason.* Minneapolis: University of Minnesota Press, 1984.

London, Herbert. "Marxism Thriving on American Campuses." *World & I* (1987):189-190.

———. "A Call To The Academy." *Academic Questions* (Winter, 1987/88, vol. 1, no. 1):3-4.

Lorde, Audre. *Sister Outsider.* California: The Crossing Press, 1984.

Lowe, Lisa. *Critical Terrains: French And British Orientalisms* Ithaca: Cornell University Press, 1991.

Lyotard, Jean-Francois. *The Postmodern Condition.* Minneapolis: University of Minnesota Press, 1984.

Madison Center for Educational Affairs 1990 Annual Report. Washington, D.C.: Madison Center for Educational Affairs.

Madison Center for Educational Affairs 1991 Annual Report. Washington, D.C.: Madison Center for Educational Affairs.

Maharidge, Dale. "Walled Off." *Mother Jones* (Nov/Dec., 1994, vol. 19, no. 6):26-33.

Marcuse, Herbert. *An Essay On Liberation.* Boston: Beacon Press, 1969.

———. *Counter-Revolution And Revolt.* Boston: Beacon Press, 1972.

Marx, Karl. "Theses on Feuerbach," in *The Marx-Engels Reader.* Ed. Robert Tucker. New York: W.W. Norton & Company, 1978, pp. 143-145.

———."For A Ruthless Critism of Everything Existing: Letter to Arnold Ruge," in *The Marx-Engels Reader*. Ed. Robert Tucker. New York: W.W. Norton & Co., 1978, pp. 12-15.

———. *The Eighteenth Brumaire of Louis Bonaparte*. New York: International Publishers, 1984.

Marx, Karl, and Engels, Friedrich. "The German Ideology, Part 1," in *The Marx-Engels Reader*. Ed. Robert Tucker. New York: W.W. Norton & Co., 1978, pp. 146-200.

McLaren, Peter. "Critical Pedagogy: Constructing an Arch of Social Dreaming and a Doorway to Hope." *Journal of Education* (1991, vol. 173, no. 1):9-34.

———. "Multiculturalism and the Postmodern Critique: Toward a Pedagogy of Resistance and Transformation," in *Between Borders: Pedagogy and the Politics of Cultural Studies*. Eds. Henry Giroux and Peter McLaren. New York and London: Routledge, 1994[a], pp. 192-222.

———. "White Terror and Oppositional Agency: Towards A Critical Multiculturalism," in *Multiculturalism: A Critical Reader*. Ed. David Theo Goldberg. Cambridge, Massachusetts: Blackwell, 1994[b], pp. 45-74.

———. "Postmodernism and the Death of Politics: A Brazilian Reprieve," in *Politics of Liberation: Paths From Freire*. Eds. Peter McLaren and Colin Lankshear. New York and London: Routledge, 1994 [c], pp. 193-215.

———. *Critical Pedagogy And Predatory Culture*. London and New York: Routledge, 1995.

———. *Revolutionary Multiculturalism: Pedagogies of Dissent for the New Millennium*. Boulder, Colorado: Westview Press, 1997.

Menand, Louis. "What Are Universities For?" *Harpers* (Dec. 1991):47-57.

Mercer, Kobena. "1968: Periodizing Postmodern Politics and Identity," in *Cultural Studies*. Eds. Lawrence Grossberg et al. New York: Routledge, 1992, pp. 424-437.

———. *Welcome To The Jungle*. New York: Routledge, 1994.

Messer-Davidow, Ellen. "Manufacturing the Attack on Liberalized Higher Education." *Social Text* (Fall, 1993, vol. 11, no. 3):40-80.

Meyer, Frank S. *In Defense of Freedom: A Conservative Credo*. Chicago: Henry Regnery Co., 1962.

Miller, Adam. "Professors Of Hate," in *The Bell Curve Debate: History, Documents, Opinions*. Eds. Russell Jacoby and Naomi Glauberman. New York: Times Books, 1995, pp. 162-178.

Miller, James. *Democracy Is In The Streets: From Port Huron To The Siege of Chicago*. New York: Simon and Schuster, 1987.

Mills, C. Wright. *The Sociological Imagination*. Oxford and New York: Oxford University Press, 1959.

Milner, Andrew. *Contemporary Cultural Theory*. London: UCL Press, 1994.

Mohanty, Chandra Talpade. "Cartographies of Struggle: Third World Women and the Politics of Feminism," in *Third World Women And The Politics Of Feminism*. Eds. Mohanty et al. Bloomington and Indianapolis: Indiana University Press, 1991, pp. 1-47.

————. "On Race and Voice: Challenges for Liberal Education in the 1990s," in *Between Borders: Pedagogy and the Politics of Cultural Studies*. Eds. Henry Giroux and Peter McLaren. New York and London: Routledge, 1994, pp. 145-166.

Moraga, Cherrie, and Anzaldua, Gloria, eds. *This Bridge Called My Back: Writings By Radical Women Of Colour*. New York: Kitchen Table Press, 1983.

Morley, David, and Robins, Kevin. *Spaces of Identity: Global Media, Electronic Landscapes and Cultural Boundaries*. New York and London: Routledge, 1995.

Morrison, Toni. "Unspeakable Things Unspoken: The Afro-American Presence in American Literature." *Michigan Quarterly* (Winter, 1989, vol. 28, no. 1):1-34.

Mowatt, Raoul. "What Revolution At Stanford?" in *Beyond PC: Towards A Politics Of Understanding*. Ed. Patricia Aufderheide. Minnesota: Graywolf Press, 1992, pp. 129-132.

Mozzochi, Jonathan. "America Under The Gun: The Militia Movement & Hate Groups in America," in *Eyes Right: Challenging The Right Wing Backlash*. Ed. Chip Berlet. Boston: South End Press, 1995, pp. 236-240.

Murray, Charles. *Losing Ground: American Social Policy 1950-1980*. New York: Basic Books, 1984.

Nagel, Thomas. *The View From Nowhere*. Oxford: Oxford University Press, 1986.

Navasky, Victor S. *Naming Names*. New York: Penguin Books, 1980.

Neilson, Jim. "The Great PC Scare: Tyrannies of the Left, Rhetoric of the Right," in *PC Wars: Politics and Theory in the Academy*. Ed. Jeffrey Williams. New York and London: Routledge, 1995, pp. 60-89.

Nelson, Joyce. *Sultans of Sleaze: Public Relations and the Media*. Toronto: Between The Lines, 1989.

Nemeth, Thomas. *Gramsci's Philosophy: A Critical Study*. Great Britain: Hervester Press, 1980.

Newfield, Christopher. "What Was "Political Correctness"? Race, the Right, and Managerial Democracy in the Humanities," in *PC Wars: Politics and Theory in the Academy*. Ed. Jeffrey Williams. New York and London: Routledge, 1995, pp. 109-145.

Norris, Christopher. *What's Wrong With Postmodernism: Critical Theory and the Ends of Philosophy*. Baltimore: The John Hopkins University Press, 1990.

———. *Uncritical Theory: Postmodernism, Intellectuals, and the Gulf War*. Amherst: The University of Massachusetts Press, 1992.

———. *The Truth About Postmodernism*. Oxford, U.K. and Cambridge, Mass.: Blackwell, 1993.

———. *Reclaiming The Truth: Contribution to a Critique of Cultural Relativism*. Durham, North Carolina: Duke University Press, 1996.

"Notes from the YAF Rally." *National Review* (March 27, 1962):190-191.

Novack, George. *Humanism & Socialism*. New York: Pathfinder Press, 1973.

Oakley, J. Ronald. *God's Country: America in the Fifties*. New York: Dembner Books, 1986.

Ohmann, Richard. "On PC and Related Matters." *Minnesota Review* (Fall/ Winter, 1992/93, no. 39):55-62.

O'Neill, John. *The Poverty of Postmodernism*. New York and London: Routledge, 1995.

Paglia, Camille. *Sexual Personae: Art And Decadence From Nefertiti To Emily Dickinson*. New York: Random House, 1991[a].

———. "Ninnies, Pedants, Tyrants, and Other Academics." *New York Times Book Review* (May 5, 1991[b]).

———. *Sex, Art and American Culture*. New York: Random House, 1992.

Parenti, Michael. *Inventing Reality*. New York: St. Martins Press, 1986.

———. *Dirty Truths: Reflections on Politics, Media, Ideology, Conspiracy, Ethnic Life and Class Power*. San Francisco: City Lights Books, 1996.

Parmar, Pratibha. "Black Feminism: The Politics of Articulation," in *Identity, Community, Culture, Difference*. Ed. Jonathan Rutherford. London: Lawrence & Wishart, 1990, pp. 101-126.

Pearson, Roger. *Eugenics and Race*. London: Clair Press, 1966.

Peck, Abe. *Uncovering The Sixties*. New York: Pantheon Books, 1985.

Perry, Ruth. "A Short History of the Term Politically Correct," in *Beyond P.C.: Towards A Politics Of Understanding*. Ed. Patricia Aufderheide. Minnesota: Graywolf Press, 1992, pp. 71-79.

Peschek, Joseph G. *Policy Planning Organizations: Elite Agendas and America's Rightward Turn*. Philadelphia: Temple University Press, 1987.

Pinar, William et al. eds. *Understanding Curriculum*. New York: Peter Lang Publishing, 1995.

Pincus, Fred L. "From Equity to Excellence: The Rebirth of Educational Conservatism." *Social Policy* (Winter, 1984, vol .14, no. 3):50-56.

Pollitt, Katha. "Culture Bores." *The Nation* (July 3, 1995, vol. 261, no. 1):9.

————. "Pomolotov Cocktail." *The Nation* (June 10, 1996, vol. 262, no. 23):9.

Poster, Mark. *Critical Theory and Poststructuralism: In Search of a Context*. Ithaca and London: Cornel University Press, 1989.

Pratt, Linda Ray. "Going Public: Political Discourse and the Faculty Voice," in *Higher Education Under Fire: Politics, Economics, and the Crisis of the Humanities*. Eds. Micheal Berube and Cary Nelson. New York and London: Routledge, 1995, pp. 35-51.

Pratt, Mary Louise. "Humanities For The Future: Reflections on the Western Culture Debate at Stanford," in *The Politics of Liberal Education*. Eds. Darryl J. Gless and Barbara Herrnstein Smith. Durham, North Carolina: Duke University Press, 1992, pp.13-31.

Prescott, Peter S. "Learning To Love the PC Canon." *Newsweek* (December 24, 1990):50-51.

Quigley, Margaret. "The Roots of the I.Q. Debate: Eugenics And Social Control," in *Eyes Right! : Challenging The Right Wing Backlash*. Ed. Chip Berlet. Boston: South End Press, 1995, pp. 210-222.

Raskin, James. "The Fallacies Of Political Correctness." *Z Magazine* (January, 1992):31-37.

Raskin, Jamin. "Affirmative Action and Racial Reaction." *Z Magazine* (May, 1995):33-41.

Rau, Krishna, and Thompson, Clive. "Hate 101." *This Magazine* (March/April, 1995):18-24.

Reed, Adolph. "Looking Backward." *The Nation* (Nov. 28, 1994, vol. 259, no. 18):654-662.

Reed, Ralph E. "Christian Coalition: An Agenda For Congress." Remarks delivered to *The Economic Club Of Detroit*, Detroit, Michigan, January 17, 1995.

Rendall, Steven, Naureckas, Jim, and Cohen, Jeff. *The Way Things Aren't: Rush Limbaugh's Reign of Error*. New York: The New Press, 1995.

Richardson, Roderic R. "The Report on the Universities." *Inter-Department Memo*, Dec. 20, 1984.

Ridgeway, James. "Behind The Curve." *The Village Voice* (Nov. 15, 1994):15-16.

Robbins, Bruce. "Tenured Radicals, The New McCarthyism and Political Correctness." *Motifs* (July/Aug. 1991):151-157.

Roche, John P. "The New Left Vigilantes." *National Review* (Dec. 8, 1989):34-35.

Rodriguez, Lisa. "Rekindling the War." *UTNE Reader* (July/Aug. 1994, no. 64):58-59.

Roiphe, Katie. *The Morning After: Sex, Fear and Feminism*. Boston: Little, Brown, 1993.

Rosen, Ruth. "New Times, Fossil Minds on the Campus." *Los Angeles Times* (January 20, 1991).

Ross, Andrew. "The Fine Art of Regulation," in *The Phantom Public Sphere*. Ed. Bruce Robbins. Minneapolis: University of Minnesota Press, 1993, pp. 257-268.

————. "Demography Is Destiny." *The Village Voice* (Nov. 29, 1994):95-96.

Rothenberg, Paula. "Critics of Attempts to Democratize the Curriculum Are Waging a Campaign to Misrepresent the Work of Responsible Professors," in *Debating P.C.: The Controversy Over Political Correctness On College Campuses*. Ed. Paul Berman. New York: Dell Publishing, 1992, pp. 262-268.

Rothman, Stanley. "Professors in the Ascendent." *Academic Questions* (Fall, 1989, vol. 2, no. 4):45-51.

Rothmyer, Karen. "Citizen Scaife." *Columbia Journalism Review* (July/August, 1981):41-50.

Rutherford, Jonathan, ed. *Identity: Community, Culture, Difference*. London: Lawrence & Wishart, 1990.

Said, Edward. *Orientalism*. New York: Random House, 1978.

————. "Intellectuals in the Post-Colonial World." *Salmagundi* (Spring/Summer, 1986, vol. 70):44-81.

————. *Representations of the Intellectual*. New York: Vintage Books, 1996.

Saloma, John S. *Ominous Politics: The New Conservative Labyrinth*. New York: Hill & Wang, 1984.

Sarup, Madan. *An Introductory Guide To Post-structuralism and Post-modernism.* Athens, Georgia: University of Georgia Press, 1989.

Saussure, Ferdinand de. *Course in General Linguistics* [first published 1915] New York: McGraw-Hill, 1966.

Sautman, Barry. "Theories of East Asian Superiority," in *The Bell Curve Debate: History, Documents, Opinions.* Eds. Russell Jacoby and Naomi Glauberman. New York: Random House, 1995, pp. 201-221.

Schrecker, Ellen W. *No Ivory Tower: McCarthyism and the Universities.* New York: Oxford University Press, 1986.

———. "McCarthyism." in *Encyclopedia Of The American Left.* Eds. Mari Jo Buhle, Paul Buhle and Dan Georgakas. Urbana, Illinois: University of Illinois Press, 1992, pp. 457-460.

Scott, Joan Wallach. "Experience," in *Feminists Theorize The Political.* Eds. Judith Butler and Joan W. Scott. New York: Routledge, 1992, pp. 22-40.

———. "The Campaign Against Political Correctness: What's Really at Stake," in *After Political Correctness: The Humanities and Society in the 1990s.* Eds. Christopher Newfield and Ronald Strickland. Boulder, Colorado: Westview Press, 1995, pp. 111-127.

Sedgewick, John. "Inside The Pioneer Fund," in *The Bell Curve Debate.* Eds. Russel Jacoby and Naomi Glauberman. New York: Random House, 1995, pp. 144-161.

Shapiro, Bruce. "Rad-Baiting Comes To Brookline." *The Nation* (May 21, 1991):705-706.

"Sharon Statement." *National Review* (Sept. 24, 1960):173.

Shaw, Peter. "The Abandonment of Literature." *Academic Questions* (Winter, 1987/88, vol. 1, no. 1):41-44.

———. "Feminist Literary Criticism: A Report From The Academy." *American Scholar* (Autumn, 1988, vol. 57, no. 4):495-513.

Shor, Ira. *Culture Wars: School and Society in the Conservative Restoration, 1969-1984.* Chicago: University of Chicago Press, 1992.

Sigal, Leon. "Sources Make The News," in *Reading The News.* Eds. Robert Manoff and Michael Schudson. New York: Pantheon Books, 1986, pp. 9-37.

Simon, William E. *A Time For Truth.* New York: Reader's Digest Press, 1978.

Sklar, Holly. "The Dying American Dream," in *Eyes Right! : Challenging The Right Wing Backlash.* Ed. Chip Berlet. Boston: South End Press, 1995, pp. 113-134.

Smart, Barry. *Foucault, Marxism and Critique.* London: Routledge and Kegan Paul, 1983.

Smith, Dorothy. *The Everyday World as Problematic: A Feminist Sociology.* Toronto: University of Toronto Press, 1987.

———. "The Out-of-Body Experience: Contradictions For Feminism." Unpublished paper, 1993.

———. "Politically Correct: An Ideological Code." in *Beyond Political Correctness: Toward the Inclusive University.* Eds. Stephen Richer and Lorna Weir. Toronto: University of Toronto Press, 1995, pp. 23-50.

Smith, Doug. "The New McCarthyism." *Canadian Dimension* (Sept. 1991):8-13.

Smith, James A. *The Idea Brokers: Think Tanks and the Rise of the New Policy Elite.* New York: Free Press, 1991.

Sokal, Alan D. "Transgressing the Boundaries: Toward a Transformative Hermenetics of Quantum Gravity." *Social Text* (1996, vol. 14, nos. 1 & 2) 217-252.

Solomon, Norman. "The Media's Favorite Think Tank: How the Heritage Foundation Turns Money into Media." *Fair/Extra* (July/Aug., 1996, vol. 9, no. 4):9-12.

Sommers, Christina Hoff. *Who Stole Feminism? How Women Have Betrayed Women.* New York: Simon and Schuster, 1994.

Spivak, Gayatri Chakravorty. "Can The Subaltern Speak?" in *Marxism and the Interpretation of Culture.* Eds. Cary Nelson and Lawrence Grossberg. Urbana: University of Illinois Press, 1988, pp. 271-313

———. "The Making of Americans, the Teaching of English and the Future of Cultural Studies." *New Literary History* (1990, vol. 21, no. 4):781-798.

Stabile, Carol. "Another Brick in the Wall: (Re)contextualizing the Crisis," in *Higher Education Under Fire: Politics, Economics and the Crisis of the Humanities.* Eds. Michael Berube and Cary Nelson. New York and London: Routledge, 1995, pp. 108-125.

Stephanson, Anders. "Interview with Cornel West," in *Universal Abandon? The Politics of Postmodernism.* Ed. Andrew Ross. Minneapolis: University of Minnesota Press, 1988, pp. 269-286.

Students For A Democratic Society. *The Port Huron Statement.* Chicago: Charles H. Kerr Publishing Co., 1990 [orig. 1962].

Suzuki, David. *Inventing The Future.* Toronto: Stoddart Press, 1989.

Talbot, Stephen. "Wizard Of Ooze." *Mother Jones* (May/June, 1995):41-43.

Taubman, Peter. "Canonical Sins," in *Understanding Curriculum As Racial Text: Representations of Identity and Difference in Education*. Eds. L. Castenal and W. Pinar. Albany, New York: SUNY Press, 1993, pp. 35-52.

Taylor, John. "Are You Politically Correct?" *New York* (Jan. 21, 1991):32-40.

Terdiman, Richard. "The Politics of Political Correctness," in *After Political Correctness: The Humanities and Society in the 1990s*. Eds. Christopher Newfield and Ronald Strickland. Boulder, Colorado: Westview Press, 1995, pp. 238-252.

"The Magazine's Credenza." *National Review* (Nov. 19, 1955):6.

The Heritage Foundation 1991 Annual Report. Washington, D.C.: Heritage Foundation, 1992.

"The Return of the Storm Troopers." *Wall Street Journal* (April, 10, 1991):A10.

Thernstrom, Stephan. "McCarthyism Then and Now." *Academic Questions* (Winter, 1990/91, vol. 4, no. 1):14-16.

Thomas, Nicholas. *Colonialism's Culture: Anthroplogy, Travel And Government*. Princeton, New Jersey: Princeton University Press, 1994.

Tomasky, Michael. *Left for Dead: The Life, Death and Possible Resurrection of Progressive Politics in America*. New York: The Press, 1996.

Tuchman, Gaye. *Making News: A Study In The Construction Of Reality*. New York: The Free Press, 1978.

Turner, Mark. *Death is the Mother of Beauty: Mind, Metaphor, Criticism*. Chicago: University of Chicago Press, 1987.

Turner, Terence. "Anthropology and Multiculturalism: What Is Anthropology that Multiculturalists Should Be Mindful of It?" in *Multiculturalism: A Critical Reader*. Ed. David Theo Goldberg. Cambridge, Massachusetts: Blackwell, 1994, pp. 406-425.

Ventura, Michael. "The Age of Endarkment." *UTNE Reader* (July/Aug., 1994, no. 64):63-66.

Vogel, Jennifer. "Throw Away The Key." *UTNE Reader* (July/Aug., 1994, no. 64):56-60.

Wald, Alan M. *The Responsibility of Intellectuals: Selected Essays on Marxist Traditions in Cultural Commitment*. New Jersey and London: Humanities Press International, 1992.

Wallace, Michele. "Reading 1968 and the Great American Whitewash," in *Remaking History*. Eds. Barbara Kruger and Phil Mariani. Seattle: Bay Press, 1989, pp. 97-109.

————. "Multiculturalism and Oppositionality," in *Between Borders: Pedagogy and the Politics of Cultural Studies*. Eds. Henry Giroux and Peter McLaren. New York and London: Routledge, 1994, pp. 180-191.

Weisberg, Jacob. "NAS—Who Are These Guys, Anyway?" in *Beyond P.C.: Towards A Politics Of Understanding*. Ed. Patricia Aufderheide. Minnesota: Graywolf Press, 1992, pp. 80-88.

West, Cornel. *The Ethical Dimensions of Marxist Thought*. New York: Monthly Review Press, 1991.

————. "Decentering Europe." *Critical Inquiry* (1991, vol. 33, no.1):22-23.

————. *Prophetic Thought in Postmodern Times*, vols. 1&2. Maine: Common Courage Press, 1993.

Weyrich, Paul. "Letter to the Editor," *Mother Jones* (Jan/Feb., 1996):3.

Wiener, Jon. *Professors, Politics and Pop*. London and New York: Verso Press, 1990.

————. "What Happened at Harvard?" in *Beyond P.C.: Toward a Politics of Understanding*. Ed. Patricia Aufderheide. Minnesota: Graywolf Press, 1992, pp. 97-106.

Wildavsky, Aaron. "The Rise of Radical Egalitarianism and the Fall of Academic Standards." *Academic Questions* (Fall, 1989, vol. 2, no. 4):52-55.

Wilden, Anthony. *System and Structure: Essays in Communication and Exchange*. London: Tavistock Publications, 1972.

————. *The Imaginary Canadian*. Vancouver: Pulp Press, 1980.

————. *The Rules Are No Game: The Strategy of Communication*. London and New York: Routledge and Kegan Paul, 1987[a].

————. *Man and Woman, War and Peace*. London and New York: Routledge and Kegan Paul, 1987[b].

Wilentz, Sean. "Populism Redux." *Dissent* (Spring, 1995):149-153.

Wilkins, Roger. "The Case for Affirmative Action: Racism Has Its Privileges." *The Nation* (March 27, 1995, vol. 260, no.12):409-416.

Will, George. "Poisoning Higher Education." *Washington Post* (April, 21, 1991):B7.

————. "Literary Politics." *Newsweek* (April 22, 1991):72.

————. "Curdled Politics on Campus." *Newsweek* (May 6, 1991):72.

————. "The Cult of Ethnicity." *Washington Post* (July 14, 1991):C7.

————. "Catechism of Correctness." *Washington Post* (Oct., 1991):C7.

————. "Literary Politics," in *Beyond P.C.:Towards a Politics of Understanding.* Ed. Patricia Aufderheide. Minnesota: Graywolf Press, 1992, pp. 23-26.

Williams, Raymond. *Culture and Society.* London: The Hogarth Press, 1993 [orig. 1958].

————. *Problems in Materialism and Culture.* London: Verso Books, 1980.

Willis, Ellen. "The Median Is the Message." *Village Voice* (Nov. 15, 1994):31-32, 34.

Wilson, John R. *The Myth of Political Correctness: The Conservative Attack on Higher Education.* Durham, North Carolina: Duke University Press, 1995.

Winant, H. *Racial Conditions: Politics, Theory, Comparisons.* Minneapolis: University of Minnesota Press, 1994.

Winter, James P. *Common Cents: Media Portrayal of the Gulf War and Other Events.* Montreal and New York: Black Rose Books, 1992.

Wolf, Eric. *Europe and the People Without History.* Berkeley: University of California Press, 1982.

Wood, Ellen Meiksins. *The Retreat From Class.* London: Verso Books, 1986.

Wright, Patrick. *On Living in an Old Country.* London: Verso Books, 1985.

Young, Robert. "Colonialism and Humanism," in *'Race', Culture and Difference.* Eds. James Donald and Ali Rattansi. London: Sage Publications, 1992, pp. 243-251.

Yudice, George. "Neither Impugning nor Disavowing Whiteness Does A Viable Politics Make: The Limits of Identity Politics," in *After Political Correctness: The Humanities and Society in the 1990s.* Boulder, Colorado: Westview Press, 1995, pp. 255-285.

Zavarzadeh, Mas'ud. *Seeing Films Politically.* New York: SUNY Press, 1991.

Zavarzadeh, Mas'ud and Donald Morton. *Theory, (Post)Modernity, Opposition.* Washington, D.C.: Maisonneuve Press, 1991.

————. *Theory as Resistance: Politics and Culture after (Post)structuralism.* New York and London: The Guilford Press, 1994.

Zeskind, Leonard. "White-Shoed Supremacy." *The Nation* (June,10, 1996, vol. 262, no. 23):21-24.

Ziedenberg, Jason. "Labour's Dirty Secret." *This Magazine* (Nov/Dec., 1996, vol. 30, no. 3):17-21.

Zinn, Howard. "How Free Is Higher Education?" *Gannett Centre Journal* (Spring/Summer, 1991):147-154.

Index

academic freedom, xiv, 31, 92–102

Academic Questions, 61, 63–64, 93

Accuracy in Academe (AIA), 6, 29

Accuracy in Media (AIM) 29, 48, 55–56, 58, 66n.3

Adorno, Theodor, 91

affirmative action, 3, 64, 102, 129n.29

African Americans, use of term, 100–2

see also Blacks, American

Ahmad, Aijaz, 162–63, 203

Alcoff, Linda, 88–89

American Enterprise Institute (AEI), 51, 54, 72n.47, 77, 114, 120, 129n.31

American Eugenics Society (AES), 117

anticommunism, 32, 36, 45

anti-feminism, 106–110

anti-intellectualism, 16–17, 147, 233n.2

Arnold, Matthew, 78–79, 126

Aronowitz, Stanley, 40, 41–42

Asante, Molefi, 150–51

Backlash: The Undeclared War Against American Women (Faludi), 104–5

Balch, Stephen, 62, 145

Bannerji, Himani, 184, 186–87, 201–2

Barber, Benjamin, 40–41, 224

Barthes, Roland, 79–80

Baudrillard, Jean, 168

Bell Curve, The (Murray and Herrnstein), 4–5, 9, 112, 113, 114–17, 119, 120, 123, 130n.39,131n.48–49

Benjamin, Walter, 1, 83, 197–98

Bennett, William, 60, 73n.52

Bernstein, Richard, 135, 156n.3

Berube, Michael, 152, 165, 171–72, 176, 211n.6

Best, Stephen, 168, 170, 193, 198, 217n.28, 219n.41

Black Americans, 44, 45, 47, 64, 69n.28, 93, 100–1, 111, 114, 117, 120–23, 129n.30, 148,172

Blaut, James, 83–84

Bloch, Ernst, 203

Bloom, Allan, 60, 62, 75, 76, 102, 103, 105, 126

Blumenthal, Sidney, 32, 33, 43, 77

Bourdieu, Pierre, 88

Bozell, Brent, 31, 36

Buchanan, Patrick, 6, 114

Buckley, William F. 31–36, 42, 68n.13, 94, 133

Bush, George, 6, 24n.40, 94, 135, 137, 156n.9

business
and American culture, 50–51
conservative policies, 47–48

Butler, Judith, 168–69, 182

Cameron, Deborah, 99–102

Campus Coalition for Democracy, 62

Campus Report, 29, 66n.3

canon, Western, 78–92, 95, 136,
146, 164, 171, 187–88
capitalism, 39, 103, 104, 194, 200
Carby, Hazel, 187
Center for Defense Information
(CDI), 20n.10
Center for the Study of Popular
Culture, 70
Cheney, Lynne, 24n.41
Chomsky, Noam, 2, 19n.4, 21n.16,
133, 147, 153, 162, 175,
211n.4
Christian Coalition, 3, 6, 56,
71n.44, 83
Christian Right, 51, 71n.43
Chronicle of Higher Education, The,
30, 229
Closing of the American Mind, The
(Bloom), 62
COINTELPRO, 70n.38
collective dreams, 203–9
Collegiate Network, 60–61
Collier, Peter, 70n.35
Committee for the Free World, 62
Committee for the Survival of a
Free Congress, 72n.51
communism, 43–44, 104
see also anti-communism
Communist Party, 43, 210n.2
Conscience of a Conservative
(Goldwater), 69
Coors, Adolph, 55
Coors family, 55–56, 58, 72n.48,
49
conservatism, 6
counterrevolution (1960s), 46–
52
history of, 30–36
neoconservatives, 43
see also New Right
cultural conservatism, 51–52, 83
culture
academic, 64
American, 6, 50–51, 86, 89
"common," 86, 88
wars, xiii, 226

Western, 52–53, 54, 65, 77, 78,
79, 83, 108, 121, 122,
127n.14, 128n.16, 205
see also canon, Western
curricula, 85, 149

Dartmouth Review, 60, 76–77
date rape, 108–9
"Dead White Males," 92
deconstruction, 152
Decter, Midge, 62
Department of Education, 51,
71n.43
Derrida, Jacques, 167, 169, 170,
211n.10, 213n.15
Destructive Generation (Collier and
Horowitz), 70n.35
dialectical interpretation, 107,
197–200
difference, 183, 184, 186, 187,
201, 202, 203, 204
Diamond, Sara, 34, 69n.23
disinterestedness, 89
Dow Chemical, 56, 60
D'Souza, Dinesh, 4, 11, 53, 55, 60,
72n.47, 76–77, 79, 81,
82–83, 84, 86, 89, 93, 94,
102,103, 104–105, 106,
107, 110, 111, 120, 121–
22, 123, 125n.5–7,
126n.8, 129n.37,
131n.49–50, 150, 155
Duster, Troy, 111, 119–20
Dyer, Richard, 188

Eagle Forum, 129n.31
Eagleton, Terry, 198, 207–8,
214n.20, 217n.29
Ebert, Teresa, 172, 174, 180, 181–
82, 202
education, xiii, 3–4, 26, 71n.43,
75–76
banking method, 84–85
and big business, 49–51
curricula, xiv, 85, 149–51, 222
influence of Right, 63–64

New Right assault on, 36
politically committed, 223–26
P.C. wars, 25–30
Ehrenreich, Barbara, 99
End of Racism, The (D'Souza), 4,
	55
Epstein, Barbara, 11–12, 160,
	168, 205
ethnic terms, 100–2
Eugenics and Race (Pearson), 118,
	130*n*.44
Eugenics Research Association,
	117
Eurocentricity, 81, 82, 91, 95,
	150–51
European diffusionism, 83–84

Fairness and Accuracy in Report-
	ing, 157*n*.15
Faludi, Susan, 104–5, 107
Falwell, Jerry, 77
Fanon, Frantz, 206, 219*n*.45
FBI, 70*n*.38
Federation of American Immigra-
	tion Reform (FAIR), 118
feminism, 11–12, 45, 47, 102,
	104–10, 128*n*.29, 129*n*.39
	see also anti-feminism
Feulner, Edwin, 56
Finn, Chester, 96
Firing Line, 68
First Amendment, 136, 153
Fish, Stanley, 94, 96, 98, 130*n*.38,
	154, 155
Foley, Barbara, 168
Ford Foundation, 150
Foster, Hal, 214*n*.17
Foucault, Michel, 168, 169,
	212*n*.11, 213*n*.13,
	215*n*.21–22, 216*n*.27
Frankfurt School, 41, 70*n*.32, 90–
	91, 128*n*.21, 162, 215*n*.25
Free Congress Foundation (FCF),
	51, 56, 72*n*.51, 73*n*.52
free speech, 68, 92–102, 135–38
	see also speech codes

Free Speech movement (FSM),
	38–39, 40, 69*n*.30
Freire, Paolo, 84, 194, 195, 206,
	219*n*.45
French philosophy, influence of,
	41, 155, 161
Freud, Sigmund, 213*n*.13
Friedman, Milton, 55

Gallagher, Charles A., 191
Galton, Sir Francis, 116
Gandhi, Mahatma, 128*n*.15
Gates, Henry Louis, 172
Gingrich, Newt, 1, 2, 22*n*.26,
	23*n*.37, 56, 228
Giroux, Henry, 19*n*.5, 21*n*.14, 41–
	42, 66*n*.7, 233*n*.3
Gitlin, Todd, 19*n*.2, 71*n*.39, 192,
	203
Goldberg, David Theo, 4, 121–2
Goldstein, Richard, 8, 146
Goldwater, Barry, 35–36, 58,
	69*n*.22–24, 129*n*.31
Graff, Gerald, 221–23, 226
Gramsci, Antonio, 6, 22*n*.19,
	67*n*.11, 90, 126, 173, 174
Gulf War, 14, 24*n*.40, 136–37, 142

Hall, Stuart, 22*n*.24, 160, 166,
	174, 195, 225
Hamerow, Theodore, 154
Harvard University, 105–6
Hayden, Tom, 37
Hebdige, Dick, 205
Helms, Jesse, 118
Hennessy, Rosemary, 174, 179,
	180
Heritage Foundation, 51, 56–57,
	61–62, 68*n*.18, 73*n*.53,
	125*n*.5
Herman, Edward S., 143, 147
Herrnstein, Richard, 4, 114, 115,
	119, 120, 123
Hobsbawn, Eric, 203, 205–6
Hoffman, Abbie, 142
Hofstadter, Richard, 16

Hook, Sidney, 43
hooks, bell, 11, 108, 165, 184,
    186, 208, 227
Horkheimer, Max, 91
Horowitz, David, 70n.35
Horton, William Robert
    ("Willie"), 21n.13
House Un-American Activities
    Committee, 144
Howe, Irving, 44–45
Hudson Institute, 73n.55
Hughes, Robert, 9, 23n.35, 99,
    101
humanism, 170, 206, 213n.14

Iannone, Carol, 64
identity politics, 15–16, 183–4,
    201, 204, 210n.1,
    216n.25, 27, 217n.51
    core presuppositions, 182–188
ideology, 178, 179, 180, 215n.22–
    23
Ideology of the New Right, The
    (Levitas), 6
Illiberal Education (D'Souza), 29,
    55, 76, 77
immigration, 215–17
Institute for Educational Affairs
    (IEA), 57–58, 59–60
intelligentsia, 29–30, 126n.8, 227–
    29, 233n.4
Intercollegiate Studies Institute
    (ISI), 34, 68n.18
IQ, 115, 130n.40
Irvine, Reed, 66n.3

Jacoby, Russell, 71n.40, 98, 99,
    164, 187
Jay, Gregory, 222–23, 226
Jensen, Arthur, 118, 119–20
JM Foundation, 58
Jordan, June 79, 204

Kellner, Douglas, 70n.32, 160,
    168, 178, 198, 219n.41
Kerr, Clark, 39–40

Kimball, Roger, 11, 28, 53, 76,
    77–79, 81, 83, 84, 87,
    103, 104–5, 106, 110,
    111, 125n.1–3, 126n.8,
    129n.35, 145, 157n.12,
    159
Kirk, Russell, 33, 88
Kirkpatrick, Jeanne, 55, 62
knowledge production, 91–92
"Know-Nothings," 7
Kovel, Joel, 209
Kramer, Hilton, 76
Kristol, Irving, 43, 45–46, 57
Kruks, Sonia, 203–4

LaBarbera, Peter, 29
Lacan, Jacques, 167, 168, 213n.13
Laclau, Ernesto, 173, 182–83
language, 92–102, 171
Last Intellectuals, The (Jacoby),
    71n.40
Left, 12–18, 23n.29, 167–68
    anticommunism of, 43
    defense of P.C., 12–17
    demonized, 10
    Disneyfication of, 165
    eclecticism, 90–91, 128n.21
    fragmentation, 188
    moralism, 11–12
    pseudo-leftists, 155
    see also New Left, Old Left
Lenkowsky, Leslie, 73n.55
Levin, Michael, 64, 73n.60, 119
Levitas, Ruth, 6
liberals, 30, 33–34, 39, 147
libertarianism, 129n.34
Liddy, Gordon G., 8
lifestyle politics, 183
    see also identity politics
Limbaugh, Rush, 6–7, 23n.28,
    133, 192, 225, 228, 229
Lind, William, 51, 84
London, Herbert, 62, 63–64,
    73n.58, 145
Lorde, Audre, 15, 184, 204, 208
ludic theory, 170, 172, 214n.17–
    18

Lyotard, Jean-Francois, 167, 168

Madison Center for Educational Affairs (MCEA), 60–62
Malthus, Thomas Robert, 116
Mankind Quarterly, 118, 130*n*.43
Marable, Manning, 190
Marcuse, Herbert, 41, 47, 52, 70, 162, 196, 230
Marxism, 128*n*.21, 151–53, 160, 161, 163, 170, 174, 175, 176, 179–80, 181–82, 183, 197, 200–1, 202, 206, 210*n*.1,3, 213*n*.12, 215*n*.25, 217*n*.29, 219*n*.46
McCarthyism, xiv, 45, 93, 141, 143, 144
McLaren, 86, 199, 205
media, 10, 156*n*.2
 anti-P.C., xiv, 9–11, 134–36, 140–43
 framing news, 140
 influence, 133–34
 objectivity, 153–154
mediation, 199–200
Mercer, Kobena, 185
militias, 2, 193
Mills, C. Wright, 41, 162, 227
Mobil Oil Corporation, 52
Moon, Sun Myung, 57, 73*n*.54
Moral Majority, 56, 71*n*.44
moral panic, 139
Morning After, The (Roiphe), 108–9
Moynihan, Daniel Patrick, 123
multiculturalism, xiv, 15, 82, 85, 88, 102, 127*n*.13, 142, 150, 187, 190–91, 194, 201
Murray, Charles, 4, 113, 114, 115, 119, 120, 123

National Association of Scholars (NAS), 13, 25, 62–63, 147–48, 149, 154

National Empowerment Television (NET), 56, 73*n*.52
National Review magazine, 30–32, 33–34, 36, 42
Neo-Nazi League, 118
New Deal liberalism, 31, 54
Newfield, Christopher, 137–38
New Left, 37–39, 44–45, 64
New Right, xiii, 126, 226–28
 attack on P.C., xiii–xiv, 134–35
 attack on education, 229
 birth of, 30–36
 business base, 48–49
 defined, 66*n*.10
 funding of, 48–51, 53–65
Newsweek magazine, 143–45, 147–52, 154, 156*n*.10
Nietzsche, Friedrich, 170, 176
Nock, Albert J., 31, 32
Norris, Christopher, 166, 177

objectivity, 88–89, 181
Oklahoma City bombing, 8, 22*n*.18
Old Left, 62, 70*n*.35, 77, 109
Olin Foundation, 43, 44, 58, 60, 62, 77, 109
O'Neill, John 176, 211*n*.11, 227, 230
Orwell, George, 135, 152
"other," the, 92, 127*n*.13, 14, 146, 184

Paglia, Camille, 107–8, 129*n*.33, 156*n*.6
Parenti, Michael, 154
Pearson, Karl, 116, 118
Pioneer Fund, 117, 118
P.C. (Politically Correct)
 anti-P.C. campaign, 62
 attacks on, xiii–xiv
 caricatured, 146–47
 epithet of Angry White Males, 146
 hysteria, 9–12
 origin, xiv, 13–14, 26–28, 66*n*.2, 151–53

Pedagogy of the Oppressed (Freire), 84
Pioneer Fund, 22*n*.22, 73*n*.60, 117–19
Policy Review, 56, 61
Port Huron Statement, 37–38, 69*n*.29
positivist rationality, 89, 90–91, 162
"post-al" theory/politics, 174, 182, 196, 198, 206
Poster, Mark, 168
postmodernism, 177–78, 212*n*.8–9, 214*n*.16–17
poststructuralism, 161, 162–63, 168, 170, 171, 174, 176, 180, 181, 196, 210*n*.1, 212*n*.8–9, 11, 214*n*.16–17
Prescott, Peter, 145, 154
Prison Notebooks (Gramsci), 67
progressives, xiii, 29
Proposition 187, 4, 22*n*.22
Public Access (Berube), 165

Quigley, Margaret, 117

racial epithets, 97–98
racism, 3–5, 110, 115, 120, 121–22, 172, 225
Race, Evolution, and Behavior (Rushton), 118–19
Raskin, James, 21*n*.13, 152
RAVCO, 36
Reagan, Ronald, 6, 36, 50–51, 57, 59, 114, 131*n*.44
Reed, Ralph, 3, 71*n*.43, 73*n*.52
see also Christian Coalition; Christian Right
religion, 20*n*.51
see also Christian Coalition; Christian Right

Religious Right, 3, 72*n*.51
Richardson, Randolph, 58–59
Roiphe, Katie, 107, 108–9
Rushton, Philippe, 22*n*.22, 118–19

Said, Edward, 90, 176
Saloma, John, 69
Sarich, Vincent, 148
Sartre, Jean-Paul
SAT scores, 111–12, 130*n*.38
Saussere, Ferdinand de, 211
Savio, Mario, 39
Scaife, Richard Mellon, 58
Scaife Family Trusts, 58
Scatamburlo, Valerie, xiii
Schlafly, Phyllis, 107, 129*n*.31
Schrecker, Ellen, 144
science, 88–89
Scott, Joan Wallach, 80, 182
See, I Told You So (Limbaugh), 6, 23*n*.28
Sexual Personae (Paglia), 107–8
Sharon Statement, 35, 68*n*. 19
Shaw, Peter, 64
Shor, Ira, 46
Silber, John, 29–30, 66*n*.7
Simon, William, 50, 57–58
Simpson, O.J., 22*n*.19, 123–24
Sixties, the
bashing, 6–7, 70*n*.35
romanticizing, 208–209
legacy of, 36–42
Sklar, Holly, 5, 19*n*.1, 4, 21*n*.17
Smith, Dorothy, 178
Smith-Richardson Foundation, 58–59, 73*n*.55
Social Text fiasco, 166–67
see also Sokal
Sokal, Alan D., 166–68, 210*n*.7
Soldiers of Misfortune (Scatamburlo), xiii
Sommers, Christina Hoff, 107, 109, 129*n*.36
speech codes, 96–99
Spencer, Herbert, 116
Spivak, Gayatri, 217*n*.27
Stabile, Carol, 166
Station for Experimental Genetics, 117
Stern, Howard, 7
Stimpson, Catherine, 24*n*.38
structuralism, 161, 210*n*.4

Students for a Democratic Society
(SDS), 37–38, 44,
69*n*.28–29, 71*n*.39
subjectivity, 170
supply-side economics, 59

Tenured Radicals (Kimball), 28,
76, 78, 105, 145
textbooks, 149
textualism, 195
theory, 166–75
Thernstrom, Stephen, 93–94
think-tanks, 48, 73*n*.55, 77
   see also Heritage Foundation;
      Smith-Richardson
      Foundation
Tomasky, Michael, 219*n*.43
totality, 198–99
Trotsky, Leon, 43
truth, politics of, 176–82
Tuchman, Gaye, 154
Turner, Terence, 193

universalism, 207
universities, 14–16, 97, 233*n*.3,
237
   admission policies, 111
   campus politics, 39–46, 48
   campus protests, 37
   Collegiate Network, 60–61
   culture, 64–65

University of California-Berkeley,
38–40, 69*n*.30, 97, 111
University of Michigan, 98
University of Texas-Austin, 148–
49

value neutrality, 90

Verbal Hygiene (Cameron), 99–100
Viguerie, Richard, 36, 49, 69
Vietnam War, 162
   protests, 39, 42–43

Wallace, George, 130*n*.41
welfare, attack on, 3, 20*n*.10, 31,
114
West, Cornel, 197, 228
Weyrich, Paul, 51–52, 56, 71*n*.44,
73*n*.52
W.H. Brady Foundation, 60, 109–
10
White Americans, 80
   males, 4–5, 8, 13, 92, 191–93
whiteness, 188–94
"white panic," 3, 21*n*.14
Who Stole Feminism (Hoff-
Sommers), 109
Whole World Is Watching, The
(Gitlin), 71
Wiener, Jon, 97
Wildavsky, Aaron, 64
Will, George, 11, 14, 24*n*.41, 149
Williams, Raymond, 126*n*.9
Willis, Ellen, 123
Wilson, Pete 3, 4, 118, 128*n*.22
women, 44, 105
   see also anti-feminism; femi-
nism
World Anti-Communist League,
73*n*.54, 118

Young Americans for Freedom
(YAF), 35–36, 42
Yudice, George, 189–90, 193, 194

Zavarzadeh, Mas'ud, 163, 216*n*.25
Zinn, Howard, 95

Studies in the Postmodern Theory of Education

General Editors
Joe L. Kincheloe & Shirley R. Steinberg

Counterpoints publishes the most compelling and imaginative books being written in education today. Grounded on the theoretical advances in criticalism, feminism and postmodernism in the last two decades of the twentieth century, Counterpoints engages the meaning of these innovations in various forms of educational expression. Committed to the proposition that theoretical literature should be accessible to a variety of audiences, the series insists that its authors avoid esoteric and jargonistic languages that transform educational scholarship into an elite discourse for the initiated. Scholarly work matters only to the degree it affects consciousness and practice at multiple sites. Counterpoints' editorial policy is based on these principles and the ability of scholars to break new ground, to open new conversations, to go where educators have never gone before.

For additional information about this series or for the submission of manuscripts, please contact:

Joe L. Kincheloe & Shirley R. Steinberg
637 West Foster Avenue
State College, PA 16801